ARTILLERY

A HISTORY

JOHN NORRIS

SUTTON PUBLISHING

First published in 2000 by
Sutton Publishing Limited · Phoenix Mill
Thrupp · Stroud · Gloucestershire · GL5 2BU

British Library Cataloguing in Publication Data
A catalogue record for this book is available from the British Library

ISBN 0 7509 2185 4

> *This work is dedicated to two women who have each touched my life
> in their own separate ways. By coincidence they are both Ethels. One
> is my late mother-in-law, who was firm but fair, and of whom I have
> many fond memories. The second Ethel is very dear and at times has
> proved to have a very profound outlook on life. This Ethel is my
> mother and I would like to say how grateful I am to her and proud to
> call her Mother.*

Typset in 10.5/15 pt Photina.
Typesetting and origination by
Sutton Publishing Limited.
Printed and bound in England by
J.H. Haynes & Co. Ltd, Sparkford.

CONTENTS

ACKNOWLEDGEMENTS

I would like to express my sincere gratitude to the following institutions and individuals for their help and unstinting kindness in putting this work together. Without such support my task would have been much more difficult. My thanks to Ian V. Hogg who listened sympathetically and offered advice; to the staff and assistants at the Royal Armouries, Fort Nelson, Fareham, Hampshire, who allowed me to roam almost at will; to the Royal Artillery Museum at the Rotunda in Woolwich, London, whose staff I wish the best of luck in their move during 2001; and to many defence manufacturers who provided a wide range of photographic material. My thanks also to the men of the re-enactment group The Brockhurst Artillery Volunteers who lay on sterling displays of First World War events at Fort Nelson; to Simon Davey and the members of The Kynges Ordynaunce who have faithfully recreated much period artillery; and to all members of The Courteneye Household and Prince Rupert's Blewcoats who have done excellent work in displaying historic artillery at special events.

INTRODUCTION

T he word artillery probably evolved from a number of earlier terms. One school of thought believes it is a combination of the Latin *arcus*, meaning bow, and *telum*, meaning projectile. A second theory attributes the term's origin to the Latin *ars tolendi*, or *ars* and *tirare*, meaning the art of catapulting or shooting. Another possible root is the Latin phrase *ars telorum*, which refers to the art of using long-range weapons. The great siege master and fortress builder Sebastien le Prestre de Vauban (1633–1707) traced the term back to the old French word *artillier*, meaning either to fortify or to arm. However, the German philologist Diez believed it was derived from the Provençal word *artilha* and that it had entered the German language as early as 1500. It seems artillery is actually an omnibus word, derived from several sources.

Whatever the true origin of the term artillery, its meaning comes down to the science of propelling a projectile at an enemy over a distance. It can be applied to machines of war fielded by the Greeks and Romans, such as the *catapulta* and *ballista*, which both used torsion power to propel their missiles and pre-date gunpowder by many centuries. During the sixteenth century, there was still some debate over how the term artillery should be interpreted. For example, in 1537 Henry VIII of England issued a charter for the Guild of St George, in which he charged its members with becoming: 'The overseers of the science of artillery . . . to witt, long bowes, cross bowes and hand gonnes for the better encrease of the defence of our realme.' Over 450 years later this charter is preserved by the Honourable Artillery Company, which is now raised as a regiment of the British Army and can trace its origins back to the Guild of St George and the year in which the charter was issued.

The reference to 'hand gonnes' in the document raises the question of when artillery and hand-held gunpowder weapons separated into two distinct types of weapon. It is very difficult to date this development with any great accuracy, but it seems likely that it came during the fourteenth century. References to 'gunnis cum telar' (guns with handles) appeared in the 1350s and mark the emergence of personal weapons. Certainly by the fifteenth century early hand-guns were being used by trained infantrymen alongside artillery. In 1411 John the Good, Duke of Burgundy, is recorded as having some 4,000 hand-guns in his armoury. These weapons would have had an effective range of some 200 metres, about the same as some of the smaller artillery pieces of the day, but the firer would have been considered fortunate if he hit his intended target. The Hussite troops of the Bohemian leader, Jan Ziska, used hand-held gunpowder weapons in their struggle against the Emperor Sigismund in 1419.

Gunpowder artillery was not available to ancient armies, but more than 650 years have elapsed since tubed artillery, which is to say conventional guns, was first recorded. The appearance of cannon proper on the battlefield in the fourteenth century signalled the end of single-handed combat and ushered in a new martial law. However, it was not until the seventeenth century that artillery was used with any great effect against enemy troops ranged in the open, rather than against a city or castle under siege. Since that time it has been deployed in a variety of roles from siege warfare to long-range coastal defence. Artillery has also been developed to perform highly specialized roles – examples include anti-tank guns, anti-aircraft guns and weapons for mountain warfare. More generally, guns have been used as field pieces in support of infantry; into this category also fall towed and self-propelled guns, which are as much part of a modern army as helicopters.

Artillery did not gain popular acceptance within the military infrastructure overnight. Its introduction was gradual. Some countries, including Japan, did try to resist the spread of gunpowder weaponry – a common reaction to any new technology, be it military or industrial. But opposition was futile and in order to survive, or at least compete on equal footing, all nations adopted artillery into their armies and navies. The motto of the Royal Artillery Regiment of the British Army is 'Ubique' (Everywhere). This refers to the fact that the regiment has served in all parts of the globe where the British Army has fought but can also be applied to artillery itself. Today it is ubiquitous.

This book charts artillery's origins and outlines some of the figures who have influenced its design and advanced the science of gunnery to make it what it is today. It concentrates on conventional artillery, because the science of gunnery is completely different to that of rocketry. There is a current trend in some modern armies towards rocket systems, for example, the American-designed Multiple Launch Rocket System and Russian-built BMW-21 multiple rocket launcher. These rocket artillery systems are designed to augment rather than replace conventional tubed artillery because they allow forces to employ the shock tactic of concentrating firepower into a designated area. Their deployment is intended as a short-term opening sequence to a barrage and is limited to an indirect fire role. Guns, on the other hand, can be aimed with precise accuracy and maintain a continuous bombardment of a target; as will be seen, this was the case during the First World War. Modern advances in computer analysis and fire control have enhanced the accuracy of artillery and thus reduced the chance of collateral damage when fighting takes place close to built-up areas.

Pieces of artillery have been given various titles over the years, including howitzer, cannon, bombard and falcon. The term cannon itself is derived from the Greek word *kanun* and the Latin *canna*, both meaning 'tube', which describes perfectly what the barrel of a piece of artillery looks like. Ancient and medieval siege engines which relied on counterpoise, torsion or kinetic energy to launch their projectiles were also called artillery. However, within this work all artillery referred to is of the gunpowder type.

A piece that has had a long and chequered history but still remains in use today, although in a much revised role and design, is the mortar. Its basic short and stubby shape, which is believed to stem from the grinding mortar of chemists, was one of the easiest to manufacture. At various times these weapons were made from different types of metal, including bronze, brass and latten, and could be cast in one piece because of their simple shape. Although the designs for early cannon were changed and improved, the shape of the mortar remained unaltered. The cannon of the day were used to fire directly at targets, but mortars were fired at elevations of 45 degrees or more and were used to 'lob' projectiles over the walls of besieged castles. However, mortars have not always been restricted to siege warfare; over the years they have also been employed as defensive weapons and in coastal defence. Some mortar designs frequently exceeded 13 inches calibre and continued in use alongside normal artillery until the nineteenth century. It was not until the First World War that mortars became refined for use by the infantry as a specialized weapon of trench warfare. This work will illustrate how early mortars were used in conjunction with conventional artillery, until they eventually fell out of favour with the gunners and were replaced by the more accurate and powerful howitzers.

The tactical roles and functions of artillery throughout history will be examined, as will the way in which these roles have been adapted to the ever-changing face of the battlefield. The changes artillery made to the way in which wars were fought were gradual – partly because in its earliest days, it was not as accurate as a longbow in the hands of a well-trained and experienced archer. However, artillery's influence did deepen the battlefield as the range of guns increased. Battles were no longer fought by armies only a few hundred metres from one another. Artillery extended the distance between them to many kilometres: new technology made the science of gunnery a precise tactic.

The introduction of gunpowder weapons on to the battlefield made it more important than ever before to train troops to a high degree of technical proficiency. Thus warfare passed from being fought by masses of relatively undrilled militia to be the occupation of more regular and better disciplined troops. Some of these sixteenth- and seventeenth-century troops were so highly skilled and experienced that they could band together and hire out their services as mercenaries to the highest bidder. This applied to all levels of troops and, of course, included gunners and their artillery. And so, it has been argued that the *raison d'être* for standing armies to defend sovereign territories was established.

This book will examine the size of gun crews, batteries and specific engagements but uniforms and the histories of individual artillery regiments fall outside its scope. The development of tools specific to the gunner's trade, such as the sextant and quadrant, will be considered. No coverage is considered necessary on pieces of artillery that could be termed 'novelty' weapons, such as the Zalinski 'Dynamite Gun' or the Zippermeyer 'Vortex Gun', which was intended to serve as an anti-aircraft weapon by shooting down aircraft with air turbulence. The reason for the omission is not that they were experimental, but simply that such designs never stood a chance of being introduced into widespread military use. Given the number and diversity of pieces that fall under the title artillery, it is inevitable that some will not appear here; this is regrettable and apologies are proffered in advance.

The basic design of tubed artillery remains the same as it has always been, but advances in ammunition, metallurgy and better understanding of ballistics, have all served to improve the overall performance of gunnery and produce weapons of reduced weight and better accuracy. Despite the increased use of rocketry on the battlefield, both guided and free-flight, it is unlikely that missiles will ever truly supplant the traditional gun of the artillery branch of any army.

Finally, the reader will find a mixture of both imperial and metric measurements throughout this work. This follows military convention: some countries have historically referred to the weight of a shell, expressed in either pounds or kilograms, and others state calibre of shell in either inches or millimetres.

ONE

WHENCE CAME THE GUNS? THE ORIGINS OF ARTILLERY, 1200–1400

N o one can say with absolute certainty when or where gunpowder was first used to propel a projectile from a tube, leading to the advent and rise of firearms and artillery. Neither is there any conclusive evidence for who made the breakthrough. Therefore, the question of where artillery began is likely to remain one of the great unanswerable military mysteries. Indeed, there is even some dispute over the origins of gunpowder. Some theorists believe it to be Arabic in origin: it could have been a by-product of early alchemy experiments. But, the hard evidence points more to its being a Chinese invention, possibly as early as the eighth century. The first known written formula for combining the three constituent compounds of gunpowder is contained in a military treatise attributed to Wu Ching Tsung Yao, written *c*. AD 1044. But there are earlier references to the use of the material by Chinese troops; its potential was chronicled in *c*. 908 when it was used to generate noise in order to unnerve the enemy and also to demolish structures.

It has also been suggested that the properties of gunpowder were accidentally discovered as a result of experiments into producing an elixir of life. Whatever its origins, one of the first recorded uses of the compound to propel a projectile from a weapon came in the form of a long-barrelled bamboo apparatus as early as *c*. AD 1132. The invention of this device is accredited to the Chinese General Ch'en Gui, the commander of the garrison of Anlu in the Hopei Province. The barrel is thought to have been bound with either rope or leather for additional strength. Despite the advanced technology which had obviously been applied to developing such a weapon, its accuracy and the safety of the user must have been seriously in doubt.

It was to be another 200 years before true gunpowder artillery – that is to say weapons with barrels manufactured from metal, capable of discharging projectiles – was to be used by the Chinese in battle. Joseph Needham, the noted historian, has named early Chinese gunpowder weapons 'eruptors'. Weapons of this type could 'pierce the heart or belly when it strikes a man or horse, and can even transfix several persons at once'. In 1341, Chang Hsien compiled a verse called 'The Iron Cannon Affair', in which he described the operation of a gunpowder or 'eruptor' weapon:

> The black dragon lobbed over an egg-shaped thing
> Fully the size of a peck measure it was,*
> And it burst, and a dragon flew out with peals of thunder rolling
> In the air it was like a blazing and flashing fire.
> The first bang was like the dividing of chaos in two,
> As if the mountains and rivers were all turned upside down.

Such a description tends to suggest that the Chinese were using gunpowder artillery with exploding shells long before the technique was developed in Western Europe.

The history of how gunpowder came to the European continent and was eventually used as a propellant there is clouded by uncertainty. The mystery is compounded by the fact that the story is sometimes populated by shady figures such as Berthold Schwartz, a German monk from Freiburg, and Marcus Graecus. It has come to be assumed that gunpowder probably arrived in Europe via the trade routes travelled by the Arabs and with it came the secret manufacturing formula. A second theory has it that gunpowder reached Europe by way of the Mongol invasion from the east in the first half of the thirteenth century. It is quite possible that the Mongols did bring the compound with them: during their epic raid into Europe in 1241–2 they are known to have used gunpowder and other types of incendiary devices, such as the *chen t'ien lei* (thunder bomb), which they had previously deployed to produce noise and confuse their enemies in lands to the east. These weapons had been acquired during the Mongol conquest of China. As they retreated to elect a new khan on the death of Ogedai in 1241, they probably left behind discarded gunpowder-based devices, such as their 'poison and smoke ball'. This military item, known to the Mongols as *tu-yao yen ch'iu*, contained sulphur, nitre, aconite (a poisonous plant related to the wolf's-bane family),

* A peck is a unit for dry measurement equal to two gallons.

oil, charcoal, resin and wax – a deadly combination that included all the constituent ingredients for gunpowder. This mixture was contained in a clay, ball-shaped receptacle. The whole weighed about 2 kilograms. It could be either hand thrown, in the manner of an early hand-grenade, or projected from a catapult siege engine using torsion energy. The writings of Miu Yu-Sun quoting Yu Wei, a minor scholar, state that in the second half of the thirteenth century a Mongol by the name of Ch'i Wu Wen, travelled into Europe taking with him the complete working knowledge of gunpowder and gunnery technology of the time.

Francis Bacon (c. 1214–94), an English Franciscan monk from Ilchester, knew of the fiery and explosive properties of gunpowder, or black powder as it came to be known, and had recorded these facts in anagrams. In 1242, when he was about twenty-eight, he wrote in cryptographic form how a portion of this mysterious powder 'no larger than a man's finger', when wrapped in parchment could be ignited to explode with a loud report. He could have learned of the existence of gunpowder through stories about a new substance left behind after the Mongols' retreat in the same year. In his *Albertus Magnus*, Bacon describes the method of manufacturing powder to produce 'thunder and lightning' and how the ingredients were to be mixed on a slab of marble, the powder to be wrapped in parchment and ignited to produce a 'blinding flash and stunning noise'. Bacon gave proportions for mixing gunpowder, and these have been interpreted as 7:5:5, saltpetre, charcoal and sulphur.

In 1267, twenty-five years after Bacon had made his notes and still during his lifetime, a revolt erupted in London, instigated by the Earl of Gloucester. The uprising threatened to unseat the regency of King Henry III. In his attempts to quell this outbreak of dissent, Henry marched on the city to rout Gloucester and it is recorded that he may have had gunpowder artillery in his train. The exact type and nature of this artillery is not known, but Grafton's *Chronicles* from the time state how the king was 'making daily assaults when guns and other ordnance were shot into the city'. Because of the uncertainty, lack of further notes and the unreliability of this reference, it could be concluded that the artillery used during this incursion was a mixture torsion-powered siege engines, such as the catapult and mangonel, both of which were still in common use at the time to launch gunpowder-filled projectiles of the types used by the Mongols. But it is also possible that Henry was in possession of very early types of *pots de fer*, or pots of fire, the full reference to which has been lost to us over the years.

At this time, the Church issued anathema condemning anyone who manufactured fiery substances for purposes of war. This blanket anathematizing of incendiary material covered Greek fire, an early type of napalm which was still in limited use. But the Church's abhorrence was reserved mainly for gunpowder. Anyone using any type of firearm was committing blasphemy by dabbling in the 'black arts'. In 1139 under Pope Innocent II the Church had issued a similar edict against the use of crossbows, but with little or no effect: gunpowder artillery continued to be developed and its use spread. However, early written works on artillery instructed men working with 'such devilish instruments of destruction', never to forget their Christian responsibilities and always to have 'the vision of God before their eyes'.

Gunpowder was termed black powder because of its colour, which was the result of the proportion of charcoal in its make-up. Another medieval name for this volatile compound was 'serpentine', but exactly why is not clear. The full danger of the powder was still largely misunderstood but it was considered 'unseemly' for gunners to stand on any that had been spilled on the ground. This was certainly not simply battlefield etiquette; it avoided the danger of accidental combustion due to the friction of the foot – the chance of explosion would have been especially high when the action was performed on a hard stony surface. An accident could result in severe burning or even the loss of a limb, depending on the quantity of powder trampled.

In his later writings during the 1260s, Francis Bacon began to refer to the existence of gunpowder more openly and mentions it as 'the powder, known in divers places, composed of saltpetre, sulphur and charcoal'. More than thirty years later, in about 1300, a book appeared claiming to have been written by Marcus Graecus (Mark the Greek). Research now supports the theory that this work, rather than being the writings of one person, is actually a compilation of many men's work. The volume is called *Book of Fires for the Burning of Enemies* and contained within its pages is a reiteration of the formula given by Francis Bacon. But the *Book of Fires* also includes another formula which gives different proportions for the constituents of gunpowder: 6:1:2 parts, saltpetre, sulphur and charcoal. It seems likely, then, that the work is indeed by several authors, each of whom had their own ideas about the make-up of the compound.

Theories on the composition of gunpowder certainly changed over time. In the fourteenth century the mixture was composed of 41 per cent saltpetre,

30 per cent sulphur and 29 per cent charcoal. And in *c.* 1400 the writer Montauban gives the proportions for mixing black powder as 70:13:17 parts, saltpetre, sulphur and charcoal. So, there was no standardized rate for mixing black powder and it is possible that the formula varied from one country to another – even from one centre of production to another in the same country. This lack of consistency continued right up the Napoleonic Wars in the first part of the nineteenth century, when there was still discrepancy concerning the actual proportions of the compounds required to produce quality gunpowder. Today the formula for gunpowder is still based on these three ingredients but has been standardized as 75 per cent saltpetre, 10 per cent sulphur and 15 per cent charcoal.

Early black powder had a tendency to separate down into its constituents because of the effects of vibration during transportation. This resulted in poor burning rates, or even complete failure to ignite when the powder came to be used on the battlefield. One method of preventing separation was to mix the three ingredients on the battlefield just before the powder was required. This was a highly dangerous job because the slightest spark or lack of concentration could result in spontaneous combustion. This hazard had been recognized by Roger Bacon when he instructed that the mixture should be blended on a marble surface to prevent accidental ignition. The handling of gunpowder on the battlefield was made more dangerous by the fact that men serving the guns had to have a fire constantly burning to provide a source for ignition. This no doubt contributed to many accidents. However, techniques advanced and changes to the method of blending powder were introduced.

One of the first significant names to emerge in the manufacture of gunpowder during the Middle Ages was Merckel Gast of Frankfurt, who rose to eminence towards the end of the fourteenth century. Gast was said to be able to manufacture gunpowder that would last sixty years by using chemicals he himself had refined. He is also understood to have been capable of restoring the explosive properties of powder which had been 'spoiled', presumably by moisture or settling during transportation. Gast also had a working knowledge of artillery and the emerging hand-guns of the time. He was able to cast the barrels of cannon and site them during battle.

Black powder was expensive to manufacture and it has been calculated that in 1346 it cost 18 pence to produce 500 grams of the substance – the equivalent of £86 per kilogram at prices in 2000. By 1376, the price had risen to £1.20 per kilo, clearly the result of an increase in demand. It should be remembered that at this time the weekly wage for a manual labourer was paid in pennies and that the brick-built Caister Castle, near Yarmouth in Norfolk, was raised between 1432 and 1435 for £1,480. The high cost of producing gunpowder was offset by the results early cannon yielded on the battlefield. The weapons spread confusion and panic among an enemy whose troops had never before encountered such weapons. Furthermore, castles and walled settlements under siege could be forced into submission with the minimum expenditure in effort and manpower.

On ignition, 500 grams of black powder will produce some 1.1 square metres of gas, which in a confined space quickly expands to produce considerable pressure. Such expanding gases had to be allowed to vent if an explosion was to be avoided. It was known that if they were vented safely, the pressurized gases could be used to impart movement to a stone or iron projectile which fitted rather loosely into a cylindrical tube. As the gases expanded, they moved the projectile forward at increasing velocity. This phenomenon must have been noted by the early gunners which explains why the side walls of thirteenth-century cannon barrels were very thick, even if at that stage the new science was not fully understood. There was no means of accurately measuring the quantity of powder that should be loaded relative to the size of the weapon; this was still very much left to the judgement of the individual gunner.

A figure called Berthold Schwartz, sometimes referred to as Black Berthold (which is a general translation of his German name), is credited with discovering the propellant properties of black powder by igniting the compound in a vessel to discharge an object. An engraving, c. 1380, purportedly shows the moment of discovery. If one takes this as the date when the foundations of artillery were laid, the whole chronology for the development of artillery would be overturned. Some references say the experiment took place in 1320, and that Berthold Schwartz was injured when his apothecary's grinding mortar exploded as he was preparing the gunpowder mixture. (It is generally believed that the expression of the use of the term 'mortar' to describe an artillery piece originated from this experiment.) However, there are a number of doubts about this mysterious figure. First, there is no conclusive evidence that Berthold Schwartz ever existed. Secondly, the term 'mortar' for a form of artillery was not to be coined until many years after the supposed incident in Schwartz's workshop. If Schwartz did exist, we know of no writings about his experiments. The fact also remains that one of the first European battles in which artillery is reliably recorded as having been used was Crecy. There, in August 1346, English troops under Edward III deployed between three and five cannon. These devices are referred to either as *roundelades* or *pots de fer*. The latter name appears to be the more popular and widespread; it was commonly used to refer to early cannon and indicates that such weapons were firmly established. This first major European deployment of gunpowder weapons predates the engraving of Schwartz's supposed experiments by thirty-four years and thereby completely dispels the theory that it was he who mastered the use of gunpowder as a propellant for artillery.

In 1852, Colonel Chesney wrote in his *Observations of Firearms:*

The Moors, according to Conde [whom Chesney says is a high authority on this subject], used artillery against Saragossa in 1118; and in 1132 a culverin of four pounds' calibre, named Salamonica, was made. In 1157, when the Spaniards took Niebla, the Moors defended themselves with machines which threw darts and stones by means of fire, and Abd'almumen, the Moorish king, captured Mohadia, a fortified city near Bona, from the Sicilians, by the same means. In 1280, artillery was used against Cordova, and in 1306, or 1308, Ferdinand IV took Gibraltar from the Moors by means of artillery. Ibn Nasan ben Bia, of Granada, mentions that guns were adopted from the Moors and used in Spain in the twelfth century, and that balls of iron were thrown by means of fire in 1331.

The term artillery had been applied to siege engines that relied on either torsion or counterpoise energy to propel their projectiles. It seemed only right that gunpowder weapons should fall under the same name. After all, these new weapons were only continuing the role catapults and mangonels had played. The only real difference between the two types of weaponry was the fact that cannon used chemical energy, generated by burning a mixture of minerals, to hurl their projectiles. It is known that in the first half of the fourteenth century, small cannon were beginning to enter service with Western European armies. An arms race had begun and no country could afford to lag behind. The use of weapons harnessing the properties of gunpowder was now more widespread in Europe than in the Far East, but

their effectiveness on the battlefield was not to be fully realized until the end
of the Middle Ages.

EARLY WEAPONS AND AMMUNITION

The first cannon recognizable to modern eyes began to appear in Europe
towards the end of the thirteenth century. They are recorded as having
arrived in Flanders by *c.* 1314 and by 1326 cannon were in limited use in
France. In 1338 a French raiding force attacked the port of Southampton,
setting fire to the town and sacking it. Among the French weaponry was a
single *ribaud* or *pot de fer* with forty-eight projectiles loaded with 1.362
kilograms of gunpowder – an average weight of only 28 grams of powder for
each discharge if all the projectiles were fired. Documents from February
1326 record that the city of Florence had set aside sufficient funds to
purchase brass cannon and iron balls and authorized the Priors, Gonfalonier
and twelve others 'for the defence of the commune, camps and territory of
Florence'. It had also appointed two men to make 'iron bullets and iron
arrows for *canones de metallo*'. By this time the properties of black powder had
been known for almost 100 years.

The earliest extant illustration of artillery in use dates from between 1326
and 1327 and appears in the manuscript *De Nobilitatibus, Sapientiis et
Prudentiis Regum* (*On the Majesty, Wisdom and Prudence of Kings*) by Walter
Milimete. This document may, in turn, be based on the reputed use of devices
referred to as *vassi, pots de feu* or *pots de fer* at the Battle of Metz in 1324.
King Alfonso of Castile is known to have made use of artillery at the siege of
Algeciras, an action also fought in 1324. Only five years after the decree of
Florence, weapons termed as *vasa* and *sclopi* were used in the attack against
Cividale in Friaul. By 1338, the French town of Rouen was deploying iron
pots in its defence in order to throw fire arrows against attackers. In his work
The Origin of Artillery, H.W.L. Hime points to the fact that Edward III of
England had already used artillery in his campaign against the Scots in 1327
and 1328, where the pieces were termed 'crakys of war'. The noise these
basic gunpowder weapons generated was like nothing the Scottish had ever
heard before, but like every early deployment of gunpowder artillery, the
tactic was not entirely conclusive for the campaign.

Within ten years of his Scottish expedition, Edward III was to enter hostilities
against a different enemy in a long, drawn-out period of conflict now known as

the Hundred Years War. The fighting between England and France began in 1337 when Philip VI of France declared all English-held territories south of the Loire to be forfeit and moved in to claim them. This action prompted a swift response from Edward III, who embarked on a military campaign with only fifteen pieces of artillery and a stock of less than 40 kilograms of black powder. Warfare was never to be the same again. Gunpowder weapons now reduced the chivalrous knight to the same vulnerable status as the common foot soldier; the castles and city walls of the pre-gunpowder age were rendered all but obsolete. Great innovators emerged during this war, including Bertrand de Guesclin, the Constable of France, who introduced the 'scorched earth' tactic as a way of denying the enemy any means of living off the land. However, despite the fact that gunpowder weapons had now begun to make an appearance on the battlefield there are remarkably few contemporary references to the presence or efficacy of such weapons.

The Battle of Crecy in 1346 was one of the most significant engagements between France and England during the Hundred Years War. At Crecy the army of Edward III of England comprised some 3,000 men-at-arms and knights, 10,000 archers and many others serving as infantrymen. The French army numbered some 60,000 troops, of whom 12,000 were heavy cavalry. Among the French troops were about 6,000 Genoese crossbowmen serving as mercenaries. It had rained briefly but intensely just before the two armies clashed. The French cavalrymen mounted one charge after another and each time they were broken by the withering fire from the longbowmen in Edward's army. Each archer was capable of shooting at least six arrows per minute (some very experienced archers maintain a rate of ten arrows per minute), presenting at least 60,000 arrows a minute. This must have been enough to shatter any charge, no matter how determined. The Genoese crossbowmen tried to engage the English archers but the distance between the two forces was too great for their short-range crossbow bolts to carry and the strings of their weapons had been dampened by the rain, further reducing their usefulness. Coming under fire from the English archers, who had kept their bow strings dry during the storm, the Genoese troops broke file and fled. The French launched fifteen or sixteen assaults before giving up. They left behind over 1,500 dead knights and between 10,000 and 20,000 men-at-arms and infantrymen.

From this brief description the battle sounds ordinary in its conduct. However, it is generally accepted as being the engagement where the English

Army deployed gunpowder artillery for the first time. An Italian chronicler, Villani, blamed the artillery in Edward's army for prompting the Genoese crossbowmen to leave their posts. Villani states that Edward sited his artillery among his archers' positions and describes its effect as being 'most fearful'. Another account says that the pieces 'with fire throw little balls to frighten and destroy horses'. But no matter how unused some of the troops may have been to gunfire, given the fact that Edward only had three or five slow-firing pieces, the Italian chronicler was probably simply making excuses for the lack of moral fibre shown by his fellow countrymen in battle. It is hardly likely that Edward III's artillery caused even a small percentage of the deaths at Crecy.

In general, gunpowder weapons deployed at this time seem to have achieved mixed results at best, frequently making little contribution to the tactical outcome of an engagement. Despite this fact, the pattern was set by which all subsequent wars would be fought. Therefore, one has to try to ascertain why artillery, which at this time was being issued with a daily allowance of gunpowder weighing barely 300 grams and producing desultory returns for the expenditure of time, effort and money involved, should have been deployed at all. It boils down to the simple fact that if one side has such weaponry, it will use it to try to influence the outcome of a battle.

The widespread use and acceptance of gunpowder weapons on the battlefield did not to come until the mid-fifteenth century at the Battle of Castillon in 1453, the last major engagement of the Hundred Years War. Here the French employed their cannon to great effect and defeated the English, securing a conclusive end to more than a century of intermittent fighting. By this time gunpowder artillery was spreading across Western Europe and having more of an impact on warfare than in the Far East where the compound had been discovered.

Early gunpowder projectors were crude by any standards and would have been very difficult to control during firing. They were no more than simple vase- or bell-shaped devices, weighing between 12 and 15 kilograms, with a thickened base into which a small hole was bored. This part of the weapon contained the powder and came to be called the chamber. The small hole in the base allowed the firer to insert a hot iron to ignite the powder charge. The devices had wide, slightly flared openings at the muzzle and were simply placed on the ground, which would have done nothing for their accuracy. They were probably used simply to produce a loud noise to startle the enemy and his horses. It has to be remembered that the loudest noises most people heard up to this time were thunder storms and the pealing of church bells. The sound of an igniting gunpowder weapon would have been quite startling.

There is evidence that the first projectiles for these early artillery pieces were no more than large arrows, the shafts of which were bound with leather to fit the barrel, which was usually between 50 and 75mm diameter. Examples of these *pots de fer* were uncovered at an archaeological site at Losholt in Sweden in 1861. The site in Scania cannot be accurately dated because of the lack of other evidence, but the objects' appearance conforms with the shape of devices shown in manuscripts. This has allowed archaeologists to set a tentative date for the site at early to mid-fourteenth century, perhaps 1350 to 1375. The weapons' users may have been killed and because other troops were not versed in how to operate the equipment, it was left where it lay. Another possibility is that once all the gunpowder had been used, there was no point in carrying a weapon that could no longer be fired. Whatever the reason, the troops using these cannon must have been most careless with them, despite the huge manufacturing costs involved in their production. These conclusions are supported by evidence from a number of such finds unearthed during battlefield excavations.

Bigger cannon had to be strapped to a trestle and pointed in the general direction of the intended target, which was usually a castle or town under siege. Another option was to secure the barrels to a board which could be angled on an earthen rampart to provide some form of elevation in a rough aim determined by line-of-sight and the gunner's eye – a technique known today as direct fire. The energy produced in the recoil of the discharging weapon, however, would knock the barrel askew and it would have to be repositioned after every firing.

The projectile, when fired at a target the size of a castle or city, would impact on one point of a fortification and destroy it by sheer weight and kinetic energy, if it struck hard enough. Initially, projectiles were shaped by masons, who used whatever stocks of stone were available at the site of the siege. Projectiles were approximately spherical, but their size was not consistent and they often fitted poorly. As a result, the stones frequently did not travel far enough or with sufficient energy to do significant damage to the target. Poorly fitting stone balls also resulted in a lot of powder being shot from the weapon without imparting any propellant force to the projectile. Furthermore, stones could shatter on contact with thick, unyielding walls.

However, less powder was needed to propel them than heavier iron projectiles. It was only when cast-iron projectiles of a consistent calibre were introduced, along with improved gunpowder with a good rate of burn, that these deficiencies were addressed.

Early gunpowder weapons must have been inaccurate and a victim would have been counted unfortunate in the extreme to have been hit directly. But the possibility of such an incident could not be dismissed entirely. Furthermore, early cannon were not entirely fail-safe and could explode on firing. This could occur when too much black powder was used by inexperienced crews during loading, which led to a build-up of pressure inside the gun and caused the weak metal to explode with great force. Such an accident happened in 1408 during the siege of Harlech Castle, Wales, when a bombard called The King's Daughter in the artillery train of Henry V exploded. The siege action was conducted by John Talbot in command of a force of over 1,000 men supported by several bombards, at least one of which fired stone balls of 560mm diameter.

Reference to The King's Daughter is made again in 1415, when it was used at the siege of Harfleur between 18 August and 4 October. It is quite possible that the piece was manufactured at the beginning of the fifteenth century as Henry IV built up his artillery train. If this was the case, Henry V would surely have inherited the piece at his father's death in 1413. The short history of this named weapon leads to the conclusion that gunpowder artillery was either so highly prized that even damaged pieces were repaired whenever possible, in order to permit continued use, or replacements were made using the same name. The theory that weapons were repaired seems the more likely because of the high cost of manufacturing new pieces.

During the 200 years after its first recorded appearance in European history, either directly or indirectly, artillery was to inflict an increasing number of notable fatalities on the battlefield. Among the prominent figures killed by gunpowder weaponry in the fifteenth century was Lord Salisbury, who was taken by cannon-ball at the the siege of Orleans in 1429. Other early high-profile casualties of cannon fire included Giovanni de Medici in 1526, and John Talbot, Earl of Shrewsbury, whose death at the Battle of Castillon in 1453 was contributed to by a cannon-ball – his horse was killed by the ball and while he was on the ground he was attacked by a man-at-arms. The exact toll that artillery fire took of ordinary men-at-arms, such as halberdiers and archers, will never be known because their lowly status made them a peripheral battlefield statistic for the chroniclers. But in due course these infantry troops would become referred to as 'cannon-fodder', a term that would last well into the twentieth century.

It must be remembered that the longbow was still very much in use at the time and, with an accurate range of 200 yards, was still very much weapon to be reckoned with. However, the trend to replace the longbow with gunpowder weapons was already beginning to gather pace. The matchlock harquebus may have only been accurate to 50 yards, but it took considerably less time to train a man to use it than it did to create a skilled longbowmen. Less skilled troops could now be armed and put in the field. Light artillery pieces called sakers could fire a 5-pound projectile out to 350 yards and a medium culverin could fire a 17-pound projectile out to 350 yards, both with some degree of accuracy – which is to say, in the general direction of the target. The heavier gunpowder artillery weapons of the period had a maximum range of 1,700 yards with iron projectiles and 2,500 yards with stone balls, which far out-ranged archers. Even when these early cannon-balls landed in open ground, their slow rolling motion belied their sheer energy. Unprotected and poorly informed infantry must have suffered broken limbs and ruptured organs when struck by such a force.

MANUFACTURE

Cast bronze *pots de fer* may have been widely used. Examples have been uncovered at various battle and siege sites, such as the Hessian Castle at Tannenburg, which itself was destroyed by artillery fire in 1399. These discoveries show just how much the design of early pieces was influenced by the shape of bells. A number of military historians, including John Keegan in *A History of Warfare*, have put forward the theory that bell foundries were used to cast barrels in the early days of artillery development. Such foundries had been established as early as the eighth century. The artisans who worked in them understood the potential problems involved in casting difficult shapes and knew how to handle large quantities of molten metal – bronze at the time. Bell foundries continued to meet orders for artillery barrels until a demand developed for larger weapons. Then foundrymen could not cope with the increased amount of molten metal required in pouring a single-piece casting.

In order to overcome the problem of supply, artillery designers turned to coopers who were skilled in the art of making wooden barrels using staves, or strips, to build up a tube-like container. Using the same principles, coopers placed billets of heated iron around a wooden former, known as a mandrel, and secured them in place with outer hoops heated to white-hot temperatures before hammer-welding the whole structure to form a tube. As the outer hoops cooled they contracted around the assembly and held everything in place. Each billet or strip of iron was worked by a blacksmith and could take many hours to forge. The process of producing a cannon by this method had to be carried out in stages and could take many days. Depending on the length of the barrel, some weapons could have between twenty-four and thirty-five outer hoops shrunk on to them and hammer-welded to secure them in place. The central mandrel was then removed and the cylindrical barrel of the cannon was ready. Known as either 'bar and bobbin' or 'hoop and stave', this stackened method of manufacturing cannon probably gave rise to the term 'barrel' being applied to this part of the weapon.

A description from 1375 of building up a hoop-and-stave barrel appears in the writings of Jehan le Mercier, a counsellor to Philip VI of France, who was instructed to organize the manufacture of 'un grand canon de fer'. This document is probably the earliest source to recount exactly how barrels were built. It says the work required the services of three master smiths, one common smith, eight assistants and one labourer. They erected three forges in the market-place at Caen, Normandy, and set to forging 2,300 pounds (some 1,000 kilograms) of iron. Mercier tells how the barrel of the weapon was built up using longitudinal bars of iron, which had been forged into shape and then welded together using heat and hammering. Hooped bands of wrought iron were then heated and fitted over the cylinder to secure the bars in place. After this, the whole was wrapped with 40 kilograms of rope, which was tightly bound, and leather hides were stitched on top. This outer covering would have guarded the gun against the elements, but the additional protection such a pliable layer would offer to the men serving the weapon if the barrel were to burst on firing should also be considered. This work was conducted at a time when iron cost the equivalent of 5 new pence per kilogram. This would put the bill for manufacturing this particular weapon at £50 for raw materials alone; there would, of course, have been an additional cost for the labour. This was a considerable sum for the period and one that only the richest and most influential men could afford.

The design of weapons of this period did not give a proper gas-tight seal at the breech end and to overcome this problem some were manufactured to be loaded from the breech, that is to say rear, end of the gun. Weapons made in this manner were sometimes referred to as bombards and varied in size and the weight of the projectile they could fire. An example of this type of weapon recovered from the moat of Bodiam Castle, Sussex, has been calculated to have used a charge of 1.36 kilograms of black powder to fire a projectile of 375mm diameter.

Cast bronze or wrought iron were to remain the only metals available for making barrels until the sixteenth century when brass was introduced. However, there was much variation in the way the metals were worked. These differences probably stem from the fact that local metal-working traditions were followed and the skill of blacksmiths varied. Bronze could cost up to ten times more than wrought iron and was difficult to work, but it did have the advantage of lasting longer.

At this time artillery was undergoing transition in China. One of the first cannon to come to light from this period has been dated to 1288 and consists of a cast-iron barrel surrounded by several strengthening bands. It is 1 metre in length, has a calibre of just over 25mm and may have been mounted on a pivot. From this design the Chinese then turned to the stackened or hoop-and-stave method of constructing cannon barrels. It is not entirely clear who copied whom in this arms development race. One Chinese piece was referred to as the 'thousand-ball thunder cannon' and illustrations of the period show such weapons being used in the same way as contemporary European ones. *The Fire-Drake Artillery Manual* (1412) mentions a Chinese cannon that weighed 72 kilograms and refers to it as the 'long-range awe-inspiring cannon'. This weapon could be loaded with a single lead ball weighing 1.2 kilograms or a sack containing up to 100 small lead balls and was fired by a charge of 250 grams of powder. The latter type of projectile must have had a similar effect to grapeshot which was at the time unknown in Europe.

BOMBARDS AND CANNON

Larger pieces of gunpowder artillery, known as bombards, were often muzzle-loaded and because of their great size were only of real use during sieges of either castles or walled towns. Such weapons were transported on horse-drawn carts and placed either directly on the ground or on a specially constructed wooden platform. The rear or breech end of the weapon butted up against huge baulks of timber which had been hammered into the ground to keep the weapon steady during firing. Dragging such artillery around the battlefield was labour intensive and was not considered tactically important to the conduct of battle. Indeed, to haul such monster weapons without the aid of a proper carriage or wheels would have been counter-productive and an extravagant waste of resources. It was not uncommon for cannon only to fire several opening shots during a battle before being silenced because fighting had developed in front of their positions. In this situation the gunners would have to hold fire for fear of hitting their own troops.

Bombards were not made to a set size and examples of this type of weapon are known to have existed with lengths between 3.65 and 5.49 metres, and bore diameters ranging from 380 to 460mm. Many fine examples are held in museums around the world and manuscripts indicate that some bombards were known to be capable of firing a 500mm calibre cannon-ball out to ranges of some 3,000 metres. The bombard was a favoured weapon design and its use continued throughout the fifteenth and sixteenth centuries. One of the most famous ever be manufactured is known as 'Mons Meg' or 'Munce' and can still be seen today in Edinburgh Castle, Scotland. This piece of artillery is believed to have been cast in Burgundy for Duke Philip the Good between 1449 and 1450. It is indicative of the type of weapons being manufactured at the time and in a style which had already been common some fifty to eighty years earlier.

One early method of breech-loading pieces of artillery – in use at the same time as the muzzle-loaders – required that removable pots be inserted into the breech opening. A stout wooden wedge would be hammered into place to secure the pot in position. After the pre-loaded pot had been inserted into the chamber, a hot wire was applied to the touch hole to ignite the powder. Among the earliest breech-loading weapons was a piece called a peterara, which used the pre-loaded pot method and was formed using the built-up hoop-and-stave method of construction. It was not an entirely satisfactory design because gas-proof sealing could not be achieved at the breech and the staves were prone to separate after a number of firings. But, even though the design was dangerous, it was to remain in service until the mid-fifteenth century when single-piece barrel casting became possible again after advances in the techniques of handling molten metals.

The *pots de fer* method of breech loading cannon is believed to have first appeared in the 1370s. The pots were pre-loaded with a charge of gunpowder and a wad between it and the cannon-ball. Such devices could be readied in advance of any actual fighting: there is a record from 1372 of a gun for which three such pre-loaded chambers, or pots, were kept in order to speed up the rate of firing. If a number of such devices were prepared in advance, and stored in dry conditions, a relatively high rate of fire could be attained – something in the order of one shot every four or five minutes, producing ten to fifteen shots per hour, which was faster than could be achieved with normal muzzle-loading types.

The pots were quite advanced castings for the day, incorporating a handle for ease of use, into which an opening for the touch hole was bored. The walls of some pre-loaded pots were as much as 1.5 times the calibre of the projectile discharged in order to prevent the breech end of the barrel from bursting, because it was at this point that the sudden build up of gas pressure would occur when the charge was fired. Another advantage of such pots was that the weapon could be unloaded for safety when not required.

Muzzle-loaded cannon were much slower to prepare for firing and required a member of the crew to place some powder into the chamber of the cannon using a long-handled wooden ladle or scoop, followed by a wad of cloth or straw. After this was rammed down, the ball, either iron or stone, was inserted and some fine priming powder poured into the vent opening. A piece of red-hot wire was inserted into the opening to fire the weapon. After firing, a member of the crew had to swab out the barrel with a bundle of wet rags or wool on a long wooden pole to remove any unburned powder and extinguish any remaining powder that might still be smouldering. The loading sequence could then be repeated. This loading and firing sequence was to remain standard practice for centuries, being refined only slightly over the years. Indeed, it was virtually unaltered when bagged charges of gunpowder were introduced at the beginning of the eighteenth century, a change that was to speed up greatly the loading process and make the handling of gunpowder much safer. However, even though breech-loaders were faster to reload, it was far more simple to make a barrel with only one opening and muzzle-loaders continued to hold sway for centuries.

Towards the end of the fourteenth century, artillery pieces were being given different names to distinguish sizes and types of gun. Some of these titles were derived from mythical beasts and others were the names of real animals, such as falcon, saker and shrimp. In England there were bombards, falcons, sakers, culverins and basilisks. In the Burgundian Army the artillery train contained weapons called *veuglaries*, intended for use in sieges, which had a barrel length in the order of 2.54 metres with a bore between 250 and 500mm. An example of this type of weapon, mounted on a wooden frame with a pair of solid wooden wheels is to be found in the display of artillery at Castelnaud, Perigord. The Burgundian artillery train also contained bombards and breech-loaded *coulverines* (perhaps a corruption of the term culverin) of cast bronze. Another type of artillery piece was termed the serpentine (not to be confused with the early name for black powder) and was in effect a larger version of the *coulverine*. Ammunition could be either stone, shaped into round balls by masons, or dart-like projectiles, the shafts of which had leather wound around them to make them fit the barrel of the cannon. Leather-bound arrows were fired from weapons sited at Artois Castle, Rihoult, in 1342. They were also used by the castle's attackers, perhaps in the vain hope of hitting an individual.

Very small pieces were sometimes referred to as minions, possibly a corruption of the French word *mignon*, meaning something tiny. This term for an artillery piece lingered on well into the seventeenth century, when it was used to describe weapons that fired a cannon-ball weighing 2 kilograms, using 1.5 kilograms of powder, out to a range stated as '1400 paces'. But it was large balls that were used with greater effect in siege operations.

In 1399, records from the Tower of London on 'artillery and other things' state that 408 springald arrows fletched with tin and 44 bronze and iron cannon were held there. Unfortunately, no sizes are given for these pieces. Names applied to pieces of artillery began to appear on clerks' lists at the beginning of the fourteenth century and continued into the fifteenth century, when it is recorded that many non-standard pieces were 'lying about the Tower [of London]'. According to one item, the term 'bastard' was being applied to any piece that did not properly fall into a recognized category.

As is often the case with technology, either military or civilian, bigger, better and more effective models were soon demanded. When traditional metallurgical methods of casting the *pots de fer* could not meet the demand for bigger weapons, new methods of manufacturing had to be adopted. It has been calculated that within fifteen years of the first illustrations of *pots de fer*, which were castings of one piece, more complicated schemes of casting to provide two sections were being developed. This change in design was intended to provide a separate loading chamber for the black powder. The forward section of the barrel could then be loaded with the ball. Next, the two pieces were screwed together for firing. Very advanced for their period, such designs were to become popular for a time during the fifteenth century, because they allowed huge calibres to be developed. Such an increase in the size and power of weapons led to artillery being refined and developed relatively quickly.

Time and money was invested in research and development and by 1377 the Duke of Burgundy had a weapon capable of firing a round stone projectile weighing over 200 kilograms. It is known to have been used at the siege of Odriuk in that same year. In 1377, the Duke also ordered another weapon that could also fire stone shots weighing 200 kilograms, which equates to a calibre of some 560mm. Among the other artillery in the train of the Dukes of Burgundy was a weapon known as the 'Dulle Griete' ('Mad Margarite'), the great bombard of Ghent, which was cast in about 1430. It was 5.49 metres in length and fired a projectile weighing between 360 and 400 kilograms, using over 30 kilograms of gunpowder for each firing.

Elsewhere in Europe, by 1380 the force of artillery in siege warfare had become clear. In this year the Venetians attacked the fortress of Borondolo and their cannon, firing cast-iron balls, breached the walls. This was a turning point in warfare. Admittedly iron projectiles were still in service in limited numbers, but the fact that they could smash through structures with better results than stone proved the case for their continued use. Illustrations of early artillery pieces in the *Chronicles* of Froissart and the *Beauchamp Chronicles* show them being used almost exclusively against castles and towns during siege operations. The 'terrifying engines' held a fascination for illustrators of the period and by 1450 were being recorded in works such as *Chronique d'Angleterre*. The accuracy of these guns during their period of emergence can only be guessed at, but when used against targets the size of a town or castle their effect must have been impressive.

TRANSPORT

Along with advances in the manufacture of guns and cannon-balls, came the innovation of mounting artillery on wheeled carriages. Using this new equipment, heavy weaponry could be moved by horses to keep pace with an army on the march. In 1382, the army of Ghent moved against the forces of Bruges and in its train it had a number of weapons termed *ribauldequins*. These were cannon of small calibre mounted on light, wheeled carts and they appear in the accounts of the city of Bruges as early as 1339. The *ribauldequin*, also referred to as *ribaude*, comprised a number of barrels, frequently as many as seven, gathered together on a wooden base, which was sometimes mounted on a wheeled carriage. On firing, either a single barrel or a whole volley could be discharged. The pieces were pulled by draught animals to the site of battle and then manhandled into position by the crew. This allowed for better mobility on the battlefield than the large bombards had, but still only provided a marginal increase in the rate of fire. An example of the *ribauldequin* is to be found at Castelnaud, Perigord; it is mounted on a wheeled-carriage and has twelve barrels, which could be fired in volleys of three.

In 1375 Owen of Wales is recorded as having been present at the siege of St Sauveur-le-Vicomte on the Normandy coast, where for the first time some forty pieces of gunpowder artillery were used to batter the walls with balls of iron and stone, with notable effect. The walls were not breached, but the fire from these pieces harassed the defenders to such a degree that they could not offer resistance. As the chronicles of the time record: 'They were so covered by the engines that they dare not go into the town or outside the castle but stayed in the towers.' One ball is reported to have pierced the walls and entered a room in which a sick English knight lay in bed and made a noise 'as if the thunder itself had entered his chamber' as it rolled around the interior. In response to the appearance of gunpowder artillery, fortifications had to evolve to survive an attack by an enemy using heavy cannon.

The age-old response of castle builders had been to build walls as high as possible to prevent them being scaled by troops. But the first bombards showed just how easily castle walls could be defeated by cannon during a siege operation. From then on builders realized that they had to incorporate special positions into their fortification plans from which cannon could retaliate against the attackers. One of the first castles in England to incorporate such firing positions was Bodiam where the walls were pierced just a few feet above ground level and the gatehouse was adapted. The work was completed by 1390. Cities were also beginning to adapt their defences to counter the effects of cannon fire. For example, between 1375 and 1381 the west gate of Canterbury, in Kent, was built with twenty specially constructed gunports. In England initially only castles and cities in the south were adapted to incorporate cannon in their defences and had their walls strengthened to withstand bombardment. Only those in the south were vulnerable to the threat of attack by France. However, as internal conflicts, such as the Wars of the Roses, split the country so these countermeasures spread to other areas. Other European countries also began to learn that castles were vulnerable to cannon fire and strengthened them accordingly.

The gunpowder and artillery revolution did not spread rapidly at first. In 1350 Petrarch described cannon as being 'as common and familiar as other kinds of arms' on the battlefield. The appearance of new artillery must have prompted exaggerated exclamations of this nature, but it must be accepted that the increase in the use of cannon was still relatively slow. Its spread was hampered by a number of factors, not the least of which was expense. Also, it took time to train men to fire the new weapons and considerable resources to manufacture and transport them. But even if the pace of change was slow, there was no turning back.

TWO

ARTILLERY TAKES SHAPE, 1400–1500

B y the beginning of the fifteenth century gunpowder artillery weapons had been deployed on European battlefields for nearly sixty years and there was hardly a state or principality on the continent without some form of this weaponry. Weapon types varied, as did their size and the numbers of pieces that an army could deploy. The most important fact was that most armies possessed artillery, which allowed any confrontation to be conducted on a relatively equal basis. Further afield, cannon had been introduced into east Asia by the Turks, who themselves were using the expertise of European gunners.

Weapon barrels were still simple tubes built up from bundles of iron bars on to which iron hoops were shrunk. But casting techniques were improving to the point where barrels, even some of quite large size, could be fabricated as a single piece. Cannon, some of extraordinary dimensions, were still being used almost exclusively for siege operations or for the static defence of fortifications. Such large pieces could only be transported from one place to another by being dragged on sledge-type mounts or wheeled ox-drawn carts. The majority of the very large weapons were still called bombards and were often fired from mounds of earth thrown up for the purpose. Sometimes bombards were mounted on specially constructed log platforms. The angle of firing, which determined the range of the projectile, was changed by simply raising the forward end of the barrel and this adjustment was achieved either by piling more earth under the barrel or by inserting wooden wedges. The huge scale of these artillery pieces rendered them unsuitable for mobile warfare on the battlefield and once they were sited during an action it was unlikely that they would be moved. A weapon was usually screened off from enemy positions by a stout wooden shield, designed to protect the gunners from archers and artillery. The shield also prevented the opposing forces from knowing a piece was ready to fire until the last minute when the wooden screen was removed.

One of the most famous named bombards of the period is Mons Meg, now at Edinburgh Castle. It has been claimed that if this weapon was loaded with

105 pounds of gunpowder, well rammed and set at angle of 45 degrees, it could fire an iron ball out to a range of 1,408 yards or a stone ball out to 2,876 yards. The weapon was cast in two sections with rectangular slots located in the front and rear portions of the chamber into which capstan bars could be inserted to unscrew the barrel for ease of transportation and to load powder into the rear chamber. Mons Meg was presented to James II of Scotland in 1457 as a gift. James was not always so lucky in the presence of artillery and was killed at the siege of Roxborough, on 3 August 1460, when one of his cannon exploded: 'ane piece of ane misformed gune that brake in the shuting'. Another account of the incident recalls how: 'While this prince, more curious nor became the Majestie of any Kinge, did stand near-hand where the Artylliare was discharged. His thigh-bone was dung in two by a piece of miss-framed gunne that brake in the shuting, by the which he was stricken to the ground and died hastilie.'

Nuremberg had a large bombard known as 'Chriemhilde'. In all probability it was built in the early fifteenth century and is known to have been loaned out to various cities and states, obviously in return for payment. The barrel of this piece weighed 275 kilograms and required a team of twelve horses to pull it. The frame on to which it was mounted for firing was drawn by sixteen horses. In 1414 Chriemhilde is recorded as having been loaned by Frederick of Nuremberg to the Teutonic Knights to breach the walls of the castles of the Brandenburg nobility. The artillery train of Chriemhilde contained four wagons each carrying eleven stone balls and a further five wagons carried ancillary equipment and gunpowder. The danger in loaning out such artillery was that the borrowers might turn the weapon against its owners. But this was a risk that several city states were prepared to take in return for income.

Bombards were to remain in use throughout the fifteenth century but innovations did emerge. In Fort Nelson, Fareham, Hampshire, a bombard dating from about 1450 forms part of the Royal Armouries' display and is one of the finest surviving examples of this early form of weapon. It was used to fire a stone shot weighing 60 kilograms to batter fortifications during siege operations. The barrel was formed by the hoop-and-stave method and tightly stackened, but the powder chamber is of a single casting or forging. Its design is believed to have been influenced by continental cannon of the period. The weapon has three lifting rings for positioning it on its firing blocks and examination of the construction reveals the skill of the craftsmen who made it. Indeed, all the medieval weapons that have survived through to the present day serve as a mark of the gunmakers' remarkable abilities.

At this time projectiles were either iron or stone, and in an age when even base metals were expensive the extravagant use of metal for such a purpose was restricted. However, iron balls did have an advantage over stone ones in that they could be retrieved and recycled. It has been calculated that even by 1530 only 100,000–150,000 tons of iron per year were being produced in Western Europe. This level of production gave very little scope for the mass-production of cannon-balls in addition to barrels for artillery and the armour (which was still worn), swords and other edged weapons manufactured for men-at-arms.

The techniques required to cut and shape stone for cannon-balls were well developed by the mid-fifteenth century and masons' services were greatly sought after. However, demand often outstripped supply and these hand-cut balls often proved to fit cannon barrels poorly because they had been prepared in haste. This lack of attention to detail in correctly fitting the ball to the barrel led to quantities of burning gunpowder being expelled from the weapon and the projectile either falling short of the target or not striking it with sufficient energy to inflict any great damage. In fact, the slow rate of fire of these bombards and their poor hitting power meant that defenders could frequently repair damaged walls before the next shot fell. A further countermeasure that the defenders could take against the effect of artillery was to drape large fascines of wood and wool in an effort to reduce the impact. The accuracy of the artillery was also poor and it was rare that two projectiles fell in close proximity.

TACTICS

One of the earliest tactics for the use of field artillery was devised in the early fifteenth century by Jan Ziska, who used *wagenburgs*, or wagon forts, during what have become known as the Hussite Wars. The Hussites of Bohemia were the followers of Jan Hus, who was burnt at the stake in 1415 at Constance for his heretical Protestant beliefs. When the Bohemians rose in revolt, the Emperor Sigismund formed a large army to crush the peasant movement and establish his authority. The Hussites rallied under the leadership of Jan Ziska, who devised a method of forming horse-drawn wagons into defensive formations when in open territory. These wagon encampments bristled with armour, and openings were left through which men could fire their gunpowder weapons. In

1419 the Hussites attacked the city of Prague and on entering it discovered four cannon in the castle. The design of the weapons impressed Ziska so much that he ordered them to be copied and distributed throughout his forces.

The Hussite *wagenburgs* were self-contained units when on the move. An illustration dated to 1430 purports to show one such unit, complete with a mobile ore crushing device for making iron, which in turn would allow the Hussites to make and repair their own cannon. The tactic of placing armed men either in the wagons or the gaps between provided all-round defence. Supported by strategically placed light cannon, they brought their combined fire to bear in the direction from which they were most threatened. Such a concentration of forces consistently defeated attacks made on the *wagenburgs* and once the impetus of an onslaught had been broken, Ziska's forces sallied forth to deliver a counter-attack, which was often pressed home with considerable zeal. One such attack mounted by the Hussites occurred during the winter of 1422, when they found themselves isolated outside their main base at Kutna Hora. On this occasion Ziska's troops mounted a night attack against their besiegers and succeeded not only in penetrating the enemy's position, but also in breaking the opposition's will to fight. After Ziska died in 1424 the Hussites' success continued. They persisted through the campaigns of 1426–7 and even pushed into Germany, where they mounted raiding parties for the next five years.

Just as religious difference prompted the creation of the Hussite forces, so it led to their downfall. At the Battle of Lipani in 1434 the more extreme Taborites were defeated by the moderates and this led to the re-establishment of the monarchy, because the moderates were ready to accept the toleration that the Holy Roman Empire offered. But that was not the end of the *wagenburg* as a tactical device, because it was taken up by the Hungarians who modified it for their own purposes in their campaigns against the Ottoman Turks. Ziska's tactical thinking did not lead to the introduction of light field artillery, but he had shown how light cannon could be used during offensive or defensive operations to support combined arms on the battlefield.

MEHOMET THE CONQUEROR

The techniques of gunmaking and the methods of handling the crude and unstable black powder mixture improved between 1400 and 1500. In addition, the use of bombards was mastered. They became increasingly effective in both the attack and defence of fortified places. Sultan Mehomet II, the Conquerer, of Turkey (1432–81) has been called the first great gunner in history. Under his tutelage the Turkish artillery train grew to such an impressive size that by the time of the siege of Constantinople in 1453 it numbered seventy pieces, of which nineteen were particularly large, including one 19-ton monster, capable of firing stone balls up to 1,500 pounds for a distance of more than a mile. This artillery train was deployed in fourteen batteries containing fifty-six guns and there were fourteen heavy cannon in support. The bombardment of the triple walls surrounding Constantinople began on 5 April 1453 and lasted fifty-five days – the first massed artillery bombardment in history. The success of the operation has been credited as much to poor Byzantine preparations for the defensive use of cannon as to the power of the Ottoman siege train. Whatever the case, the outcome was impressive enough to justify Sir Charles Oman calling the action 'the first event of supreme importance whose result was determined by the power of artillery'.

Because the effects of weapon recoil during firing were still misunderstood and because of the need to put the cannon back in position after each shot, some large weapons could fire only seven or eight rounds per day. Estimates on the expenditure of ammunition during the great siege varies, but the figure of 4,000 balls fired is perhaps the most accurate and gives an average of ten shots per gun per day for the duration of the fighting. The first breach was made in the walls on 18 April, but it was not wide enough for the attacking Turks, who were repulsed by the defenders, and the damage was hastily repaired. It appears that treachery, rather than artillery, opened the way into the city in the end: an insider was persuaded to open a small unguarded postern gate, thereby allowing the forces of Mehomet to enter. The historian Edward Gibbon remarked that: 'after a siege of fifty-three days . . . Constantinople, which had defied the power of Chosroes, the Chagan and the Caliphs, was irretrievably subdued by the arms of Mohammed the Second'. Under the continued leadership of Mehomet the Turks were able to advance on all fronts, even reaching into Italy by 1481, the year of his death.

In the East only the Ottomans paid significant attention to developing and refining gunpowder artillery at the time, even resorting to the use Western experts, such as gunner Master George, who assisted in the siege of Rhodes in 1480. For unknown reasons, George deserted his Turkish masters and went over to the Christian side, where he was hanged on charges of being a spy. At Rhodes, however, the defenders of the city put up such stout resistance that the Turks abandoned their operations and were not to return until 1522. The defenders of Rhodes were not the only ones to successfully withstand the might of the forces of Mehomet II. In July 1456 the Turks besieged the city of Belgrade in Hungary, but were beaten off by the actions of John Hunyadi, a Transylvanian nobleman who had exceptional experience of war. The forces led by Hunyadi even succeeded in capturing some artillery from the Turks, who either could not or would not return until 1526.

A number of guns in service with the Turkish artillery train are believed to have been the work of Urban, a gun-founder working in either Wallachia or Hungary, who is understood to have cast some weapons at Adrianople. Some of these artillery pieces can be termed 'super-bombards', each requiring sixty oxen to move them. They rested on a wagon formed from thirty carriages. Over 200 men were required to keep these weapons on the road and serve as guards. A further 250 were employed as labourers to level the roads along which they were to travel and effect repairs where necessary. Moving these guns was a slow process and records indicate it took two months to transport one 200 kilometres, an average of just 3.3 kilometres per day. These cannon could fire balls weighing 500 kilograms with a diameter of 760mm, but it took between two and three hours to load and prepare each piece for firing. This included having to put the weapon back on the frame from which it had fallen during firing.

The Turks realized early on that it was not always practical to haul such large bombards over long distances, unless the objective could not be achieved without them. They were, however, ready, willing and able to transport large quantities of metal ore to the site of a siege and cast the weapon in camp. One such piece was cast in two pieces by Munir Ali, who produced a weapon that could be screwed together by means of capstan bars for firing and then unscrewed for loading powder into the chamber and for ease of transport, in the same way as Mons Meg. Three years after the Turks cast this massive 18-ton piece, the history of how it came into being was recorded by Kritoboulos. He recounts how Munir Ali first gathered together a mass of the purest clay which was made malleable by many days of kneading by a host of workers. To this were added lengths of hemp and linen for strength. It was then formed into the mandrel for the weapon's bore, which tapered to one-third the size at the chamber. This mandrel was then set up like a pillar, around which was moulded another layer, with a dividing space of 240mm between the two surfaces, to give a cylindrical shape. The cylinder was then supported by a framework of timber and earth. Two furnaces were in constant use for three days and nights to melt sufficient bronze for casting the great barrel. The molten metal was poured into the clay mould and the mandrel was covered to an extra depth of 800mm. On cooling the bronze contracted from the clay covering, which was broken away, and the barrel was then ornately decorated and polished.

As part of the preparation for firing, the gun was mounted on a heavy timber framework which butted up to a solid wall because the gunners believed, erroneously as it transpired, that the recoil would upset the gun's already inaccurate aim. After loading a powder charge of 136 kilograms the gunners tamped in tightly fitting wooden plugs, which could only be removed by firing the great weapon. Then a stone cannon-ball of 294 kilograms was rolled into the barrel. The ball could be shot out to ranges of 1.6 kilometres. The weapon was called Elipolos, the 'City-taker', and it was claimed a single shot from it could reduce a castle tower. The great cannon, which was the seventieth ranged against the walls of Constantinople in 1453, now resides in Fort Nelson, Fareham, Hampshire, where it is part of the Royal Armouries' display.

An interesting adjunct of the great weapons of Mehomet II is that in 1807 an English fleet under Sir John Duckworth was sailing through the Dardanelles in an attempt to invest Constantinople when it was fired on by great guns sited at the forts of Kilid-Bahr and Chanak, to the north and south of the straits respectively. Several ships in the fleet were damaged by these guns which were of 350 years vintage. The lesson to be learned is that guns might be old, but they can still be dangerous, a fact that has been reiterated many times, including during the twentieth century when artillery pieces dating from the First World War were used again between 1939 and 1945. In 1868 Britain's Board of Ordnance acquired examples of Mehomet's cannon, one of which is thought to have fired on Sir John Duckworth's fleet and now resides in Fort Nelson, Fareham.

Another type of artillery piece that Mehomet deployed during the great siege of Constantinople was a huge mortar. It was used to fire shot indirectly into the city's interior at a very high angle of trajectory, where the plunging effect would cause considerable damage and injury. Most mortars at this time were no more than large metal pots secured to a firm wooden base. They are known to have been used against enemy shipping venturing too close to shore, although they were more likely to scare the vessel away rather than achieve a direct hit. It is understood that Mehomet's huge mortar scored at least one direct hit on a ship as it lay at anchor off the Golden Horn, but this was more by luck than judgement. Ranging was determined by observing the fall of shot and varying the amount of gunpowder used to propel the projectile. Mortars were also being used in Europe at about this time, but they were referred to as bombards.

An experimental German-designed artillery piece from the mid-fifteenth century appears in the Codex Germanicus 600, which is held in the Staatsbibliothek, Munich. This manuscript shows a man standing by a turntable on which are mounted four short barrels set at 90 degree angles to one another. It is believed that each piece would be loaded and spun into action for firing, thereby providing four shots in quick succession. A device at the base of the turntable gives the impression that the platform could also be angled to alter the range and thus engage targets at varying distances. It is a rather fanciful notion and does not appear to have been seriously pursued.

MANUFACTURING AND TESTING

By the fifteenth century most cannon were designed as muzzle-loaders, which is to say that the whole process of loading the powder and ball was carried out at the front of the cannon using long-handled wooden tools. Breech-loading bombards were also still in common use, where their relatively high rate of fire was considered useful during sieges. These breech-loaders remained notoriously prone to exploding and tearing themselves apart. This was the result of hairline fractures, which were faults present during manufacture either by casting or by the stackened method of hoops and staves; the cracks were further weakened during firing. Molten metal, often no more than lead, was sometimes poured into these fractures in an attempt to seal the barrel of the cannon. Other accidents were caused in part by a lack of adequate sealing at the breech (or obturation as modern artillerymen call it); this allowed propelling gases to escape to the rear. Their unreliability soon led to such weapons becoming unpopular. Barrels were all smoothbore at this time but there is some evidence to indicate that early attempts at rifling may have been conducted in Germany by the end of the fifteenth century.

The strength of a cannon barrel could not be known. Some had inherent defects from the time they were built and others weakened during service to the point where they could self-destruct with terrible consequences for the men serving them. Frequently a cannon was tested for strength simply by being loaded and fired with ever-increasing charges to the point where it was operating to greater tolerances than it had been designed to withstand. If it survived this test it was passed as fit for normal service.

The records for Basle show that in 1375 a gun was tested in such a manner outside the city walls in an area set aside for proving. In England cannon under trial were referred to as 'weak, broken, noisom, used up and broken and wasted in trials and assay'. It was essential that cannon barrels were tested to their limits, because failure in battle could mean the difference between defeat and victory. Cannon that had been proved were given a special 'proof' mark on the barrel. This usually incorporated the sign of the recognized proving authority or the arms of the town where it had been cast and tested. Some less scrupulous proving bodies merely examined the barrels by sight and did not bother to go to the trouble of conducting a scientific examination.

Improvements in the method of manufacturing gunpowder put increasing pressure on barrels. The means by which the compound was produced became known as 'corning' and was developed in France sometime during the fifteenth century. The 'corning' method involved mixing the three constituent ingredients together into a wet paste, which was then allowed to dry into flat 'cakes'. These 'cakes' could be milled into crumb-like granules using wooden rollers. The granules were then graded according to size. The process allowed regular-sized grains to be produced and this meant the efficiency of the powder was greatly improved because burning rates were constant. But improved gunpowder did not solve the problem that a lot of the chemical energy released on firing was lost either as propelling gases vented forward around the projectile, an effect known as windage, or as still-burning gunpowder blasted from the cannon. These defects were to be partly redressed when iron projectiles of an almost standard calibre replaced roughly hewn stone balls.

Men serving the artillery now began to have special titles. As early as 1411 the French were referring to them as *cannoniers*, an expression that was adopted by several other countries. They were, in effect, the master gunners of their day. At the turn of the fourteenth into the fifteenth century the crewmen of a cannon were referred to as bombardiers, a term believed to have been derived from the Latin *bombus*, meaning a muffled sound. In fact, bombardier is a title still used in many artillery branches of armies around the world today, including the Royal Regiment of Artillery in the British Army.

During the 1400s the Dukes of Burgundy – Philip the Good and his son, Charles, formerly the Count of Charolais and called Charles le Téméraire

(Charles the Bold) – took the lead in incorporating a regular unit of artillery into the army structure. To command this branch of the army they began to appoint noblemen as *maitres d'artillerie*. Such appointments were quite logical: men of high office would have had a better education and thus would have been more capable of understanding the workings of these new weapons of war than the average man-at-arms. Another move the Dukes made was to site all their cannon together instead of placing solitary weapons around the battlefield without thought to tactical advantage. They realized that by grouping artillery in batteries they could increase firepower and make cannon more effective against an enemy. But despite their superior artillery, the Burgundians were to prove no match for the Swiss, who had their own ideas about artillery deployment and support, and enjoyed great mobility on the battlefield.

As the fifteenth century progressed so too did the skill of the artillerymen and the quality of the cannon. During this period the art and craft of designing guns, and the manufacture and employment of artillery was usually handed down from gunsmith to apprentice. This meant the circle of the initiated was kept intentionally small and knowledge was transferred by word of mouth and hands-on experience. But all this was to change with the appearance of the first books on the subject. By 1420 the first written works on artillery and methods of casting barrels for cannon were beginning to appear, but they were not to be universally circulated until more than 100 years later. One work of this time is the *Firework Book*, written in Germany, which explains how a master smith should be a 'thoughtful employer, and should be able to make all the chemical products appropriate to his craft, as well as firedarts, fireballs and other pyrotechnic devices that could be used to kill or deter an enemy'. It was obvious to most military minds that the accurate use of artillery was already too much for a single man to remember. The master gunner had to be skilled in mathematics, reading and writing. At this period few people had sufficient technical or mathematical skills and competence: gunners were in great demand but few were freely available, most being in the direct employ of either a city or state.

Printing from movable type was invented in Germany in about 1455 and with its introduction the availability of books on the subject of gunnery grew wider. Reference works on the otherwise obscure secrets of the gunner's art spread and allowed military ideas to disseminate. Works on artillery were written by Valturius in 1472, Pliny in 1476 and Frontinus in 1480. It is safe to assume that these books would have been read and digested by scientific minds of the day, including Leonardo de Vinci. In fact, in his own *Codex Atlanticus*, da Vinci claims to have a working knowledge of the art of war. He lays out plans that he may have seen from other sources, as well as his own original ideas. It is true he must have been aware of the types of artillery deployed by Mehomet II at the sieges of Constantinople in 1453 and Rhodes in 1480. Some rather fanciful designs created by other theorists also appeared, including the use of horses to *push* a cart, on which was to be mounted one or several weapon barrels. In the years to come books would ensure the spread of the art and practices of gunnery.

THE HUNDRED YEARS WAR

Serious improvement in very heavy siege artillery took time, but the latent power of the weapons was ably demonstrated by the artillerymen of Henry V of England during the king's campaigns in France between 1415 and 1422. The size of some of the artillery pieces in question was quite extraordinary. Examples of stone balls measuring 600mm in diameter, which were fired during the time of the siege of Falaise, have been uncovered. Fighting erupted in 1415 when Henry V attacked Calais and captured the town through the use of artillery.

At the siege of Harfleur between 18 August and 4 October 1415, a defending force of only 400 French manned the walls surrounding the town. There were twenty-six towers set into the walls at intervals and each of these was pierced with openings through which artillery and hand-guns could be fired. An English account of the siege reports how the towers were equipped 'with narrow chinks and places full of holes through which they [the French] might annoy us with their tubes, which we in English call "gunnys"'. Henry V himself is understood to have sited his great siege guns ringing the town. He then retired to a nearby hill to watch the proceedings, which were conducted by his brother, Humphrey. The King's Daughter, along with other pieces of artillery, inflicted some damage on the walls, but the rate of fire was so slow that the defenders could repair the damage at night. However, the English then introduced a shift system to serve their artillery and were able to maintain the bombardment of the city day and night. With no relieving force, the town was left with no option but to surrender to Henry's army, which at the beginning of the siege had numbered over 10,000. The English had suffered some 2,000 losses, mainly to disease, and a further 2,000 men were dismissed as being too sick to carry on the campaign. He moved his army to engage the French at Agincourt on 25 October, an action that brought another triumph of the English longbowmen over the finest French cavalry. It is now believed that the French probably had some artillerymen in their lines at the battle, with some historians suggesting they were located among the crossbowmen. If this was indeed the case, the densely packed ranks of ordinary men-at-arms must have prevented the guns from being used properly, and like the earlier English use of cannon at Crecy in 1346, the effect of these weapons on the field of battle goes largely unrecorded.

Henry V's artillery train was to see extensive action during several sieges in the Normandy region. In 1417 Henry and his brother the Duke of Clarence besieged Caen, which at the time was one of the greatest towns in France. Its capture was important to Henry's strategy, because it controlled the entrance to the River Orne. In July Henry encircled the town with his batteries of artillery, and earthworks were thrown up in front of the weapons to protect the gunners from the French. The artillery opened fire on the walls. By elevating the barrels, the gunners were able to fire iron and marble balls into the town where the force of their impact crushed buildings and smashed equipment. Using incendiary projectiles, Henry's artillery was also able to start fires and smaller English weapons were brought closer to the town so they could fire along the gaps between the buildings. The French artillery was lighter, but had a higher rate of return fire and was far more accurate. Nevertheless, it could not match the sustained fire of the English guns. They tore great rents in the town's walls, which had been built in a pre-gunpowder age, and breaches were made at several sites. But, again, artillery did not decide the outcome of the siege. After a number of calls for surrender were rejected by the French, Henry assaulted the town from one direction while Clarence attacked from another. Caen was entered and a great slaughter ensued, until Henry called a halt to the senseless killing of the civilian population.

Richard Beauchamp, Earl of Warwick, was with the forces at the siege and the chronicles he compiled are both enlightening and illustrative, because they provide a glimpse, albeit small, of how artillery was used in the time of Henry. For example, a silverpoint drawing made either during or shortly after the siege shows a breech-loading cannon being armed with a pre-loaded pot. The man loading the weapon is depicted in full armour and appears to be receiving instruction from a second man, who is also in full armour. The barrel of the weapon rests on a wooden board which is simply laid directly on the ground and protected to the front by a wooden palisade. Such weapons firing at low angles would have weakened a town's walls by undercutting them to the point where they would collapse under their own weight. This standard tactic was employed by artillerymen many times to breach walls. Other towns invested by Henry's artillery included Rouen in 1418; it had defensive artillery of exceptional quality and was able to hold out for five months. The siege of Cherbourg in 1419, despite the best effort of Henry's gunners, was to last six months.

The greatest advances in gunmaking and gunnery during the fifteenth century began in France in about 1440 and were instituted by brothers Jean and Gaspard Bureau. They made great strides in the evolution of artillery and examined how it could best be used on the battlefield. The Bureaus used their cannon to batter down the walls of English-held castles with amazing rapidity. Jean was the more eminent of the two and is described as 'a citizen of Paris, a man of small stature but of purpose and daring, particularly skilled and experienced in the use of artillery'. However, his work in the field of artillery was not always in the interests of his French masters: he is known to have served with the English in the role of master of artillery. This mercenary service with the English must have given him an understanding of their ways of conducting war and he was able to use this knowledge to his advantage. Under the direction of the Bureau brothers the sieges conducted by French forces during the reconquest of Normandy in 1449–50 were relatively brief affairs. At the siege of Harfleur in 1449 a single shot from one of the Bureaus' cannon went straight through the ramparts of the castle. The French siege of Bordeaux, following the English defeat at Castillon in 1453, was prosecuted by the full might of the French artillery train under Jean Bureau. It lasted some ten weeks between late July and October 1453. During this time the Bureaus' artillery was deployed at no fewer than sixty sieges and the power of their pieces became legendary. They provided Charles VII with an 'irresistible' artillery train with which to recover his kingdom. The campaign was largely financed by Jacques Coeur, who supplied money and credit, no doubt with an eye to profit in the future.

By the end of the century, artillery had rendered traditionally built medieval fortifications all but obsolete. The tall, straight walls were prime targets to be attacked by gunners and such designs left nowhere in which large cannon suitable for counter-battery operations could be sited.

Meanwhile, on the battlefield at Formigny in 1450, the French showed they had learned many lessons. They abandoned the tactics used at Crecy and Agincourt and deployed well beyond the range of the English archers. They moved up two culverins, long-range weapons of relatively light design, and deployed them to cover the flanks of the English Army of 5,000 men, commanded by Sir Thomas Kyriel and Sir Matthew Gough. Some culverins could fire a 17-pound shot 400 yards with a degree of accuracy and the ball could carry out to a maximum range of 2,500 yards, which greatly out-ranged the English longbow. The French artillery force was also armed with bombards, which had earlier been emplaced for siege operations and were now resited to cover the directions from which English reinforcements might approach. When these weapons opened fire on English positions, artillery achieved a significant outcome on the battlefield for the first time. The English forces attacked the guns and succeeded in seizing and holding them for a while, but a French counter-attack drove the English off and recaptured the weapons. Further attacks by the French carried the day and some 4,000 English were left dead on the battlefield. Artillery, no matter how inaccurate it might be against infantry in the open, was now a force to be reckoned with, and over the following three years its importance to the French Army was to grow. By 1453 Bordeaux had been regained by the French and the Hundred Years War was finally at an end, leaving only the town of Calais in English hands.

The Battle of Castillon fought on 17 July 1453 is of particular note because it was one of the last set-piece encounters of the Hundred Years War and proved the superiority of French artillery. At this engagement Jean Bureau assembled a French artillery park containing 300 guns deployed in an area 640 metres wide by 183 metres deep. The English commander Sir John Talbot, supported by at least 700 hand-gunners, impetuously charged this mass of artillery and during the course of the action he lost his life. A cannon-ball struck his horse which fell, pinning him to the ground. Then, according to chroniclers, Talbot was killed by a man-at-arms with an axe. The English attackers were repulsed with great loss of life.

French victory in the Hundred Years War is often attributed to their advanced development and incisive use of gunpowder weapons. This is apparent both in the use of heavy siege artillery, which the Bureau brothers supplied to King Charles, and at a tactical level in engagements including Formigny and Castillon, where artillery out-ranged the English longbow which had dominated the battlefield for so long. But it could also be argued that the English refusal to change tactics contributed as much to their final defeat as the French artillery.

INNOVATIONS AND DESIGN

This period in the development artillery truly belongs to the French, for they took the lead in designing the new field pieces that were to be widely used on the battlefield by the final decade of the fifteenth century. According to C. Duffy in his book *Siege Warfare*:

> French craftsmen and bell-founders . . . evolved a cannon that was recognizably the same creature that was going to decide battles and sieges for nearly four hundred years to come. The heavy 'built-up' bombard, firing a stone ball from a wooden platform that had laboriously to be lifted on to a cart whenever it changed position, had been replaced by a slender homogeneous bronze-cast tube, no more than eight feet long, its proportions carefully calculated to absorb the progressively diminishing shock of discharge from breech to muzzle. It fired wrought iron balls, heavier than their stone equivalents but, because of that, of three times greater destructive effect for a given bore.

These designs began to appear in about 1460, when relatively light cannon of cast bronze were mounted on two-wheeled carriages pulled by horses. The cast bronze barrels, although expensive, were much safer to use and the design soon replaced the older welded-and-bound iron cannon. The two-wheeled carriages that replaced earlier four-wheeled versions also allowed the gunners to manoeuvre the weapons more easily by hand. Charles VIII of France took a force of between 266 and 300 such cannon to Italy in 1494; of these, 70 were exceptionally big. They were used to considerable effect against various targets, including high-walled castles. One of the first fortifications to fall to the French artillery was the Neapolitan castle of Monte San Giovanni, which had withstood a siege conducted by traditional methods for seven years. Within three hours of the opening shot, the castle had fallen to the forces of Charles VIII. Within three months, Italy was in his grasp.

Italian architects, such as Giuliano da Sangallo, had been preparing for such an eventuality and since the 1480s had been laying down advanced defensive measures. One of the first of the new designs was a feature called the 'angle bastion', which was incorporated into the defences at the Poggio Imperiale in Tuscany. It comprised thick walls that were squat in shape and had broad, triangular platforms, on which counter-battery artillery could be sited. These bastions were well angled to present glancing surfaces from which, it was hoped, the cannon-balls of attacking artillery would ricochet. A city ringed by such defences supporting one another presents a formidable target that has little or no 'dead' ground at the base of its walls.

The French gunners' favourite tactic was to fire cannon-balls, preferably made of iron, at the base of castle walls in order to smash gaping holes in them. When the holes were large enough, the weakened walls collapsed. This technique was so effective in breaching defences that it continued to be used until well into the sixteenth century. But the angle bastion defences at the Poggio Imperiale demanded a new approach. Long-range artillery fired at the defences, permitting the infantry to move in while engineers and pioneers moved the lighter field pieces closer to the walls. Then an assault could be made. The campaign was described by Niccolo Machiavelli as being conducted 'chalk in hand', because whatever Charles VIII marked on the map, his gunners soon secured for him.

The rate of pay for French gunners at this time was some five to six *livres* per day. The French force has been described as the 'first modern army' because all three service arms – infantry, cavalry and artillery – cooperated on the battle-field in coordinated tactics and were supported by pioneers and engineers.

With their field artillery mounted on wheeled carriages, the French had the mobility necessary to deploy weaponry around the battlefield and unlimber it with considerable ease. The speed with which this newly developed type of artillery could be brought into action from a column of march was displayed at the Battle of Fornovo in 1495, along with another simple but effective device known as the trunnion. Forming an integral part of the barrel, trunnions are horizontal axles that protrude from either side and rest in recesses on the carriage, thereby supporting the weight of the barrel and allowing the force of the recoil on firing to be passed into the wheeled carriage, which would then roll back. The design of the trunnion allowed for the mounting of cannon on permanent wheeled carriages and gave improved aiming and accuracy in ranging because, for the first time, the barrel could be elevated independently of the carriage. This was a marked improvement on earlier, awkward methods of raising and lowering the muzzle or breech of the weapon. The idea caught the attention of gunmakers in other countries and it soon became universal practice to cast barrels with trunnions as part of the design. Older barrel designs were updated by retro-fitting devices called trunnion rings. In effect these were hoops with trunnions which were shrunk on to the barrels to adapt them for use on a wheeled carriage.

The French were not the only ones mounting cannon on wheeled carriages: it seems that as early as 1456 the Scottish mounted at least two cannon on vehicles, referred to in an act of the Scottish parliament as 'carts of war' for conveying light artillery. However, rather than having two separate barrels these weapons may have been double-barrelled cannon, looking like a giant double-barrelled shotgun like those in Castle Wemyss in Fife, Scotland, which houses forty-two weapons of this type. These muzzle-loaded pieces are of very simple construction and vary in calibre and barrel length. They were all manufactured by the same method, that is from wrapped wrought iron banded with iron rings for strength. Some are fitted with trunnions and there is some speculation that they may have been made by a very capable local blacksmith, perhaps even working within the castle grounds.

Other European countries, including Austria, should not be overlooked in the story of the development of artillery at this time. Bombards used by the Austrian Army were referred to as *Steinbuchse*. A surviving example is the weapon known as 'Der grosse Pumhardt von Steyr', which is understood to date from around 1425. It was made using the hoop-and-stave method and is, in effect, a massive siege perrier capable of firing balls of nearly 900mm in diameter. It has a narrow powder chamber and is believed to have been fired from the ground, being propped up at the muzzle end of the barrel by blocks of wood to give a rudimentary form of elevation. The 'Pumhardt' in some ways resembled the mortars that were to appear later in the period. It is fitted with lifting rings to facilitate loading on to a wagon for transportation and weighs almost 10 tons.

The introduction of lighter weapons mounted on wheeled carriages from which they could also be fired, as in the case of the French developments, went some way towards easing transport problems. However, moving really large pieces of artillery, some of which were truly cumbersome devices, was still extremely difficult. Some English cannon were so large at this time that they required an average of fifty horses to haul them. It was no mean feat of logistics to shift these massive weapons around the battlefield and the problem was compounded when great distances had to be traversed on campaign. In addition, fifteenth-century roads were little more than well-worn tracks along which passed all manner of traffic. During the summer, the surfaces of these routes were firm and could be travelled fairly easily, but in wet conditions they became quagmires, made worse by the thousands of passing feet and wheels of an army on the move.

Artillery was by now an accepted part of many armies and the men serving the cannon had gained recognition as professionals. However, the drivers who handled the transport of the cannon were still civilians under contract to the army. This arrangement often led to complications. If the campaign appeared to be becoming too dangerous, the civilian drivers, who also owned the draught animals, would often decamp, taking all transport and their assistants with them, which left the artillery stranded. This contractual arrangement with civilians was not to end until late in the sixteenth century, when drivers began to be enlisted as part of the army and were paid a soldier's wage.

The men serving the cannon were obliged to march alongside their weapons, which meant that a slow walking pace was the best speed artillery trains could make. Horses were used as draught animals to haul the guns, but their progress was slowed by pulling many tons over poorly maintained routes. Oxen were more hardy beasts of burden, but their speed was poor. It was difficult for the master of artillery to choose between horse or oxen as draught animals and he often used what was most readily available. Oxen did have an additional use to the army because they could be slaughtered for food if necessary.

Ammunition and gunpowder were transported in separate wagons and, depending on the capabilities of the transport teams, artillery could filter onto the battlefield or siege site long after the main elements of the army had deployed.

The construction and maintenance of wheeled wooden carriages demanded the skilled services of carpenters and labourers. The first gun carriages were very similar to those used for other purposes, except in size, and were fitted with large wheels. At first these were solid in design and only later became spoked. The two-wheeled gun carriages increasingly used during the fifteenth century had to incorporate light weight with strength so that cannon could be moved around by men alone and yet survive the stresses induced by firing. The carriage for a cannon firing a 4.5 kilogram shot comprised 'cheek' or side bracket pieces that took the direct weight of the barrel when mounted. These had interstices on their inner faces which aligned with lugs on the piece of the vehicle known as the trail: the latter rests on the ground as a point of balance and the gun is towed from the trail end. The bed, which formed part of the trail, allowed the axle-tree, to which the wheels were fitted, to be secured in place. All the wooden components were shaped by hand and interlocked fully. They were strengthened at the joints by metal bands and bolted into place. These carriages were eventually to evolve into three distinct types to deal with the three types of land warfare: garrison, siege and field.

By looking at the sizes and weights of fifteenth-century artillery, it has been calculated that some 15,000 horses with 3,000 wagons would have been required to move an artillery train containing 100 cannon and 60 mortars. The best speed such a mass could make would be in the order of 3 kilometres per hour and it would be stretched out over 24 kilometres of road. The whole column would therefore take many hours to pass one spot.

It is not difficult to believe that an artillery train of such size existed at this time. At the Battle of Morat on 22 June 1476, the Swiss are thought to have deployed some 10,000 culverins of various calibres, including some hand-held types, when they fought the Burgundian Army. At this engagement, Charles the Bold, leading a Burgundian Army of 20,000 men, besieged Morat, near Bern, and Fribourg. The Burgundians constructed palisaded defensive positions and dug trenches. However, because of poor weather conditions, the Burgundians entrenched only one-fifth of their army, the remainder being encamped nearby. The Swiss Army of 25,000, supported by 1,000 German and Austrian cavalry, attacked with great rapidity and inflicted losses of between 7,000 and 10,000 on Charles's forces. The two sides clashed again on 5 January the following year at the Battle of Nancy, where Charles the Bold was killed. The war continued until 28 December 1478, when another Swiss victory at the Battle of Giornico concluded the campaign.

During the war the Swiss made great use of captured Burgundian artillery. They acquired from the enemy large numbers of wrought-iron field guns mounted on two-wheeled carriages. The barrels of these guns were bound with iron hoops for strength, had an average length of 1.58 metres and a calibre of 75mm. The overall length of each weapon was 3.6 metres and they were light enough to be hauled by only two men using ropes attached to the trail of the carriage. Elevation of the cannon was achieved by means of a bracket on the side of the carriage into which could be fitted pegs to support the framework on which the barrel was directly mounted, thereby allowing it to be pivoted up and down. It was a simple but effective means of elevation and would almost certainly have been recognizable to the artillerymen of the Napoleonic Wars 350 years later.

Just before war between the Swiss and the Burgundians erupted, Charles the Bold had conducted the desultory siege of Neuss from 20 July 1474 to 13 June 1475. The Burgundian Army of 30,000 had what was generally regarded as the best artillery train in Europe and used it to invest Neuss, near Dusseldorf, the rebel city of the Archbishop of Cologne. The city had 3,000 'stout defenders with good artillery' who organized themselves into 'shifts', fighting, eating and sleeping in rota. The besiegers settled down to starve the city out, but the defenders went on to strict rationing, strengthened walls and moats and even stripped the lead covering from roofs to cast into cannon-balls. A relieving force approached the city in May 1475 but did not attack, and the Burgundian Army withdrew two months later, contented that honour had been satisfied.

The Dukes of Burgundy had not only the Swiss to contend with, but also the French. In his book *A History of Warfare*, John Keegan states that:

In 1477 Louis XI of France further extended his area of control over his ancestral lands by using cannon against the castles of the dukes of Burgundy. By 1478, as a result, the French royal house was fully in control of its own territory for the first time since Carolingian days six centuries earlier, and ready to erect a centralized government – supported by a fiscal system in which cannon were the ultimate tax-collectors from refractory vassals.

Castles and fortified towns were now being built or remodelled with defence against cannon in mind. The most common defence technique was the creation of cannon-ports in the lower floors of towers and the provision of smaller guns, some of which were fitted on swivel mounts in the upper levels of the castle. These swivel-mounted cannon, sometimes called slings, were usually of the breech-loading type using the pre-loaded pots which were secured in place by a transverse wedge. They were fitted with a tiller-like projection at the breech-end to aid aiming and could be 1.5 metres in length. They served mainly in an anti-personnel role. Such weapons were still to be found in use in the Far East during the seventeenth century. In an effort to reduce vulnerability to cannon fire, walls were made thicker at the base, and permanent outworks were constructed at a distance from the main walls, where cannon and lighter firearms could be emplaced by defenders during a siege. These modifications were not universal and were generally rare outside France and Italy. But in England it was not deemed necessary to strengthen existing castles, apart from those along the English–Scottish border. However, this thinking was to change within two years of the end of the Hundred Years War as the English turned on themselves and entered into a civil war for the throne. The ensuing series of battles has come to be known as the Wars of the Roses.

It was not just in the wars of large European countries that artillery had an impact. The Channel Islands, a handful of English territorial possessions lying just off the coast of northern France, were considered to be extremely vulnerable to attack and were armed accordingly. Between 1435 and 1436 the fortification known as either Gorey Castle or Mont Orgueil on the island of Jersey was repaired and strengthened, possibly to accept cannon. The French did attack and seize the island, holding it from 1461 until 1468, during which time Pierre de Breze, Count of Maulevrier, Grand Seneschal of Normandy, ordered that Guy de Briouse, Governor of Gorey Castle, draw up a list of the castle's ordnance. This catalogue, compiled in 1462, states that he inspected 'often all the armaments of the place, cannon, culverins, crossbows, cannon-balls and powder'. The island was secured once more for England in 1468 by Vice-Admiral Richard Harliston and Philip de Carteret, and the Harliston Tower was built to guard the entrance to Mont Orgueil Castle and was designed to allow for cannon to be mounted within it.

DEVELOPMENTS IN CHINA

Even though they were operating in almost complete isolation, fifteenth-century Chinese artillerists came up with new designs that paralleled some European achievements and at times even overtook them. During the sixth year in T'ien Sun's reign, 1462, it is recorded that 1,200 gun carriages were built. Only three years later, in 1465 during the first year of Ch'eng-Hua's reign 500 carriages for cannon were built and 300 'great general guns' were manufactured. Such figures, along with other statistics, lead to the conclusion that Chinese methods of manufacturing artillery were more advanced than in Europe and capable of output on a scale that could almost be called mass-production. The Chinese cannon termed the 'great general gun' is described as follows in *The Fire-Drake Artillery Manual* of 1412:

Among the large firearms there is none that is greater than the 'great general gun'. Its barrel used to weigh 80 kilograms, and was attached to a stand made of bronze weighing 600 kilograms . . . Yeh Meng-Hsiung changed the weight of the gun to 150 kilograms and doubled its length to 6 feet [almost 2m], but eliminated the stand, and it is now placed on a carriage with wheels. When fired it had a range of 800 paces. A large lead shell weighing 3.5 kilograms is called a 'grandfather shell' and the next shell of medium size, weighing 1.8 kilograms, is a 'son shell', while a smaller shell weighing 600 grams is a 'grandson shell'. There are also 200 small bullets each weighing 60 grams to 90 grams, contained in the same shell and called 'grandchildren bullets', while the saying is that the 'grandfather' leads the way and the 'grandchildren' follow. They are supplemented with iron and porcelain fragments previously boiled in cantharides beetle poison. The total weight of the projectile is some 12 kilograms. A single shot has the power of a thunderbolt, causing several hundred casualties among men and horses.

By using such weapons the Chinese were able to defend their borders against barbarian invaders.

The Chinese also developed a double-barrelled cannon known as 'Mr Facing-Both-Ways'. It comprised two cannon joined together at the breech-ends. After one barrel had been fired the weapon was quickly rotated to allow the crew to discharge the second. A Chinese account states: 'Immediately after firing the first gun the second is rotated into position and fired, each one being muzzle loaded with a stone projectile. If the gun is aimed at the hull of an enemy ship below the waterline, the cannon-balls shoot along the surface and smash the side into splinters. It is a very handy weapon.' By the fifteenth century, a single battalion of the Chinese Army was equipped with 40 batteries of cannon, 3,600 'thunder-bolt shells', 160 'wine-cup, muzzle-loading general cannon', 200 large and 328 small 'continuous bullet cannon' firing an early form of grapeshot, 624 hand-guns, 300 small grenades and almost 4,000 kilograms of gunpowder and over 1,050,000 bullets. Such weaponry led historian Joseph Needham to remark in *Science and Civilisation in China*: 'this was quite some firepower, and the total weight of the weaponry was reckoned to be 29.4 tons'.

China's vastness meant successful gunpowder artillery had to be developed rapidly to ensure the country's security. Its isolation in the east also meant that such advances in gunpowder technology remained hidden from the West for some time. But over time and through trade the news of developments in any technology passed from one civilization or country to another.

THE RISE OF THE TUDORS

In England a political power struggle was developing between the aristocratic houses of Lancaster and York, both of whom claimed regency of England through descent from the sons of Edward III. The war, which raged for more than thirty years, saw a number of minor engagements and sixteen major battles. It began with the first Battle of St Albans on 22 May 1455 and ended at the Battle of Bosworth in1485. Both sides employed artillery at various engagements with varying success. The Yorkists, with over 4,000 troops, opened the Battle of Tewkesbury, 4 May 1471, with an artillery bombardment. The fighting was bloody and the Lancastrians left 2,000 dead on the battlefield from their original force of 3,000.

The war continued for a further fourteen years before culminating at Bosworth on 22 August 1485. At this engagement Richard III, leading a Yorkist force of 12,000 men supported by some artillery, attempted to intercept Henry Tudor, who had inherited the Lancastrian claim to the throne and was marching on London. The Lancastrian force numbering 10,000 was fired on by Richard's artillery, but the weapons did not contribute much to the way the fighting developed: both sides were still using longbowmen. The two armies closed and Richard was cut down as he attempted to fight his way through to Henry, presumably to engage him personal combat. When the Yorkist Army received a flanking attack its spirit gave way and it fled the field, leaving behind some 900 dead. Lancastrian losses numbered only 100 and the victory established Henry Tudor as King Henry VII of England.

In 1495, ten years into Henry's reign, a list of artillery returned to the Tower of London was made by Sir Richard Guilford. It included a bombardelle, a curtow, a demi-curtow, serpentines and falcons, which fired balls ranging from a maximum of 120 kilograms for the bombardelle down to 0.45 kilograms for the falcon.

The Tudor dynasty was to rule England and Wales until 1603, during which time the country's fortunes were to ebb and flow. The most enigmatic of all the Tudor monarchs, Henry VIII, brought England's artillery train to new heights of power in the sixteenth century.

THREE

INTO A NEW ERA, 1500–1600

O n mainland Europe the sixteenth century started just as the fifteenth had ended, with Spain and France at war over the question of Italian conquest. The problems facing the sixteenth-century artillerymen engaged in this conflict were not new and stemmed from the fact that there had been no resolution of the problem of how best to combine mobility with long-range firepower. The French had made a number of improvements to artillery mobility, but had made no great advances in improving the effective range of cannon. It was obvious to most practitioners of the science of artillery that increases in range, accuracy and firepower were most likely to be achieved by weapons which had a barrel length of 20 calibres or more. That is to say, that if the diameter of the barrel was 200mm, then the length had to be 20 × 200mm or 4 metres. The barrels of these new cannon also had to have walls that were thick enough to withstand the pressure built up by detonation of a large powder charge. Experiments using artillery pieces with thinner barrel walls and loaded with reduced powder charges showed that they could fire equally heavy projectiles, but with a significant reduction in accuracy and range. Even so the lightest of these was still clumsy and difficult to move. Some of pieces of the time still required a team of twenty-four horses to move them and could not be readied for action with any great speed.

HENRY VIII AND THE ARMING OF ENGLAND

Henry VII may have emerged victorious over Richard III and may have reigned as king of England for twenty-four years, but on his death he bequeathed to his son an army that had fallen into stagnation. When Henry VIII ascended the throne in 1509 aged eighteen, continental European armies were already beginning to take steps towards becoming professional forces and were making further advances in artillery and other gunpowder weapons. Henry VIII had great military ambitions and the thought of

England being weaker in arms than other European nations stung him to the quick. Within four years of ascending the English throne, he was embarking on his first continental military expedition.

Under Henry VIII's direction, artisans with gunfounding skills were brought from all over England and even from the continent to cast cannon. These weapons were intended to equip new artillery forts being built at sites along England's southern coast, including Deal and Walmer in Kent and Portland and St Mawes, in Dorset and Cornwall respectively. Henry attracted the services of artisans such as Peter Baud from France and Arcanus de Arcanis from Italy. (The latter may also be Francesco Arcana, who was known to be casting sakers for Henry in London from about 1529.) They not only cast cannon for the king but also instructed others in the art of gunfoundry.

Henry also imported many cannon and mortars from Germany, France and the Low Countries. Mortars became more widely used in the early sixteenth century, when their usefulness in lobbing balls and shells filled with gunpowder in high arcs over defensive walls was recognized. An illustration of the siege of Munster in 1530, after an engraving by Erhardt Schoen, depicts a battery of four cannon of various sizes; it shows shells filled with gunpowder and fitted with a simple fuse being used from early mortars.

Peter Baud (sometimes spelled Bawd) along with his counterpart, Peter van Collen, cast mortars up to 11 inches in calibre and 19 inches in diameter for Henry. The shells of these weapons were loaded with 'wild fire or fireworks and a match [fuse] that the firewoork might be set on fire for to breake in smal peeces, whereof the smallest peece hitting any man would kill or spoile him'.

In an attempt to keep labouring costs as low as possible women were employed for some of the manual work. Bristol merchant Thomas Badock recorded how women were used to dig the pit into which the gun mould was placed, carry wood for the furnaces to melt the metal and dig out the barrel after casting. When the barrel was cool enough, they dragged it from the casting pit to the site where it was test- or proof-fired. For their services these women were paid in cherries, bread, wine and cider. It goes without saying, that men involved in gunfoundry were paid in money.

At this time a smith called Savadyng de Varte used a central mandrel of metal covered in clay to cast the barrel of cannon. After the mandrel was removed, the interior of the barrel was polished and smoothed with special borers, weighing 7.3 kilograms and fabricated by de Varte himself, using iron supplied by the very capable Thomas Badock. The moulds for de Varte's cannon were prepared by an artisan referred to as 'the king's fondidor', and known to us through the pages of history simply as 'Jacobo'. He fashioned the royal arms out of wax, along with other embellishments and garnitures, to decorate these barrels.

Robert and John Owen were members of a family of brass founders and cast both cannon and balls. Henry VIII employed them from 1536; they continued to work for the Tudor monarchy and were still casting cannon for Edward VI, Henry's son. Bronze cost ten times more than iron but a large number of artillery pieces were nevertheless cast in the metal. This was because bronze, an alloy of tin and copper, has a lower melting-point than iron, making it easier to work. Furthermore, it does not produce a large number of air bubbles during its molten stage, a problem in the casting process that can produce a weakening of the finished weapon.

Henry VIII continued to order great numbers of artillery pieces from the continent until he had a well-established industry in England. The first iron cannon cast in England by an Englishman is believed to have been made by Ralph Hog of Buxted, Sussex, in 1542. Cast iron had been known about since the fourteenth century, but it was only by the sixteenth century that metallurgy had advanced to the point where it could be worked to any degree approaching usefulness. (The 58th (Sussex) Field Regiment of the British Royal Artillery claimed descent from the cannon foundries sited in Sussex.)

Some cannon barrels were by this time being cast as solid pieces. The chamber was bored out using a new technique called reaming. The reamer was fitted with a three- or four-pointed head, which could be either square or round in section. These heads were made from hardened metal on a long rod and acted by literally scraping out the interior of the barrel's chamber. They were powered by treadmills and eventually waterwheels; series of cogs and gears often allowed two or three barrels to be reamed out at once. As the head of the reamer drilled into the metal, the barrel, which was mounted on a sledge-like platform, was drawn onto the tip of the borer by the gunsmiths in a controlled manner. Once the barrel was bored out, the touch hole was drilled. After finishing with hammers to flatten and smooth out the exterior surface of the barrel, the weapon was ready for proof-firing. Barrels of all gunpowder weapons were manufactured using this method and many military thinkers of the day expressed a preference for weapons made in this way. They understood that manufacturing accuracy was greatly improved and believed artillery could be improved likewise. Barrels could now be cast with trunnions and any other embellishment before they were reamed. Cannon-balls were beginning to be cast in clay moulds which had been prepared with grease. Some moulds allowed several balls to be cast in one pouring. Taken as a whole, artillery production had been greatly speeded up and output increased.

In September 1523 an inventory of artillery at the Tower of London was drawn up Geoffrey Hughes, who records seventy-four cannon, including seven large bombards, which fired cannon-balls weighing over 113 kilograms with a charge of 36 kilograms of gunpowder, each of which was hauled by twenty-four horses. There were also a number of the small pieces known as 'falconets'. The gunners serving these weapons were paid according to the power of the gun; 2 shillings per day for the bombards and 8 pence per day for the falconets. (This differentiation in pay was not unique: in 1559 the garrison at Gorey Castle on Jersey comprised thirty-eight soldiers, each of whom was paid 2 pence per day, and twelve gunners, each of whom received 2.5 pence per day.) In 1547, the year in which Henry VIII's artillery and cavalry gained victory over the Scots at the Battle of Pinkie on 10 September, another inventory was made of the military stores kept within the Tower of London. The stock is listed by the chronicler Hall as including, among other weapons: '5 great curtalls, 2 great culverynges, 4 sakers and 5 serpentynes, as fayre ordnance as hathe bene, beside other smal peces'. This inventory included some cannon taken from the Scots at the Battle of Flodden in 1513.

The iron guns mentioned made up only a small part of the total of artillery pieces available to Henry's forces and a not inconsiderable number were cast on the continent. Henry was 'indefferent' to hand-guns, but on the matter of cannon he took a personal interest and even went as far as establishing an officer of state, the Master of the Ordnance, with his own department to attend to the provision and storage of artillery and ammunition for land forces and the navy. In 1537, Henry VIII established the Guild of St George to be 'overseers of the science of artillerie' and that artillery was to make the greatest contribution towards the defence of England. The artillery train that Henry VIII had at his disposal was by no means the largest in Europe, but it was certainly one of the most impressive.

Political upheavals, the break with the Roman Catholic Church, and the annulment of Henry's marriage to Catherine of Aragon, the aunt of Emperor Charles V of the Holy Roman Empire, prompted Pope Paul II to issue a bull excommunicating Henry in December 1538. That in itself was of no consequence to the king, but when the Pope managed to unite the empire and France in an alliance in mid-1538 against Henry and began to preach that the English king was comparable to the infidel Turk, it became clear that war was imminent. Preparations had to be made. In early 1539 England prepared itself for the expected invasion. Defensive measures included the construction of fortifications at vulnerable sites along England's southern shores. They were built with remarkable speed and included castles at Deal and Walmer in Kent and Sandown on the Isle of Wight. All three were largely complete by 1540. Calshot Castle was also started at about this time, but was not finished until 1544. They were of a new design and were the first true artillery forts to be built in England.

Unlike European fortifications of the time which used ramparting and retired bastions in the 'Italian trace' design, Henry's new forts comprised a series of interlocked round towers arranged in a sexfoil design. The castles at Deal and Walmer were built partially below ground level, thereby presenting a low silhouette to attacking artillery, while at the same time providing the site with a dry moat that any attacking enemy would have to cross. The new defences, termed blockhouses or bulwarks, were linked by a series of earthworks and were designed to protect the area of the Downs in Kent. The plans for these new fortifications have been attributed to the Bohemian engineer Stefan von Haschenberg, who may have in turn been influenced by similar designs drawn up for the defence of Antwerp by Albrecht Dürer between 1520 and 1521. They incorporated curved parapets to deflect cannon-balls and were tiered to allow batteries of artillery to be sited at varying heights. The site at Deal is equipped with 145 embrasures for firearms, and artillery could be mounted on three levels behind low parapets. The new fortifications were equipped with special vents to take away the smoke of gunpowder during firing – this would otherwise have choked the gunners and hampered their vision. Construction of the forts was completed quickly because of the level of resources devoted to the project. At Sandown, for example, a typical daily workforce consisted of 630 men, of whom half were skilled craftsmen.

The first garrison at Deal was a force of thirty-five men commanded by Thomas Wynkfelde of Sandwich. The exact number of artillery pieces sited at the castle is not reliably recorded, but the weaponry is believed to have included demi-cannon firing 27-pound balls. At Calshot Castle, overlooking the Solent towards the Isle of Wight, the complement of artillery by the end of the 1540s is recorded as being thirty-six pieces. However, by 1559 this number had been reduced to ten. In the end these defences were built to repel an invasion that never came. But over the following centuries they were to be pressed into the defence of England's shores on more than one occasion. They were not complete follies.

By the mid-sixteenth century gunpowder had been in use on the battlefield for more than 150 years, but not all strategists thought of artillery as the great leveller of forces that it was fast becoming. One detractor, Sir Roger Williams, wrote: 'The fury of all batteries are past at the first.' But by now he was one of the few militarists who did not fully understand the power of gunpowder weapons and therefore dismissed them. In fact, in the previous 100 years artillery had brought decisive conclusions to many battles that would otherwise have degenerated into long slogging matches as each side tried to out-match the other in manpower and tactics.

Fortunately for the gunsmiths and gunners, Sir Roger Williams' voice was virtually lone against a chorus of those who knew better. Not long into his reign Henry VIII began to make serious attempts to reclaim English possessions lost to France in the fifteenth century. One his first forays came in June 1513, when he landed at Calais, at the time still an English territory, with a force of 28,000 troops, against which the French deployed 15,000 men who harassed the English but refused battle. On 16 August 1513, the two armies met on the field at the Battle of Guinegate. The French, who had hoped to surprise the English, had the tables turned on them: they were routed from the field. The English seized Therouanne on 22 August after a siege in which Henry's artillery saw action. During the siege of Therouanne (also spelled Terouenne) a soldier recalled in a letter how: 'The walls of Turwyne [Therouanne] are sore beaten with gunnes and many houses broken and destroyed. Our gunnes lie within a birdbolt shote to the wallis and our miners are also near them.' Some thirty years later, in 1543, the town was again besieged, but this time by the Burgundians, who were engaged by the defenders' artillery in what was the first recorded use of indirect artillery fire. The Burgundians had sited their artillery in a valley which was obscured from the town by the crest of a hill. The defenders sent out observers on the flanks of the crest and these men indicated the fall of shot through a system of signalling. The Burgundians were taken completely by surprise and suffered heavy casualties.

At the time of Henry's incursion into France, the Earl of Surrey was to the north of Henry's kingdom. He met and defeated the Scots at the Battle of

Flodden on 9 September 1513. The battle had opened with an artillery duel and the bold, if somewhat foolhardy, English attacked the Scottish forces strongly sited on Flodden Hill. English tactics carried the day and King James IV of Scotland and many of his principal nobles were killed.

CONTINENTAL CONFLICT

With his northern borders now secure, Henry VIII was free to enter into an alliance with the empire, Spain, the Italian states and the Pope, with the aim of driving France out of Italy. Henry was to become involved in a decades-old dispute.

In the 1490s French and Spanish forces had clashed several times, resulting mainly in Spanish victories. On 21 April 1503 the two sides met at the Battle of Cerignola. The Spanish force of 6,000 men under the command of Hernandez Gonzalo de Cordoba had marched out of Barletta and positioned themselves on a hillside behind a palisade of sharpened wooden stakes and a ditch. Cordoba's artillery was rendered useless when its store of gunpowder exploded. The French, led by the Duke de Nemours, were supported by their artillery. They advanced their cavalry and Swiss pikemen in a frontal attack. Spanish harquebusiers were well sited and took a deadly toll of the opposition, including the Duke de Nemours. The French were thrown back in confusion. The battle has entered the pages of history as the first military engagement won entirely by the use of gunpowder weapons. Cordoba has been termed the 'father of trench warfare' as a result of this and other actions. The lesson was not lost on the French who copied the Spanish methods of fighting and tried to create countermeasures.

The Battle of Ravenna in 1511 has been described as the first confrontation between two truly modern field armies. It was one of a series of engagements between Spain and France during the struggle for Italy. The war lasted from 1495 until 1559, with this particular phase being known as the campaigns of Gaston de Foix. The Count Gaston de Foix, the new Duke de Nemours, became the French commander at the age of only twenty-one and led his forces with tireless energy. His campaign started well with the capture of Bologna on 13 May 1511 after which he fought off the allied army. Marching northwards he then defeated the Venetians at Brescia and captured the city. By early 1512 most of northern Italy was under his command. Gaston then turned south to invest Ravenna, reaching it by March that year with a force of 32,000 men, including some 8,500 mercenaries, supported by 54 cannon. They encountered a Spanish force of 18,000 men with 30 cannon led by Pedro Navarro, a military engineer by training. The Spanish were deployed with their rear protected by the River Ronco and their flanks well entrenched, as Navarro planned. An artillery duel began during which the Spanish cavalry were heavy assaulted, but the infantry in their trenches were almost untouched. Using the cover of his artillery, Gaston transferred two cannon over the River Ronco to fire at the rear of the Spanish positions. Unnerved by this and a French frontal assault, the Spanish broke, fleeing their trenches. In the open they were easy targets and the battle cost more than half their total force. The French lost 4,500 men, including their commander Gaston de Foix.

An engagement of particular note in the dispute over Italy was the Battle of Marignano, 13–14 September 1515. The French were equipped with artillery, but such was the suddenness of an attack by Swiss mercenaries, that they were unable to bring their weapons effectively to bear. The Swiss were in turn counter-attacked by a French force led by Francis I in an action that lasted five hours. After a period of reorganization the battle resumed with typical ferocity on the part of the Swiss. By now the French had organized their artillery, which comprised 140 cannon – a ratio of five guns per 1,000 men. The weapons ripped into the Swiss and inflicted heavy losses. The French lost some 5,000 men and the Swiss 6,000, with the result that the Swiss never fought outside of their national borders again as a fully organized army – a state of affairs that was to last until the French Revolutionary Wars of the late eighteenth century. Francis I occupied Milan. Switzerland negotiated peace, soon to be followed by the Pope. The anti-French alliance had collapsed and France was in control of Lombardy.

The Battle of Marignano was a lesson to every military thinker that monarchs needed to improve their gunpowder weaponry and tactics even further. The Battle of La Bicocca, 27 April 1522, drove the lesson home. The engagement was part of the continuing territorial dispute between Charles V, the Holy Roman Emperor and King of Spain, and the French king, Francis I. The French forces commanded by Marshal Odet de Lautrec, numbering some 25,000 with 10,000 allied Venetians, advanced on Milan in April 1522. Italian forces under the command of General Prosper Colona and numbering 20,000 were well entrenched in a strong defensive position at Bicocca, when the two sides clashed. The Swiss mercenary force, after some indecision and impatience at waiting for the French artillery to be sited, entered the battle in a headlong charge on entrenched positions; they suffered 3,000 casualties in less than thirty minutes. Lautrec was forced to withdraw eastwards into allied Venetian territory to recover. The morale of the Swiss had been dealt a severe blow and, coupled with their mauling by the French at Marignano seven years earlier, it meant that never again would their mercenary units use the old-fashioned tactic of frontal assault to attack positions defended by harquebuses.

Mercenaries hired their services out to the highest bidder, but despite this they were formidable, well-trained fighting forces with a strict code of conduct. The Swiss were considered the best mercenaries at this time but the German *Landsknechte* were also sought after. Such forces, under their own rules, could plunder and take prizes of war and loot, but they could not take gunpowder or artillery. These items of ordnance had to be handed over to the field captain.

Between January and February 1525, French forces under the command of Francis I and numbering 28,000, including 4,000 Swiss mercenaries, armed with 53 cannon, besieged the Italian city of Pavia. The city's defending garrison numbered some 6,000. A relieving Imperial force of 23,000 with 17 cannon, under the command of Marquis of Pescara, attempted to fight its way through to the city in January but found its path barred by French entrenchments and an unfordable river. Unable to advance, the Imperial forces dug trenches and both sides engaged in an artillery bombardment, which achieved little. On the night of 24/25 February, in an attempt to break the deadlock the Imperial forces moved northwards under cover of a storm and artillery bombardment. Pescara's troops crossed the river and attacked a walled park on the left flank of the French positions. The French had few men in the trenches but, although surprised, they mounted a spirited counter-attack. At first they gained ground but Spanish harquebusiers began to open accurate fire, which took a heavy toll. The garrison of Pavia launched an attack on those French troops left in the trenches and destroyed them. The French artillery could not support the attacks because of the speed at which the battle had developed. In less than two hours the siege had been lifted and the French had lost 13,000 killed and wounded and all 53 pieces of artillery captured. The Imperial forces had suffered only 500 killed and wounded.

After his campaign of 1513, Henry VIII was to return his forces twice more to France – first in October 1523. On the first sortie of this new attack, his artillery was ranged against the walls of the town of Bray. The action lasted a mere two hours between 4.00 a.m. and 6.00 a.m., when 'a gap as broad as a cart' was made in the walls. A week later at the town of Montdidier Henry's huge siege guns were sited only 12 metres from the walls. Four volleys were enough to complete the work of levelling the defences 'hard by the myghtie strong bulwerke, the strongest that evyr I saw'. Smaller pieces of artillery in the train were used in an anti-personnel role, where they wrought terrible casualties against infantry and horses massed together in the open.

Dummy guns made from materials such as wooden barrels would sometimes be constructed during this period and used to fool defenders into believing that larger numbers of artillery pieces existed than were actually present, in an effort to make the town or castle surrender without fight. Neither was it unknown for the appearance of monster guns to persuade defenders to surrender and prevent unnecessary loss of life and damage to a city. This underhand show of force did on occasion force a surrender. Such false tactics were not solely for use by attackers. At Craithes Castle, near Aberdeen, Scotland, built in the second half of the sixteenth century, carved stone cannon are incorporated into one of the towers, no doubt intended to intimidate and scare off any would-be attackers.

Henry's last attack on the French came in 1542 and resulted in the capture of Boulogne, but he was forced to withdraw his forces through lack of funds. An interesting illustration of Henry's artillery in action at the siege of Boulogne, in an engraving of 1788 copied from a lost sixteenth-century wall painting in Cowdray House, shows the artillery train being mainly comprised of culverins and sakers. The gunners in the picture are shown performing the loading sequence of cannon at the time: ramming and ladling powder and shot into the barrel using long-handled wooden implements.

THE BEGINNINGS OF STANDARDIZATION

Gunmakers and military thinkers were gaining experience all the time and experimenting with new designs and new bore diameters. Attempts were made to reduce the thickness of barrel walls, improve powder charges and standardize projectile weights. Initially, this period of trial resulted in almost as many different types of artillery as there were weapons. As a result, the regular supply of standardized ammunition became an almost impossible task, which in turn contributed to a partial decline in the importance of artillery in field operations. It was a trend that could not be left unchecked. By the mid-sixteenth century Charles V, the Holy Roman Emperor, had ordered the standardization of all artillery weapons into seven types. Following this example, Henry II of France ordered the establishment of six standard models for French artillery. Further experimentation followed and other types of artillery were added to the basic models, but these introductions were more restrained and entered service in a more orderly and systematic manner. Prince Maurice of Orange-Nassau went one step further than the French and ordered that Dutch artillery be reduced to just four calibres: 6, 12, 24 and 48 pounds. These pieces could be interchanged on carriages of standardized construction. These early attempts at standardizing cannon were not universal. By the end of the sixteenth century the Spanish use of artillery and the harquebus was to emerge as one of the powerful forces in Europe, even though it was still deploying no fewer than fifty different types of cannon in some twenty various calibres until the time of the Thirty Years War (1618–48), which must have made resupply a logistical nightmare. Indeed, some thinkers disapproved of the move towards standardization because they believed it allowed for little in the way of advancement.

Torn apart internally by the Wars of Religion in the mid-sixteenth century, the French were to lose their superiority in artillery construction. For a time the lead was taken by the more imaginative German gunmakers. Few actual changes were made to German artillery design – innovative efforts were concentrated on hand-guns and the wheellock was just beginning to enter service – but there were significant improvements in the techniques used to make artillery pieces. The Holy Roman Emperor Maximilian's main cannon foundry was at Innsbruck. The emperor took a keen interest in his artillery and is known to have visited foundries to view his new pieces being cast. But he also received bronze cannon, cast by artisans such as Poppenruyter and Remy de Hallut, from the southern provinces of the Low Countries, where the emperor exercised power.

Maximilian's arsenal was prepared between 1504 and 1508. From 1515 to 1519, it was catalogued by Wolfgang Reisache. The German court painter and architect, Jorg Kolderer, illustrated the arsenals from 1507 until 1512. He shows the Imperial artillery on the march with bronze cannon forming up on the field, weapons of the siege train drawn by teams of eight horses. He also depicted bombards, which were called *Hauptstucke* in Germany, and even a small falconet on a carriage pulled by a single horse. Kolderer's illustrations also reveal what appears to be a four-wheeled wagon serving as a mobile stamping mill for 'corning' or 'mealing' gunpowder on campaign.

Maximilian's arsenal was soon to be pressed into service by his successor, Charles V. In 1525 a peasants' rebellion quickly spread in Germany. The uprising had been prompted by Archduke Ferdinand of Hapsburg's increasingly severe demands for punishments under the feudal system of rule that existed in Germany at the time. The peasants formed forces of up to 40,000 and soon became well armed with artillery, which included pieces loaned to them by city states. Rothenburg, for example, hired out two large artillery pieces with balls, powder and gunners. The peasant forces at Lake Constance took the towns of Marktdorf and Meersdorf, which gave them thirteen pieces of artillery and 16 tons of gunpowder. The rebels realized they could not take on the very large cities, such as Nuremberg, but in open battle their large numbers could bring them victory. For example, in July they captured the entire artillery train and its ammunition from the Styrian nobility. But it was not all one-sided: armies massed under the League of the Swabian cities and Imperial forces compelled the peasants to give battle under terms which were better suited to the professional soldier. This engagement came at Upper Allgau where the peasant army was destroyed by concentrated artillery fire. The rebellion disintegrated and by 1526 had been entirely crushed, but the episode showed how powerful weaponry, even in the hands of peasantry, could contribute to civil war and provide victory against the state.

Just before the build-up of Maximilian's arsenal, a gargantuan gun called 'King of Cannon' was made in Russia, which was ruled by the militarily experienced Ivan III. The weapon was a true milestone in sixteenth-century barrel-casting techniques. It was cast in 1502 from bronze and was 5.2 metres in length. This huge cannon was the largest built to that date, had a calibre of 915mm and could fire a stone ball weighing over 1,000 kilograms. It rivalled the huge guns cast for Mehomet over forty years previously. Later Russian cannon included the Tsar Puschka (Great Gun of Moscow) cast in 1586, which was of similar dimensions to the King. But such monstrous weapons had to have a practical purpose and were not cast for their novelty value. The King of Cannon was used in siege warfare.

The Spanish were to excel in the use of gunpowder weaponry on the battlefield and maintained their superiority for most of the sixteenth century. The Spanish reputation for well-managed artillery was based in large part on the outcome of the Battle of Ravenna, fought with France on 11 April 1512. However, in the wake of this engagement it soon became clear to most military thinkers that the use of other gunpowder weapons, such as the harquebus, was just as important as artillery. Nevertheless, artillery was not completely usurped on the battlefield. It still retained a place in the order of battle, including the attack and defence of fortifications, and it was also beginning to grow in importance in naval warfare. Like the Spanish, the leaders of most European armies were beginning to understand how the use of combined arms could bring them victory or halt an enemy's advance.

AMMUNITION AND AIMING

Advances were made in the types of ammunition that were available. The term 'ammunition' relating to projectiles fired from cannon is believed to originate from this period and is possibly a corruption of the French term *munition*. The most common type of projectile to be fired from cannon was the cast-iron round shot. Trials now began into developing hollow cast-iron projectiles that could be filled with gunpowder and were known as shells. They were crude attempts at creating explosive ammunition that could be fired to burst among the enemy. Not always successful, these bombs were put to their best use when fired from the mortar-style weapons. Their lack of reliability resulted from problems with fusing. A basic wick-like fuse was fitted to the earliest types, which were sometimes lit at the time of loading. Timing was the essential element here, because if the shell were ignited too soon, it would detonate prematurely before reaching the target and thus have no effect. If the fuse was lit too late, the shell might land and either fail to explode or, if it fell on soft ground, some of the force of the explosion could be absorbed. Later, shells were loaded into the barrel in such a way that the fuse was positioned so that when the main propelling charge was ignited, the flame it produced would also ignite the fuse of the shell. This still did not resolve the ambiguity surrounding timing, but it did make handling the shell much safer. The problem would not be solved until the late eighteenth century.

Another experimental type of projectile was the canister round. This was a particularly nasty type of ammunition that dated back to at least 1410 and consisted of a can filled with small projectiles. The projectiles could vary from small lead balls of the type used in the harquebus to odd bits of metal, including old nails. The round was intended for use in a close-range, anti-personnel role. The third type of ammunition being developed for use in cannon was grapeshot, which consisted of a cluster of iron balls. This, too, had a mainly anti-personnel role but was effective at longer ranges.

Development in types of ammunition did not coincide with progress in transportation methods. This still came down to moving ammunition around in wheelbarrows, horse-drawn carts or even on a man's back. The gunner still walked beside his cannon and it was his pace that set the rate at which field artillery made it into battle. In effect, nothing about this area of the science of artillery had changed in more than 100 years.

One of the most important sixteenth-century artillery developments came in 1571. In that year an English gunner called John Skinner, one of 'the Queen's Majesty's men', is credited with devising the elevating screw, which was placed beneath breech end of the barrel and gave the gunner fine control over the degree of elevation imparted to the barrel. In fact, an engraving of 1527 by the engraver and military thinker Albrecht Dürer records a cast bronze cannon of the Renaissance fitted with a similar device and mounted on a two-wheeled, wooden carriage. But whoever was responsible for the introduction of this idea, it made elevating the barrel much easier and was eventually to replace the old method of hammering wooden wedges under the breech end to impart elevation, which, while it worked, did not afford the same degree of adjustment as the elevating screw. However, sighting was to remain by direct line of vision and targets could normally only be fired on if they were visible – the Theroanne experiment was one of a kind.

By now a number of the most experienced artillerymen were reaching an advanced age. In fact, during the reign of Queen Elizabeth I of England, it is recorded that several of the gunners at the Tower of London were over ninety years old.

Elizabeth's sister Mary had shown little interest in warfare. On 6 January 1558 English-held Calais fell to the French after a siege lasting only days. Neither money nor troops were released for the relief of the city. The blame for this must be shared between Mary and her husband Philip II of Spain, who dominated her. Elizabeth was made of sterner material. Pieces, such as bronze falcons, were cast at the Tower of London throughout her reign. In 1580 work was supervised by Henry Pitt and the Tower foundry was to continue in operation until the reign of Charles I. It was also during Elizabeth's reign that the English at last decided to declare the longbow obsolete. After a long drawn-out debate a royal ordinance of 1595 declared the longbow no longer useful on the battlefield: the English Army became the last European army to accept the harquebus firearm as the official weapon for troops.

THE QUEST FOR MOBILITY

A piece of sixteenth-century artillery nicknamed 'Queen Elizabeth's Pocket Pistol' has an interesting history. It was cast in 1544 in Utrecht by Jan Tolhuys, and is a 12-pounder brass basilisk. It was actually presented to Henry VIII, Elizabeth's father, by the Emperor Charles V. It is known to have been sited at Dover Castle, Kent, by 1613 and is still there. It is 7.3 metres in length, has a calibre of 120mm and could fire a shot some 11 kilometres. It is known to have been used during the English Civil War where it formed part of King Charles I's artillery train at the siege of Hull in 1643. It was captured by the Parliamentarian forces who then turned the weapon on its former owners at the siege of Sheffield. On the barrel is inscribed the legend 'Breek scrvret al meur ende wal bin ic geheten doer berch en al boert minen bal van mi germeten'. This has been translated as: 'Breaker my name of rampart and wall, Over hill and dale I throw my ball'. The first line may be a direct reference to pieces of artillery known as 'wallbusters' (*muurbraeckers*). Another part of the inscription on this piece reads 'Load me well and keep me clean, I'll carry my ball to Calais Green'.

Such mottos were quite commonly inscribed on weapon barrels and may have been intended to inspire the morale of the men firing the gun. The barrels of several sixteenth-century artillery pieces in the Army Museum, Paris, have similar mottos. One, German in origin, dated from around 1528 and weighs 12,589 kilograms. It bears the inscription: 'My name is the Griffon. I serve my gracious Master of Treves. Whenever I go into action I break down doors and Walls'. This too may be a reference to it being a 'wallbuster', particularly considering the fact that it was cast in Germany where such weapons were popular. Another German barrel in the same museum, but dating from the latter part of the century, introduces itself as follows: 'My name is Catherine; don't trust my contents. I punish Injustice . . .'. Solemn words indeed.

These large artillery *muurbraeckers* or wallbuster pieces were still widespread in Germany, but in other European countries the trend was towards more mobile weapons, such as sakers and culverins, which fired shots of 2.5 kilograms and 6 kilograms respectively.

By the end of the sixteenth century cast cannon were in use with virtually all armies, and there was also some degree of standardization in calibres and sizes to the point where certain guns were given specific names, many taken from fifteenth-century tradition. One type was the robinet, which had a calibre of about 37mm and fired a shot weighing 500 grams. A large robinet of Austrian origin, dated *c.* 1570, is on display at Fort Nelson, Hampshire. It was actually taken by the allies during their occupation of Paris in 1814, following the abdication of Napoleon Bonaparte. The barrel is inscribed 'I am forsooth an uncouth peasant – who tastes my eggs won't find them pleasant', a reference surely to its ammunition. The falcon had a calibre of some 65mm and fired a 1.5-kilogram shot; the saker was of approximately 80mm calibre and fired a 2.5-kilogram shot; the culverin had a 140mm calibre and fired an 8-kilogram shot. At the top of the tree was the cannon, 203mm in calibre and firing a 27-kilogram shot.

Still lacking full battlefield mobility, guns could often be captured and recaptured with every charge. Sometimes the turnaround was not so quick: in November 1529 Sultan Suleiman returned to Constantinople two huge cannon that the Hungarians had captured from the Turks under Hunyadi during an earlier Turkish campaign into Hungary. For the artillerymen serving the cannon, the threat of being overrun added to the danger of an already difficult business. In an effort to protect the gunners, units of bodyguards, which would eventually become known as fusilier companies, were now raised and deployed. On occasion, however, the role of these troops was to prevent the gunners from running away as the enemy closed in, rather than protecting the men from the attentions of the enemy. The overall commander of artillery was usually a soldier but the transport staff and drivers were still hired under contract and therefore had a civilian's attitude towards war. Some gunners were fortunate to be in a position where they had their own pieces of artillery for mercenary hire. These men, too, were basically under contract with no special allegiance to anyone in particular. Their main concern was for their pieces of artillery and their lives, which would be forfeit if and when their positions became overrun by the enemy.

THE TURKISH CAMPAIGN

In 1522 the Turks under Suleiman the Magnificent, the great-grandson of Mehomet II, began a campaign against the Christians in the Mediterranean and lay siege to island of Rhodes, on which was a fortress garrisoned by the Knights Hospitaller of St John. The siege began on 25 June when the Turks made an unopposed landing of up to 100,000 men, including siege engineers and artillery. Within a month the Turkish forces were in full siege positions with their artillery in place. Repeated assaults were made on the garrison and in one month alone the Turkish artillery fired more than 3,000 cannon-balls into the fortress. Both sides suffered horrendous losses during the siege but peace negotiations, tabled by Suleiman, broke down and fighting resumed. By December the Turks had penetrated the city's outer defences but were then repulsed with heavy losses. Suleiman once more offered terms of peace to the defenders and guaranteed their safety. He wished to end the siege which was gradually becoming a war of attrition that neither side could win. His proposals were accepted and 180 knights and 1,500 other troops, many of whom were wounded, evacuated the island out of an original force of 700 knights and 6,000 other troops. The operation had cost Suleiman between 50,000 and 100,000 men from a force that eventually totalled 200,000.

On mainland Europe, over the next three years Suleiman conducted border warfare with Hungary. In 1524 he agreed to a neutrality pact with Poland which left the way open for him to attack Hungary with his full force. In April 1526 Suleiman left Constantinople for his campaign into Hungary with 300 cannon in his artillery train, collecting more from border posts en route. Between May and July Suleiman's forces advanced, bringing his artillery up the River Danube by boat, while the Hungarians prepared for war. By 28 August the two sides were forming up their forces, with the Turkish Army numbering 300,000 men to the Hungarians total of 25,000 men with about 20 pieces of artillery. They joined battle on 29 August at a site called Mohacs, close to the Danube. The Turkish victory was a forgone conclusion, but it did not come without great loss of life. The Hungarians were routed, leaving 15,000 dead on the battlefield. The prisoners taken by the Turks were decapitated; with their leaders dead, the Hungarian resistance crumbled.

Suleiman's campaign continued with an advance into Austria in 1529, all the time using his powerful siege artillery to reduce towns and cities. Between 27 September and 15 October his forces besieged Vienna but hostilities reached an impasse and he withdrew from the city. The defence of Vienna had been directed by Marshal William von Roggendorf, who instructed the

Austrian artillery in counter-bombardment against the Turkish guns and disrupted the Turkish forces' forming-up areas.

By 1533 Suleiman's attentions were turning towards Persia and peace was concluded between his empire and Hungary. Eleven years later in 1544, he was forced to return to Hungary in the face of civil war. King Ferdinand of Hungary and Bohemia had raised an army to fight the Turks and his artillery train included 60 siege cannon and 80 field pieces with 200,000 cannon-balls and 500 tons of gunpowder. The whole assembly was moved by over 1,000 horses. Suleiman was once again victorious and Ferdinand was forced to pay tribute for the small strip of northern and western Hungary which he was allowed to retain.

CATEGORIZATION

By the end of the sixteenth century the methods used in manufacture had advanced to a point where range, power and the structure of major types of guns were to hardly change over the next 300 years. Modifications made to artillery in the next century would be mainly concerned with improving its mobility, organization, battlefield tactics and field gunnery techniques. By the late 1500s, artillery was organized and categorized into three distinctive types of weapons. Fundamentally, these definitions are still in use today.

Artillery of the first class consisted of long-barrelled pieces, usually about 30 calibres in length. The barrels had thick walls and the pieces in this category were designed to fire accurately at long range. Included in this range of weapon was the culverin type, which is roughly comparable to the modern self-propelled medium field gun.

Class I: Culverin types 25–44 calibres in length

Type	Weight of piece (pounds)	Weight of shot (pounds)	Bore (inches)	Length (feet)	Effective range (yards)	Maximum range (yards)
esmeril (or robinet)	200	0.3	1.0	2.5	200	50
serpentine	400	0.5	1.5	3.0	250	1,000
falconet	500	1.0	2.0	3.7	280	1,500
falcon	800	3.0	2.5	6.0	400	2,500
minion (or demi-saker)	1,000	6.0	3.3	6.5	450	3,500
pasavolante	3,000	6.0	3.3	10.0	1,000	4,500

Type	Weight of piece (pounds)	Weight of shot (pounds)	Bore (inches)	Length (feet)	Effective range (yards)	Maximum range (yards)
saker	1,600	9.0	4.0	6.9	500	4,000
culverin bastard	3,000	12.0	4.6	8.5	600	4,000
demi-culverin	3,400	10.0	4.2	8.5	850	5,000
culverin	4,800	18.0	5.2	11.0	1,700	6,700
culverin royal	7,000	32.0	6.5	16.0	2,000	7,000

The second class of artillery consisted of lighter, shorter pieces that were designed to fire relatively heavy projectiles but over shorter distances, thereby sacrificing range and some degree of accuracy. However, these two factors were traded off in order to achieve more mobility with little or no loss in damage-producing power when the projectile struck its target. These are the so-called cannon types of weapon, with barrel lengths of some 20 calibres on average. This class is roughly comparable to the modern howitzer.

Class II: Cannon types 15–28 calibres in length

Type	Weight of piece (pounds)	Weight of shot (pounds)	Bore (inches)	Length (feet)	Effective range (yards)	Maximum range (yards)
quarto-cannon	2,000	12.0	4.6	7.0	400	2,000
demi-cannon	4,000	32.0	6.5	11.0	450	2,500
bastard cannon	4,500	42.0	7.0	10.0	400	2,000
cannon serpentine	6,000	42.0	7.0	12.0	500	3,000
cannon	7,000	50.0	8.0	13.0	600	3,500
cannon royal	8,000	60.0	8.5	12.0	750	4,000
basilisk	12,000	90.0	10.0	10.0	750	4,000

The third and final class of artillery consisted of shorter pieces with relatively thin barrel walls. These weapons were used to fire heavy projectiles for shorter ranges in high angles of elevation. Included within this group were two sub-categories. First, there were the pedreros; they fired a stone projectile that was much lighter than an iron projectile of the same diameter. This meant that the barrel of the pedrero could be between 10 and 15 calibres in length with quite thin walls, yet still be capable of firing a rather large stone cannon-ball almost as far as a cannon could send an iron one. The second sub-category covered the emerging mortar. Early mortars were short, with a barrel length of 10 calibres or less, and fired relatively large projectiles at short ranges but in a high, parabolic trajectory to shoot over the walls of fortified towns and cities. These weapons are essentially in the same class as mortars in use today.

Class III: Pedrero and Mortar types*

Type	Weight of piece (pounds)	Weight of shot (pounds)	Bore (inches)	Length (feet)	Effective range (yards)	Maximum range (yards)
pedrero (medium)	3,000	30.0	10.0	9.0	500	2,500
mortar (medium)	1,500	30.0	6.3	2.0	300	750
mortar (heavy)	10,000	200.0	15.0	6.0	1,000	2,000

*It should be noted that variations to weapons in this last group were encountered, but pedreros were usually of 10 to 15 calibres in length and fired projectiles weighing in the order of 50 pounds. Some mortars could have a barrel length of only 3 to 5 calibres but still be capable of firing projectiles up to 200 pounds in weight.

DEFENCE AND FORTIFICATION

There was a revolution in fortification at the beginning of the sixteenth century. High masonry walls of even the most massive medieval fortifications had been shown to be vulnerable to the smashing power of heavy siege guns. Defenders tried to reply to bombardments in kind, but their cannon mounted on high walls were too light and had insufficient power even to harass the men serving the long-range attacking guns. Heavier weapons were sometimes tried, but moving them to the top of ramparts was time consuming and absorbed a great deal of manpower. Even when such pieces had been laboriously manhandled into place, their use soon proved to be counter-productive. The force of the recoil from the cannon during firing threatened to shake the walls' foundations to the point where they became dangerously weak, leaving them easier targets for the enemy's artillery to breach. In the sixteenth century, fortifications were massively remodelled to incorporate gunpowder weapons and withstand their attack. On the Channel Island of Jersey Mont Orgueil (Gorey) Castle was all but rebuilt to accommodate cannon. The bowmen were replaced by harquebusiers and hand-gunners, and 'cannoneers' serving under master gunners, operated the culverins, sakers, falcons and mortars that took the place of the medieval springalds, mangonels and ballistae.

By 1531, the garrison of Gorey Castle included a lieutenant in command, a gentleman porter, an armourer, three cannoneers, four watchmen and eighteen soldiers. The military officers, cannoneers and most of the retinue were Englishmen, with Jerseymen making up the rest of the garrison. An inventory of the artillery from this time reveals the castle was armed with twenty pieces of small ordnance comprising one fowler, one short fowler, one three-quarter sling, three half-slings, two quarter-slings, eight serpentines, three double-serpentines and one half-serpentine. The list of equipment also includes ancillary items related to artillery, for example, 29 moulds for cannon-balls, 400 lead and iron balls, 450 'other sorts of cannon-balls', two hammers 'for making stone cannon-balls' and various other tools.

The new walls of fortified sites were now lower, thicker and with proper emplacements for defending artillery. This move was intended to make the breaching process more difficult for enemy siege guns. Many new fortifications were constructed with broad walls from which protruded triangular bastions called Italian traces, after the country where they are first known to have been incorporated into defensive designs. The Italian traces were extended as far as practicably possible to permit the defending artillery to cover all of the approaches to the castle or fortified city. Older fortifications were modernized by the erection of new walls and bastions of this type, with some existing walls being lowered, broadened and covered with an earthen embankment to absorb the shock of the impact of the cannon-balls.

The rest of the century was to see an ongoing struggle to improve fortifications against an increase in the power and range of siege artillery. Weapons such as the great basilisks and cannon royal could still breach the new walls but only by prolonged and concentrated fire. In an effort to overcome strengthen defences still further, the ditches surrounding fortifications were widened and were in turn protected by a counterscarp wall. At this point light artillery pieces could be sited beyond the ditch to try to keep the great siege guns at bay. Clear fields of fire were provided for the defender's artillery and small arms weapons on the counterscarp. Earth excavated from the ditch was spread in front of the counterscarp wall to create a gradually sloping terrace or glacis, which afforded the attackers no cover. This open slope, descending from the counterscarp, added to the strength of the low wall, while at the same time further complicating the aim of the attackers attempting to bring effective fire to bear on the counterscarp's defenders.

During the sixteenth century the first real artillery towers took shape. Some were completely new buildings, others were incorporated into the remodelling of medieval fortifications, such as the one at Castelnaud, Perigord. Standing on a promontory commanding a view of the surrounding Dordogne countryside, Castelnaud certainly had artillery sited within its grounds in the fifteenth century. But the first purpose-built artillery tower was added to its structure towards the end of the sixteenth century. It is at the southern end of the castle's outer defences and is circular. It is 30 metres high and has a diameter of 15 metres; the outer-facing walls are 5 metres thick at their base. It is very advanced in design, having an interior hoist to allow loads to be transferred from one level to another through a series of trapdoors. These openings also vented smoke from the artillery. In addition, the tower contains a small room between the second and third levels which has been identified as a powder magazine. It is located outside the walls of the artillery tower and abuts against the natural rock on which the castle is built. This design reduced the risk to the tower should the powder have exploded.

The new scientific approach to fortification advanced more quickly than artillery development and sieges once again became long, drawn-out affairs. Warfare was in danger of becoming a series of sieges, punctuated by battles only when some combination of manoeuvring skill, confidence or logistical pressure forced the opposing sides to meet face to face in the open. This led strategists to devote serious effort to improving siegecraft.

One potential solution to the challenge posed by the counterscarp and the power of defensive artillery was to devise a method whereby the attacking artillery and small arms could be brought close enough to the defences to bring effective fire to bear. Clearly, medieval apparatus like mantelets and siege towers would be totally useless against defenders with gunpowder weapons. But the old-fashioned method of digging one's way towards the target was still a choice open to the attackers. After all, it had been good enough for the Turks at the siege of Constantinople in the fourteenth century. By the end of the sixteenth century this method of approaching by series of entrenchments was quite well developed. However, it was not to be carried out scientifically until the seventeenth century when strategists such as Vauban refined the tactic to the point where it would invariably produce results.

The sixteenth-century method of approach by entrenchment was to conduct the work under the cover of protective fire from long-range culverin-type guns. The attacking engineers and infantry simply dug trenches towards an identified weak point in the defences and inevitably suffered casualties in doing so. Once the trenches came to within range of the attackers' artillery, thick earthen walls, known as parapets, were built up in front of the wide but shallow trenches to provide some protection to the men serving the siege guns directed at the counterscarp. In an effort to reduce losses among artillerymen, the weapons were not brought into position until nightfall. The defenders knew what was happening, but could do nothing except maintain harassing fire. Once in place, the attackers' artillery could fire on the defenders. The whole process was repeated until, finally, under cover of artillery fire, the infantry could storm the positions of the counterscarp defenders. If the city or fortification had not surrendered by this point, the attackers once more moved their big guns forward, knowing that they now had time to concentrate on the main fortifications. The tactic was the best available at the time, but it was a long and laborious affair which sapped manpower. However, it did achieve its objective: to bring about a surrender.

DEVELOPMENTS IN GUNPOWDER

Gunpowder had become more expensive and more powerful because of the newly developed French technique of 'milling' or 'corning'. The drawback to using the more powerful gunpowder was that it was more likely to burst the barrels on some of the older designs of cannon built using the hoop-and-stave method of construction. This hazard, coupled with the expense of the new powder, prevented it from being fully accepted for some time. But the introduction of corned gunpowder did help encourage the development of cannon fitted with stronger barrels.

The storage of powder also became a cause for concern. It still had to be kept near to the cannon on the battlefield and lighted matches had to be on hand at all times to ignite the guns, but new methods for handling it were developed. The powder was transported in wooden barrels bound with rope stays into which a leather liner could be inserted to keep the powder dry and cut down on spillages. After firing, the barrel of the cannon was swabbed out.

Such techniques cut down the number of accidents but it remained inevitable that injuries and even fatalities would occur. The highly volatile substance could ignite with alarming ease, even under the most apparently safe circumstances. When this happened the gunners serving the weapons were often horrendously burned. In 1536 after the French attack at Milan, Ambroise Paré, a leading medical practitioner, witnessed firsthand the methods for dealing with men badly burned in a gunpowder accident: 'Beholding them with pity there came an old soldier who asked me if there was any means of curing them. I told him no. At once he approached them and cut their throats gently and, seeing this great cruelty, I shouted at him that he was a villain. He answered me that he prayed to God that when he should be in such a state he might find someone who would do the same for him, to the end that he might not languish miserably.'

THE ARTILLERYMAN'S ART

Artillerymen, who were not enlisted as true soldiers, were organized into guilds of masters, gunners and apprentices and gun-servers. A prince or king might supply the actual cannon for firing, but the artillerymen had to supply their own tools of the trade, such as quadrants, levels and gauges. Some of these tools were made to have a dual purpose, for example a quadrant in the form of an axe. A gunner's quadrant of this type is displayed at the Royal Armouries Museum at Fort Nelson, Fareham, Hampshire. It was made in Germany in about 1585 and is known to have been used by Julius, Duke of Brunswick.

More books on the subject of artillery and shooting began to appear at this time, including William Bourne's *The arte of shooting in great Ordnaunce*, published in London around 1587. It is well illustrated and shows a gunner how to align the bore of an artillery piece according to the required range, as well as indicating where the bore lay in relation to the outer lines of the muzzle and breech. Bourne described how this was done using a rule and plumb lines.

Another author on the subject of artillery was Vannoccio Austino Luca Biringuccio, a mine manager and metalworker from Sienna, whose *Pirotechnia* was posthumously printed in 1540, two years after his death. Published in

Venice by Venturino Roffinello, the work ran to ten volumes and included all the details of the practice of metalworking as it then stood. Biringuccio was widely travelled in Europe and had learned his craft from many sources. His writings were eventually translated into several languages, including French and English. Biringuccio conducted experiments into devising a cannon which was of light weight, but with enough strength for use in battle. He also refers to the absence of standardization in artillery pieces, but remarks that some cannon-founders were beginning to show some consistency with regard to the thickness of the walls of their barrels. He noted they were also displaying some thought concerning the relationship of calibre to barrel length and the impact this had on ensuring all the powder was burnt before the ball had left the muzzle on firing. In addition, Biringuccio expounded how much better iron cannon-balls were than stone ones, because they permitted the gunner to fire with better accuracy and greater power. However, he records that he did not have any great faith in the weapon known as the mortar.

Niccolo Tartaglia (1506–59) has entered the pages of artillery history as the 'father of ballistics'. Born in Brescia, Italy, he was a lecturer in Verona before becoming a professor of mathematics in Venice. He wrote extensively on ballistics. Indeed, it was his work on projectile ranges that rightly earned him his sobriquet. He is credited with the invention of the gunner's quadrant, a device used to set the angle of elevation and thereby the range of a weapon. The quadrant staff was simply inserted into the end of the barrel so that the quadrant faced down and the attached weighted cord cut across it. The gunner then elevated or depressed the barrel until the cord crossed the scale at the point corresponding to the required range. As Tartaglia himself said of the quadrant: 'This instrument will help us to judge of all the variable positions or elevations that may happen in any peece of artillerie whatsoever . . . The whole square [right angle] shall contain 144 equal parts which I call minutes'. Twelve of Tartaglia's minutes were equal to 'one point': for example, 72 minutes gave 6 points of angle or 45 degrees. However, it should be noted that in England these angles were divided into right angles of 90 degrees, a universal measurement today.

Nuova Scientia, or *New Sciences*, is the best known of all Tartaglia's works. He was a man of peace by nature, but nevertheless concerned himself with matters of fortification and 'Colloquies concerning the arte of shooting in great and small peeces of artillerie, variable randges, measure and waight of leaden, yron, and marble stone pellets, mineral saltpeeter, gunpowder of diuers sortes, and the cause why some sortes of gunpowder are corned and some are not corned'. He also calculated ranges for various artillery pieces, such as the 'Faucon' (falcon) and the 'Saker', which he describes as having point blank ranges of 320 yards and 360 yards respectively. He also lists their 'Utmost', that is to say extreme, ranges as 1,280 yards and 1,440 yards respectively.

Tartaglia also expounded theories that might have led to his being ridiculed by his contemporaries. Among these notions was his idea that the second shot from a cannon would carry further than the first because 'it doth find the air not only wholly stired with the pellet of the first shot, but also much tending or going towards the place to which it is shot'. Tartaglia showed he understood the rudimentaries of ballistics and realized that a projectile fired from a cannon did not travel directly to its target; 'a piece of artillery cannot shoot one pace in a straight line'. Tartaglia may have been familiar with the works of Biringuccio, but it is doubtful if those writings had any influence on his own theories surrounding ballistics.

EXPLORATION

The sixteenth century was a period of discovery, particularly for the Spanish and Portuguese. The men who went on expeditions to the New World took gunpowder weapons with them for protection and for the subjugation of native peoples. The use of artillery and harquebuses spread to other continents. In 1518, Hernan Cortes, a Spanish nobleman and officer, landed on Hispaniola, the island now known as Cuba, which had been discovered by Christopher Columbus in 1492. Using the island as a stepping-off point, he headed further west and into Mexico to conquer the Aztec Empire. Cortes had a force of 570 men, 16 horses, which were hitherto unknown in those parts, and 10 cannon. In only three years he brought the Aztec Empire to its knees. By 1522 Cortes was advancing into modern-day Honduras and Guatemala, with his force now increased to 850 men, 86 horses and 15 cannon. He called the newly conquered area Nueva Espana (New Spain). Eleven years later, Francisco Pizarro, another Spanish soldier-explorer, arrived on the continent. In 1533 his force comprised 180 men, 27 horses and 2 cannon; he went on to conquer the Inca Empire in what is now Peru.

The Spanish had brought two completely alien entities to South America: horses, which gave them mobility, and gunpowder weapons in the form of artillery and harquebuses, which allowed them to destroy large numbers of people at a distance and at a single stroke. Using these methods Gonzez de Jeliauesada had also brought Colombia into the Spanish fold.

Portuguese explorers were now entering Africa, taking with them artillery and other gunpowder weapons to facilitate expansion by force. But such was the nature and vastness of the terrain that massed artillery in the European style could not be employed. Local tribes gave battle in a manner alien to European tactics and the power of gunpowder in a culture with no experience of such things meant they were very quickly subdued in much the same way as the Central and South American peoples.

By this time artillery was also beginning to make an impact on the Indian sub-continent by way of Portuguese explorers, although some believe that the Indians may already have known about the use of gunpowder weapons and artillery. If they did not, they were certainly quick to learn. For example, within fifty years of the arrival of the Portuguese, at the Second Battle of Panipat on 5 November 1556, Akbar, the grandson of Babur the first Mughal emperor, scored a victory over the forces of Hindus and rival Muslims, whose combined forces amounted to 100,000 men and 1,500 elephants. Akbar's forces included 20,000 horsemen and a well-served artillery park. An even earlier engagement at Panipat had occurred on 21 April 1526, when a Mughal force of some 10,000 men led by Babur clashed with the much larger force of the Delhi Mohammedans, led by Ibrahim, and supported by 1,000 elephants. The strength of Sultan Ibrahim's army has been put at 100,000 men. But it was Babur who eventually carried the battle which 'lasted till mid-day, when the enemy were completely broken and routed'. Included among Babur's forces were a number of *feringi* (foreign) cannon which he lashed together with rawhide and placed in front of Ibrahim's war elephants. Babur's victory marked the end of the Afghan dynasty of Delhi and established the Mughal Empire.

In barely 200 years gunpowder weapons had spread across all the known world and they were being used not only to forge empires but also to destroy them.

FOUR

THE GUN TAKES THE FIELD, 1600–1700

The seventeenth century was to witness many developments in the way artillery was deployed on the battlefield. There were also significant changes in its deployment and use in battle. In addition, it was at about this time that artillery began to become known by the collective term 'guns'.

The first half of the century was a decisive period in the history of artillery, particularly in mainland Europe. Henry IV of France (1589–1610) was one of the first monarchs to realize that gunpowder weapons had enormous potential and accordingly set about exploiting their power. In 1600 he appointed Maximilian de Bethune, Duc de Sully, as Master-General of France and it was the duc who oversaw the creation of new French artillery, which included a force of 400 specially cast field pieces, and its organization. By the end of the century the French Army had a separate Royal Regiment of Artillery, which was raised in 1693. At the time of Bethune's appointment the French Army numbered only an estimated 15,000, but by 1690 it had been increased to some 400,000 drawn from a population of about 20 million.

During the seventeenth century pieces of artillery were cast in China with a calibre of 5.5 inches or 6.3 inches and in India by 1685 huge 40-ton behemoth weapons were being made, including the 'Moolk-I-Meidan' (sometimes spelled 'Mukh-el-Maidan'), which translates as either Master of the Field or the Master of the Plain. There was also the great brass gun of Agra known as 'Dhool Dhanee' (The Scatterer), which had a calibre of 23.5 inches. In 1832 this piece of artillery was broken up and sold for the value of its metal. These weapons were comparable to the pieces the Turkish sultan Mehomet II commanded in 1453 and at the time nothing in the region could match them for power. Turkish influence is known to have been responsible for the casting of great artillery pieces in India as early as 1548. Under the supervision of a Turkish expert 'The Great Gun of Beejapore' was cast at

Ahmednuggar; it had a calibre of 28.5 inches and was capable of firing a projectile weighing 1,000 pounds using a charge of 80 pounds of gunpowder. Meanwhile, in Portugal, guns of a more modest 8.7-inch calibre were being cast in bronze in about 1627.

By the end of the seventeenth century a series of influences both on and off the battlefield meant that a more scientific approach was being applied to the way in which guns were grouped to support other arms during particular phases of hostilities. By 1700, projectiles of between 30 and 200 pounds were being fired out to ranges of 2,000 metres. The main type of ammunition was still solid shot, but gunners also used hollow cast shells, referred to as bombs, which were filled with gunpowder and fused to explode in the air or on landing. These were usually deployed in sieges against fortifications, where their high angle of trajectory could get them over the walls.

During a rather minor action at the siege of Elfsborg, Sweden, by Danish and English forces in 1612 it is recorded that:

> Parts of the English forces came before Elsborough Castell in Sweden on Thursdaye the 14 of Maye and landed on Satterdaye the 16 of the said month. Then was the ordnance planted, and on Frydaye the 22th by 7 a clocke in the morning the King [James I] began to playe with 7 peeces upon one of the towers of the castell contynually tyll ten a clocke, at which tyme he had beaten downe parte of the tower, having spent 200 shot. . . . at 2 a clocke the same daye . . . he commaunded the cannon to playe agayn, and before 5 a clocke (having drawne downe more greate peeces) he had with 286 shott made a breache for 3 to enter abrest.

This is probably a reference to England's involvement as a mediator in the War of Kalmar involving an alliance of Norway and Denmark versus Sweden. War had broken out in 1611 precipitated by rivalry in the Baltic and by Swedish attempts to gain control of Finnmark (modern Finland). King Christian IV of Denmark sent forces to the mouth of the Gota and to Kalmar, which they laid siege. In January 1613 the Peace of Knarod was recognized, which was a result of mediation by James I of England. James's involvement leads to the conclusion that English mercenaries rather than regular soldiers supplied by England may have been participating in this war.

By 1617 there were only nineteen men on duty at Gorey Castle in Jersey, including a master gunner and his mate and sixteen soldiers. The average

age of the garrison was forty-four years. Between 1617 and 1619, the castle was given its finishing touches. 'A perfect inventorie taken by Sir Edward Conway and Sir William Bird, Knights, His Majesty's Commissioners' on 13 May 1617, lists: 'Brass Ordnance, Mounted– 1 Demi-cannon. 1 Whole Culverin. 1 Demi-Culverin. 2 Falcons. 1 Falconet. Iron Ordnance, Mounted– 1 Demi-Culverin. 6 Sakers. 2 Falcons. I Falconet. 1 Mortar. Iron Ordnance, Unserviceable– 2 Mortars. 1 Perrier. 2 Portuguese Basilisks. 4 Fowlers.' The list continues with an inventory of the types of shot available for the guns. This includes: 100 shots of 32 pounds for the demi-cannon, 200 of 16 pounds for the whole-culverin, 250 of 9.5 pounds for the demi-culverin, 300 of 6 pounds for the sakers, 80 of 2 pounds for the falcons, 120 of 1 pound for the falconets. The shot for the fowlers weighed 15 pounds and there were 180 barrels of powder in the store. This was quite an arsenal for such a small island only 45 square miles in size, but it reflects how much England wanted to preserve Jersey from the French. In 1640, a list of artillery held in the castle is recounted by Prynne as fifteen cast pieces. And forty years later, Captain Richard Leake, Master Gunner of England, prepared: 'An accompt taken of all the Ordnance, etc. in Mount Argile Castle'. His was a more complete listing and actually mentions where each piece was mounted. At the same time as compiling the inventory, he made recommendations regarding the rearmament of the castle. He advised that the existing guns be replaced with two culverins and twenty-two demi-culverins.

GUSTAVUS ADOLPHUS OF SWEDEN

One of the influential figures in the development of gunpowder weaponry in the early seventeenth century was Gustavus Adolphus, King of Sweden from 1611 to 1632. He was deeply interested in artillery and, like his French counterpart Henry IV, he made truly astonishing changes to the construction of artillery and its deployment. These changes influenced the way other European armies viewed their artillery and its use on the battlefield. Gustavus's personal involvement in the evolution of weaponry earned him the title 'the father of modern field artillery'. He devised the concept of using massed, mobile artillery fire. He was motivated to make changes because he deplored the fact that artillery's heavy firepower potential could not support infantry and cavalry manoeuvres on the battlefield. One of his first moves was to reduce the weight of artillery pieces by decreasing the amount of metal in the barrel; after a series of trials and experiments, this was achieved by shortening the barrel's length and reducing the thickness of its walls. Then Gustavus oversaw the introduction of improved and standardized gunpowder, which burned at a uniform rate. This permitted greater accuracy even though gun barrels were shorter; it also restored the ballistic power lost by making the tube lighter.

Following the example set by Prince Maurice of Orange-Nassau in the previous century, Gustavus allowed only three standard calibres: 24-pounder, 12-pounder and 6-pounder guns. A long series of experiments under the king's personal supervision led to the production of a fourth piece by 1629, the so-called 'regiment piece'. This was a light but sturdy 3-pounder regimental gun. It generally required two horses to move it but could be pulled by one horse if necessary, or even be handled by two or three men. The cannon-ball was directly wired to a bagged charge of gunpowder, called a cartridge, which gave unprecedented rapidity of fire because it was loaded as a single round of ammunition rather than two separate items. The regiment pieces, sometimes referred to as battalion guns, were produced as high priority weapons. They were Gustavus's so-called 'leather guns'. The barrels were cast from iron with a lining of brass, an alloy of copper and zinc, to produce a weapon that weighed just over 620 pounds, little more than 280 kilograms; they were bound with rope and leather for reinforcement.

At the time of Sweden's emergence as a military power, a number of foreign thinkers were being drawn to the country by its advanced military organization. Among them was Melchior Wurmbrandt, a colonel in the Austrian Army, and he is understood to have shown a design for a lightweight piece of artillery to the Swedes in 1625. Wurmbrandt's design may have been based on a similar idea he had seen in Zurich, Switzerland, in about 1622. Gustavus realized the important role such a weapon could play and placed an order with Wurmbrandt for guns firing shots of 3 pounds and 6 pounds; but it was the 3-pounder that became the more widely used and most famous. Enough of these weapons had been made to allow their deployment at the siege of Wormditt in October 1627. In siegework the new guns were too light, but they could be moved quickly and easily over ground for redeployment elsewhere on the battlefield. In 1628, Gustavus's troops took at least eight with them to the mouth of the Vistula river. There they manhandled them over rough terrain to fire on a Polish fleet and inflict severe damage. In 1629 the Swedes lost ten of these guns to Polish forces at the Battle of Honigfeld, after which the secret of their design was out.

An English account of the new Swedish guns dated August 1628 states that they were:

> as good and better service than his Copper Cannon: for as fast as the souldiers are able to march, the Cannon is convayed along with them, having but one horse to draw but the biggest of them, and three or foure men can carry the biggest of them on their shoulders over any straight place, or narrow Bridge whatsoever, so that the Polls are not aware ere the Cannon play upon them, for it will shoot as great force as any other: which make the Palonians say, his Maiestie useth Devilrie: but that is all untrue: for I my selfe have heard those Cannon severall times shot with as great force as any other.

Gustavus was to take over eighty of these lightweight weapons to Germany in 1630, with many others being brought up by the resupply column as it followed in the wake of the army. By 1631 every one of Gustavus's infantry squadrons within a regiment had two or three regiment pieces attached to it. A combination of fire from infantry weapons and canister from the guns was used to tear into the enemy. The new piece was light enough to support the infantry and to be moved quickly to anywhere it was needed on the battlefield. Gustavus Adolphus's artillery was to number 9.4 guns per 1,000 men by 1630. Earlier this figure had been 1 gun per 400 men, but even then it was better than the many other European armies, such as the Holy Roman Empire's, which could deploy only 1 gun per 1,000 men. In order to ensure effective command and control over the weapons, Gustavus abandoned the old system of hiring civilian contract gunners and in their place established military units of cannoneers, who were disciplined and trained to the same standards as his infantry and cavalry.

The Battle of Breitenfeld, 17 September 1631, was fought between the forces of Gustavus Adolphus, which numbered 40,000 men with 60 to 70 guns supported by an allied Saxony force of some 40,000 men led by John George, the Elector of Saxony, against 31,000 Imperial Catholic troops under Count Johan Tilly, totalling 32,000 and supported by 30 guns. This was only one action in a period of hostilities known as the Thirty Years War, which lasted from 1618 until 1648. The conflict essentially began over religious issues generated by a power struggle between Roman Catholics and Protestants in Germany. But what started as a religious war soon dissolved into a political struggle, in which many European countries fought. The phase of the war in which Sweden was involved has become known as the Swedish Period and lasted from 1630 to 1634. By the time of Breitenfeld, Gustavus Adolphus had been leading his men on campaign for fourteen months.

At Breitenfeld Tilly's guns were of the 24-pounder type, which required twenty horses apiece to move them and a further twelve animals to haul each of the supporting equipment wagons. Heavy and cumbersome even in the best of conditions, they became even more difficult to shift in wet weather or during an actual battle. The object of this particular engagement was to recover Leipzig for the Protestants from the Imperial-Catholic faction. The Swedish forces were drawn up with the infantry in the centre and the cavalry on the flanks with musketeers supporting them. The infantry had the support of forty-two regiment guns each served by two men. These guns were sited in ranks one behind another with their attachments. A small reserve artillery force was held in the rear and brought forward to support the final attack. The battle opened at noon with an exchange of artillery fire. Tilly's Imperial cavalry attempted to take the Swedish right flank but was prevented from doing so by the Swedes' simple expedient of extending the flank under attack. The fighting ebbed back and forth for nearly three hours, during which time the Swedish muskets and guns achieved a firing rate three times that of the Imperial artillery. Gunpowder weaponry of all types took its toll. The Swedish troops managed to take back the Saxon artillery which had been lost in the battle and turned the pieces on the Imperial troops. Gustavus Adolphus's troops, secure in the knowledge that they had superior artillery firepower, could now go completely onto the offensive.

The outcome of the battle assured the future of German Protestantism and the ascendancy of Sweden as a major military power. Breitenfeld showed how cavalry could be thrown back by firepower which combined flexibility and mobility, both elements of Gustavus's force. Tilly, who was badly wounded in the action, lost 7,000 men killed and had 6,000 others taken prisoner. Gustavus Adolphus lost 2,100 killed and wounded, with his Saxon allies losing about 4,000 men.

At the Battle of Lutzen, 16 November 1632, the Swedes were to prove conclusively that their artillery was the finest of its type in existence. Some 19,000 Swedish troops led by Gustavus Adolphus himself deployed east of

Lutzen and were supported by 20 guns. The Imperial forces of about 19,200 commanded by General von Wallenstein and supported by 30 guns, faced them across a ditched road. The Swedish Army attacked the enemy's right flank but was driven back by the arrival of Count zu Pappenheim. Gustavus charged Count Heinrich Holk's Imperial cavalry, forcing them back onto their own artillery, and drove the musketeers into the ditch. Wallenstein launched a surprise cavalry charge which threatened the Swedish centre. Gustavus attempted to rally his troops but was mortally wounded in the fray. Pappenheim launched another attack which forced the Swedes back, but he too was killed. The Swedes continued to fight and succeeded in gaining a victory, despite the loss of their king. Their cavalry drove Wallenstein's troops off and seized the Imperial artillery. The Imperial forces had lost 12,000 men and the Swedes about 10,000 in one of the bloodiest battles of the entire war.

The Swedish artillery is known to have been deployed more than once to support various manoeuvres at the Battle of Lutzen. But with the inspired leadership of Gustavus Adolphus gone, Swedish artillery soon fell into decline. Only two years later at the Battle of Nordlingen on 6 September 1634 the Swedes lost 10,000 men killed and 6,000 prisoners to an Imperial army of 40,000 led by Ferdinand of Hungary, who also captured 80 valuable pieces of Swedish artillery.

Neither every commander nor every army was convinced of the effectiveness of the new Swedish guns and some nations still opted for the traditionally cast bronze cannon. A reason for their reluctance to introduce regiment guns might be the fact that they were known to become overheated during prolonged use in battle and charges could spontaneously ignite on loading if the barrel was not properly swabbed out between shots. But even so, the voices of resistance had to take into account changing tactics in cavalry and infantry deployment.

Artillery in use with the English Army in the 1630s had changed little over the previous thirty years or so, with few, if any, positive advances being made. The Scots, however, were prepared to adopt weaponry that could give them an advantage against the English during periodic exchanges along the border. Among the Scots were well-known and highly regarded mercenaries, many of whom had seen service with Gustavus's forces in Europe. In 1640 the Scots used versions of the Swedish leather guns to good effect against the English at the River Tyne. Then, during the English Civil War, the Royalist Army produced a version of the 'galloper-gun', which was a small brass piece mounted on a two-wheeled carriage with the gunners riding alongside. It is believed to have been developed by Prince Rupert, the nephew of King Charles I, whose military thinking had been influenced by Gustavus Adolphus.

Before Sweden's irruption into Germany, artillery had been consigned to a largely static function on the battlefield. During battles it was invariably placed in the open field and at the front of the battle order. In this position batteries of artillery could be used to fire on the opposing side before the movement of battle closed in front of the guns' positions, thereby preventing them from being used for fear of firing on their own troops. But in this location the guns were at risk of being overrun by the enemy – as the Swedes had overrun Imperial weapons at the Battle of Breitenfeld. During siege warfare the defenders fired their guns from ravelins or hornworks and in turn the attackers used their artillery to batter fortifications from positions protected by field works and erections such as gabions, which were large wickerwork baskets filled with earth. For the time being, then, this was the only way in which artillery could be used because its size and weight rendered it virtually immobile in battle. Not until about 1680 when trail wheels began to be fitted universally to gun carriages was manhandling on the battlefield made easier. These additions were simply a pair of wheels onto which the trail could be hooked, thereby distributing the weight over four wheels instead of only two. The development did lead to an increase in weight but this was largely offset by the increased mobility afforded by the articulated joint. The device was to evolve into the limber, in which ammunition was carried 100 years later.

VAUBAN AND SIEGECRAFT

The Vauban system of siegecraft which emerged during the seventeenth century provided the means for the systematic approach of attackers and their artillery to a fortification via a series of entrenchments. The main aim of the Vauban system was to enable attackers to bring their siege artillery to a range where it could easily force a breach in defensive walls and provide covering fire for an infantry assault. In some instances the infantry assault could be made without waiting for heavy siege artillery to breach the walls because the mining work conducted by engineers and pioneers had already demolished the defences. Siege work could often proceed rapidly, but typically lasted no more than six to eight weeks.

Marshal Sebastien Le Prestre de Vauban came from a humble background in Burgundy and joined the army serving as a volunteer under the rebel Prince of Condé in 1651. He was taken prisoner in 1653 and opted to serve the Royalist cause after being converted to it by the French statesman Cardinal Mazarin. Vauban then served an apprenticeship as an engineer under the Chevalier de Clerville, whom he succeeded in 1678 as the Commissaire Generale des Fortifications. He was promoted to the rank of lieutenant-general in 1688 and became Marshal of France. In his career, Vauban conducted fifty sieges and drew up plans for 160 fortifications. His ideas on military thinking came to dominate developments in the opposing sciences of siegecraft and fortification. Through him these arts approached the ultimate possible for military forces limited to muzzle-loading weapons and black powder. His innovations were extremely important in a century in which sieges were among the most common form of combat. By using new techniques, Vauban was able to consolidate the experiences and practices of over 100 years of fortification and siegecraft, achieving more in this area than any other single person of his age.

The method of approach employed by Vauban was eventually to become standard practice. A first a parallel trench was dug some 600–700 metres out from the fortification, often completely encircling the target. Along this trench, which was just out of reach of the defenders' artillery fire, points were selected from which an assault or several assaults were to be made. The engineers then dug a series of 'saps' toward the fortification using a zig-zag method of approach because this prevented the defenders from firing down the length of the trench. Throughout, the spoil from the digging was thrown up to form earthworks to add height to the parapets and further protect the troops. The length of a sap was usually fixed because it was close to the maximum effective range of defending and attacking artillery of the age and was set at about 300 metres. Under Vauban's directions a good sap might be pressed forward at the rate of about 146 metres in 24 hours. Then a second parallel trench was dug, with additional earthworks being thrown up in front to serve as protection for siege artillery emplacements which were now brought forward. Under cover of fire from these guns the attacking engineers began to dig further saps towards the fortification. All the time the siege guns would be firing against the ramparts in an effort to force the defenders to take cover, thus reducing the effects of the defenders' artillery. If a breach was made in the wall at this point the attackers could assault and storm the position. However, there was always the possibility that the defenders might rally, counter-attack and force the attackers to withdraw. Under such circumstances the attacking force might pull back after spiking its guns, which is to say nails or metal spikes were forcefully hammered into the touch holes or vents of the artillery pieces. This action rendered the weapons useless to the enemy, but it also meant that should the pieces somehow be retaken, their owners could not use them either.

In a siege attackers had to be ready for any eventuality and strong infantry forces were maintained constantly in the parallels to protect the guns and cannoneers against any sallies that defenders might launch. Should the defenders continue to resist then a third parallel would have to be dug and again artillery pieces would be brought up. The types of artillery deployed at this stage could include mortars, which would be used to lob bombs at high angles inside the defences. Vauban wrote on the use of mortars at the site of a siege in 1672, where they were loaded with up to two wheelbarrows-worth of stone or scrap iron at a time: 'The stones fly through the air in a cloud and then flog the ground with a force that can only be compared with that of pikes landing point-downwards.' Usually it took no more than two days bombardment from this third parallel to break the defenders' resolve.

The fortress designs drawn up by Vauban emphasized the role of artillery in defence. He produced three different systems, including the bastioned trace, and massive designs that incorporated bastioned towers, covered redoubts in the ravelins and recessed curtain walls with casemates, which would remain immune from fire until the last moment. But Vauban was not alone in his field and among contemporary theorists was the Dutchman Menno van Coehoorn (1641–1704). The Marquis de Montalambert (1714–1800) also had important ideas. Indeed, the latter realized that a siege at this time was no more than a prolonged artillery duel. He, therefore, proposed that fortresses should be huge multi-storey gun-towers from which the defenders could dominate the firing artillery of an attacker. Should attackers wish to take the city with the minimum amount of damage, the gunners could use a method of dispatching their projectiles known as 'ricochet' fire, from the French ricocher, meaning to bounce. Gunners had to fire cannon-balls at an angle low enough just to graze the parapet of the wall and head off on a bouncing trajectory into the interior of the defences. Cannon-balls fired in such a manner could inflict terrible injuries and even decapitate several men at once.

RESISTING THE SPREAD OF ARMS: JAPAN AND EGYPT

During the seventeenth century many big guns were successfully cast in iron from sources including the excellent Swedish ore. Bronze, however, was still the preferred metal for field guns, despite the costs involved, because it was not prone to bursting during firing. Artillery trends spread eastwards along trading routes and oriental countries were soon producing guns of Western design. Jesuit priests were widely engaged in helping China to improve its development in casting guns. From 1699 bronze weapons were being made by local Sinhalese craftsmen at Jaffnapatam, Indonesia, for the Dutch East India Company.

The Japanese lord Minomoto Ieyasu wrote 'guns and gunpowder are what I desire more than gold brocade', but the Japanese elite did not always embrace artillery. Portuguese explorers brought gunpowder and gunpowder weapons to Japan as early as 1542. The introduction of such weaponry into the realm of the Japanese, where ritualized combat was akin to the tactics of the twelfth-century European crusaders, must have produced reactions comparable to those felt by knights at the Battle of Crecy in 1346. It was not long before leaders such as Oda Nobunga trained their troops to fire all gunpowder weapons in volleys. At the Battle of Nagashino in 1575, for example, he decisively defeated his enemies through the use of gunpowder weapons. The control of gunpowder weapons rested in the hands of the warlords, and rather than their use becoming widespread, the reverse happened. Strict control of weapon production was instituted and by the end of the seventeenth century only a handful of armourers knew how to make and cast cannon and those cannon that did exist all dated from before 1620.

With no influences from outside, Japan was more fortunate than European countries and was able to centralize cannon founding. In 1607 all gunfounders and gunsmiths were ordered to take their workshops to the city of Nagahama. There the four chief gunsmiths were elevated to samurai status, which guaranteed their loyalty to the upper, sword-bearing classes. Orders for gunpowder weapons could only be placed by the Commissioner of Guns and he only placed such orders if instructed to do so by the state. Eventually the Japanese armouries were full of weapons that would hardly be used and did not become broken or worn out. Weapons control had been introduced. The Japanese status quo remained in place until 1854 when an American, Commodore Perry, appeared in Tokyo Bay with his 'black ships' and forced the country to open its doors to the world.

The Japanese were not the only ones to find the use of gunpowder weapons repugnant. The Mamelukes in Egypt had also rejected their use during the sixteenth century. Thus when they were confronted by the Ottoman armies at the Battles of Marj Dabiq in August 1515 and Raydaniya in January 1516, they were completely routed.

THE GUNNER'S TRADE

By now gunners were equipped with more or less standardized tools of the trade. There were one or two exceptions, however, such as in Italy where some artillerymen used an item called a *stiletto*, a finely bladed dagger. The example held at Fort Nelson in Fareham, Hampshire, dates from about 1650 and shows how highly elaborate such special daggers could be. Markings on the blade allowed a gunner to use it as a ruler for measuring the calibre of a weapon and converting the measurement to weight of shot; this proves that the knives were employed for purposes other than display and self-defence. Other tools included the linstock, a shortened spontoon-like pole arm, but which lacked a blade. Curved arms held the burning ends of the slow-match (a slow-burning wick impregnated with saltpetre) which the gunner could then apply safely to the vent-piece of the gun. During the loading drill, when the powder was rammed into the breech via the muzzle, a member of the gun crew was detailed to 'serve the vent', which entailed him placing his thumb over it to stop air being blown through the hole, thereby preventing any smouldering powder or fragment from the wadding being ignited. The tell-tale sign that a gunner was involved in this operation was a split thumb. To prevent this painful condition vents-men were issued with thumbstalls, a small leather tube which was slipped over the thumb and tied around the wrist. This continued to be standard issue until the nineteenth century and was not phased out until the introduction of breech-loading weapons with a moveable breech-block.

The 'port-fire' or quick-match was a tube filled with flammable material that could be applied to the vent hole when the gun was to be fired. The firer lit his port-fire from the slow-match held by the linstock sited between two guns; this practice reduced the number of linstocks being used in the vicinity of gunpowder but still allowed the same number of guns to be fired at once. The filled port-fire tube quickly burned through and was applied to fine gunpowder placed in the vent. After use, the burning end could be cut off using a port-fire cutter. The small port-fire device greatly improved safety, but did not entirely replace the method of applying the linstock with the slow-match into the vent for firing the gun.

Another device was the gunner's rule, which began to be used in England during the seventeenth century. This instrument had a number of purposes, including the calculation of shot weight from calibre. It also allowed the gunner to determine the size of a proof charge for a particular gun. Other implements included equipment that had long been in use without alteration, such as the rammer, which was used to push the powder charge and cannon-ball firmly into the breech end of the cannon. The sponge was for swabbing the barrel out between shots, the worm was employed for clearing obstructions, such as bits of swabbing, and the powder scoop was a long-handled wooden ladle. These items varied in design but were in universal use among gunners around the world.

By 1620 master gunners were beginning to benefit significantly from the achievements of innovators such as Tartaglia and new written works on the gunner's art continued to appear. Francis Markham's *Five Decades of Epistles of Warre* was published in London in 1622. He believed that the primary duty of a master gunner was to relieve the master of ordnance of some of his burdens. Markham said that junior gunners should be supervised in order to establish whether they were adept and 'skilful, ready and carefull in Charging and Discharging, Levelling, Mounting and Guarding their peeces'.

Although thinking on the operation of artillery and the deployment of gunpowder had developed, some gunners persisted in beliefs that should have been consigned to legend. Progress mingled with tradition. For example, one published work recommended that a gunner eat and drink before discharging a gun because the fumes of the powder might otherwise be 'hurtful to his brain'. The same work suggested that a gunner prepare his gunpowder charges of even weight in cloth bags before a battle instead of scooping them into the barrel, roughly estimating quantities using a wooden ladle. So, although artillerymen were more aware of the dangers of gunpowder, there was still much they did not understand. They did note that whether the 'air was thick or thinne' (moist or dry) would influence the distance a cannon-ball would travel, and that if the wheels of the gun carriage were not levelled the shot would not hit the intended target. They had experience built up from years of observation, but did not understand the physics. Markham relates a story he heard of a fatal accident involving a 'Canoniere' who was the worse for drink and had dropped his linstock, the lighted match for igniting priming powder on a cannon, into a barrel containing gunpowder. The accident happened on board a ship and not only rendered the vessel short of gunpowder, but also damaged it and reduced the gun crew by one member.

Other books on military thinking in general and artillery in particular included *The Principles of the Art Militaire*, which was published in about 1643. It concerns tactics, employment of weapons and advances in artillery. A shortage of trained gunners had recently become all too obvious, particularly during a recent Irish rebellion. None of the English attackers at the siege of Limerick in 1642 knew how to place charges to blow up the houses which the enemy were using as cover and artillery had to be used. It was also during the Irish rebellion that an overloaded cannon blew up on the battlefield, killing Master Gunner Beech and his mates. This accident highlighted how inexperienced some gun crews were; efforts were made to train new gunners and eliminate ignorance among those already serving the guns. Manuals appeared, including Thomas Eldrid's *The Gunner's Glass* (1647). Some were up-to-date and contained highly technical instructions, while others were no more than reiterations of earlier works, containing all the old errors without any attempt at correction.

By this time some gunners understood that a constant relationship between the weight of the charge of gunpowder loaded into the chamber and the degree of elevation given to the barrel determined how far the cannon-ball travelled when fired. But they knew that in order to achieve any degree of accuracy the powder charge had to be carefully measured and the angle of elevation strictly determined using a quadrant. Gunners were increasingly converted to using proper drills and formal calculations. The quadrant, in its staff-like form with divisions or points marked off, was an invaluable tool.

The method of moving the barrel of the gun remained very rudimentary because the elevating screw was still not in widespread use. Handspikes and wooden wedges, called quoins, were inserted between the rear portion of the carriage and the breech end of the barrel to adjust the elevation of the muzzle. But aiming was still a question of merely pointing and firing the gun in the general direction of the target. It was often achieved by manoeuvring the gun carriage on its wheels; the final position would be determined by sheer brute force as the gunners used handspikes to lever their piece into the arc of fire.

'Bagged' charges of gunpowder, as developed by Gustavus Adolphus, had not won acceptance either and gunners were still required to ladle the loose gunpowder into the barrel; it was them rammed down tight into the chamber. A wad of old rag or cloth was inserted in an attempt to reduce the effect of windage and the cannon-ball was also rammed down. When the firer had calculated the range and elevation and then sighted along the barrel, a small measure of finely corned gunpowder was poured into the vent hole. The slow-match on the linstock was then applied and the gun fired. Recoil was still not fully compensated for and the gun had to be resited after every shot.

At this time the infantry began to accuse artillerymen of conceit and adopting superior graces. For their part the gunners took great pride in themselves and their weapons. A typical field gun at the time of the English Civil War was operated by a crew of at least three men: the gunner, the gunner's mate, still called a mattross, and an assistant who was used for fetching and carrying. Gunners had to operate their pieces to a strict set of rules. For example, there were thirteen commands for the use of the sponge and ladle. Scooping out the incorrect load of powder for a cannon was deemed a 'foul fault for a gunner to commit' and if he spilled gunpowder on the ground he was ordered not stand on it – 'it being a thin uncomely for a gunner to trample powder under his feet', a dictum that had not changed in nearly 200 years. A gunner was also expected to 'set forth himself with as comely a posture and grace as he can: for agility and comely carriage in handling the ladle and sponge doth he give great content to standers by'.

MANUFACTURING

Pieces of artillery known as 'culverin-drakes' were cast in iron by Thomas Ffoley and George Brown in England in 1652 during the period known as the Commonwealth. This was the time of Oliver Cromwell's rule in England. Cromwell is known to have preferred to order iron guns on the grounds of economy: the metal was still much cheaper than bronze. There is an example of this type of weapon on display at Fort Nelson, Fareham, Hampshire; it has the calibre of 140mm and the ball weighs 9 kilograms. The word 'drake' apparently refers to the interior design of the gun, which narrows down at the breech to form a reduced powder chamber instead of following an even cylindrical bore all the way down. This design creates 'shoulders' on which the ball rests instead of being directly in contact with the powder.

At the Battle of Nantwich, 25 January 1644, the Parliamentarian Sir William Brereton opened fire with his drakes using 5-pound balls which 'caused more terror than execution'. The cannon-balls struck hard flinty surfaces which sent up great shards of stoney splinters, thereby causing the Royalists to turn away shouting: 'Let us fly, for they have great ordnance.' At Chester in 1643 a drake firing a 5-pound ball was recorded as killing sixty of the king's party with one shot. Other artillery in use during the English Civil War could be just as effective, for example, at Rowton Heath, an action fought on 24 September 1646. In this engagement the Royalist artillery fired a 29-pound ball at a Parliamentarian infantry regiment and 'made such a line through them that they had little mind to close again'. Another contemporary statement on the efficacy of artillery records how: 'The English cannon shoot further and with greater force.'

An illustrated work entitled *Modern Fortification* or *Elements of Military Architecture* (1673) by Sir Jonas Moore shows a number of barrels of artillery pieces, including a mortar and a cannon petrieroes, with the internal features of the culverin drake. Other artillery barrels such as the culverin, which is referred to in the work as a 'culvering', and a cannon for battery fire both had a more uniform barrel diameter. Sir Jonas also includes an example of a cannon which he calls a 'Brass Basis or Petrieroes A Baga', which is accompanied by a device called a 'Mascolo' and is identical to the early pre-loaded pot-shaped breech pieces used on some of the earliest forms of artillery. It is likely that this piece was of either Spanish or Portuguese influence or design. It shows how some older, tried and tested methods were still being resorted to in an attempt to increase the rate of fire. These plans support the discovery, made by Antonio Gonzales in about 1680, that by reshaping the powder chamber from a uniform cylinder to a tapered shape, a much smaller charge could be used to generate the same range and penetration, thereby opening the way for dramatically lighter pieces. This development also meant that gunpowder could be used to better effect and more sparingly.

The techniques for casting cannon barrels had not advanced that much since the sixteenth century and still involved pouring molten metal into a mould of the correct shape and size, after which it was allow to cool and solidify. The first stage in gun foundry was to make an exact replica, or pattern, of the gun. This was done by winding rope on to a wooden core, on top of which the barrel shape was modelled in clay, followed by a coating of wax. The mould was made by covering this pattern with clay, which after it had dried and been strenghtened with iron bands, was carefully removed. The mould was then stood upright and supported in a casting pit in front of the furnace mouth. The molten bronze or iron was run into it. After the bronze had cooled and solidified the mould was hauled out of the pit and broken away from the casting. If all looked well and the gunsmiths were satisfied, the barrel was taken to the boring factory workshop. Gunsmiths such as Verbruggen used this solid casting method and bored out the chamber. The bored-out material generated by this method of manufacture could be re-used for further barrels.

The seventeenth century saw renewed attempts to produce multi-barrelled cannon. One of the leading exponents of this design was the Italian Antonio Petrini who designed a double-barrelled weapon, the tubes of which were joined together at an angle of 30 degrees. They were intended to fire simultaneously two cannon-balls linked by a length of chain. This experiment had similar elements to designs created by the gun-founder Peter Baud, who worked for Henry VIII at Houndsditch in London between 1528 and 1546. Petrini claimed that his gun could produce 'the greatest destruction'. But as anyone with a sense of timing will understand, trying to get two barrels to fire at exactly the same time and at the same velocity is like trying to make water run uphill. Petrini faded into obscurity.

From the seventeenth century the Board of Ordnance in England employed a master carpenter to oversee the manufacture of gun carriages in government and private contractors' workshops. (This arrangement was to last until the nineteenth century when all such work was moved to the Royal Carriage Department established at Woolwich, where quality control checks could be carried out at every stage of manufacture.) By the seventeenth century, gun carriages were almost universally fitted with two wheels connected by an axle with 'cheeks' to support the barrel by its trunnions. The trunnions, and therefore the barrel, were kept in place by metal fittings called capsquares, which were bolted to the frame of the carriage and prevented the barrel from simply jumping off when moved at speed over rough terrain. The carriage was formed into a trail by two rearward-facing arms which rested on the ground to support the weight of the gun and act as a type of rudimentary shock absorber for the recoil on firing. This part of the carriage had fittings to which horses could be harnessed.

IMPACT OF THE ENGLISH CIVIL WAR

By 1642 the relationship between King Charles I and Parliament had deteriorated to such a degree that fighting broke out. The English Civil War was really a series of cavalry actions supported by massed ranks of pikemen and it could be argued that artillery had little decisive effect on the conflict, except at a handful of engagements. For example, in autumn 1642 an early skirmish between the two sides at Southam, Warwick, was described by Sergeant Nehemiah Wharton of the Parliamentarian forces. It started as a cavalry skirmish but:

> In the morning early our enemies, consisting of about 800 horse and 300 foot, with ordnance, led by the Earl of Northampton, the Lord of Carnavon, and the Lord Compton . . . We went to meet them with a few troops of horse and six field pieces; and being on fire to be at them we marched through the corn and got the hill of them whereupon they played upon us with their ordnance, but they came short. Our gunner took their own bullet, sent it to them again, and killed a horse and a man. After that we gave them eight shot more, whereupon all their foot companies fled.

Throughout the Civil War artillery was mainly reserved for use during sieges. Some of these were rather minor affairs, but larger and more important actions were conducted at Bristol, Leicester, Leeds, Worcester and Lincoln. One of the lesser sieges that quickly got out of control was at Old Wardour Castle, Wiltshire. In April 1643 the castle was held by Blanche, the sixty-year-old wife of Sir Thomas, 2nd Lord Arundell, who was in Oxford campaigning with the king, and a garrison of twenty-five, including female servants. A Parliamentarian force of some 700 horse, commanded by Sir Edward Hungerford, approached the site with the view to seizing it. Hungerford called for reinforcements, which eventually numbered 1,300 supported by two cannon. The castle was fired on for several days. However, little damage was done to the fabric apart from bringing down one chimneypiece and breaking all the glass in the windows. By 8 May the siege had ended, but it demonstrated just how easily a small-scale engagement could degenerate into an action which absorbed large quantities of troops and equipment. Most of those castles destroyed by artillery fire during the English Civil War were largely obsolete and therefore were not replaced. Indeed, fortified sites were frequently 'slighted' by Parliamentarian forces when they were captured. This involved placing casks of gunpowder under the walls of the castle and simply igniting them. The resulting explosion tore the walls apart. This was the fate of Donnington Castle in Berkshire, Caerphilly in Wales, Basing House near Basingstoke and, to a lesser degree, Farnham Castle in Surrey.

Artillery was also used in siege actions in the Channel Islands during the Civil War. Jersey, the largest island in the group, declared for the king, and Guernsey, the second largest island, declared for Parliament. In early October 1651 a Parliamentarian force landed on Jersey and Gorey Castle surrendered on 27 October. However, the island's other fortification, known as Elizabeth Castle and sited on a rocky promontory and cut off from the main island by the sea at high tide, managed to hold out. Between 28 October and 2 November 1651 several batteries of artillery were sited on the island facing the castle. The largest contained 36-pounder guns and was located on South Hill, which had commanding views of the area surrounding the Bay of St Aubin. According to the diarist Jean Chevalier, the largest of the artillery mortars used 10 pounds of gunpowder to fire a projectile weighing 450 pounds with an explosive filling of up to 40 pounds. A smaller mortar used 8 pounds of gunpowder to fire a projectile of 250 pounds with an explosive filling of 25 pounds. A third mortar used 4 pounds of gunpowder to fire a shell of 36 pounds containing 12 pounds of explosive. Each of these mortars was supplied with 300 projectiles. The late Brigadier-General W. Evans, CMG, DSO, Secretary of the Royal Artillery Institution, estimated the calibres of these weapons to be 18.75 inches, 14.75 inches and 4.25 inches respectively. The massive mortars fired on the castle using projectiles filled with musket balls, but when these did not achieve the desired effect the crews launched shells filled with gunpowder. Over the twelve days from 5 to 17 November it is believed some thirty-eight mortar projectiles fell in or around the castle. Mid-way through the bombardment, on the night of either 9 or 10 November, one fell on the old abbey church within the castle; it destroyed twelve barrels of powder and great quantities of other supplies, killed sixteen men and wounded a further ten. The defenders were called on to surrender but they held out until 5 December. Writing in 1685, the Jurat, Philip Dumaresq, believed that some 500 projectiles were fired at the castle during the entire siege. The bringing together of such a force of artillery to attack a small castle may seem like an overreaction, especially when the besieged garrison could have been starved out.

The Parliamentarians' New Model Army came into being on 15 February 1645 with Sir Thomas Fairfax in command and Oliver Cromwell as Lieutenant-General of Horse. The original strength of this force was 14,000 infantry and 7,600 mounted, which left only 400 to serve with the artillery. There had previously been no standing artillery force in England and it had been left to the Ordnance Department to raise trains of artillery as required, along with hired horses, civilian drivers and supporting services. Even now, the artillery arm of the Parliamentarian forces was regarded as unimportant; it was equipped with older, heavier guns and its reorganization was considered unwarranted.

Artillery trains at the time of the English Civil War were not of a standard size; they consisted of what was available or needed. From the beginning of the war the Royalist Army was at a disadvantage because it had fewer artillery pieces than the Parliamentarian side. The disparity was only partially remedied when the Royalists captured forty-nine pieces at the siege of Lostwithiel, 21 August to 2 September 1644.

Even though artillery was largely deployed in siege actions during the Civil War, it did also appear on the battlefield and artillerymen were often greatly exposed. For example, at one point Parliamentarian cavalry overran Royalist artillery at the Battle of Edgehill, 24 October 1642, and cut down the gunners – an action, no doubt, intended to prevent their further participation in the battle further. The Parliamentarian commander, the Earl of Denbigh, had declared that he would 'rather lose ten lives than one piece of my artillery'. Victory was claimed by both sides, but the Royalists seized several guns from the Parliamentarians and could technically claim to have taken the day.

In his book *The Seven Ages of the British Army*, Field Marshal Lord Carver states that: 'In a typical battle, the first exchange of fire would be from the artillery, aimed at breaking up the enemy's battleline. However, it does not seem to have been very effective and in some cases, for instance the Battle of Preston [17–19 August 1648] neither side had any artillery as it had failed to keep up.' The New Model Army had few gunners and the Royalist Army at one time could only count fifty pieces of artillery in its train – and these required over 1,000 horses to move them. Royalist artillery was able to support cavalry during the engagement at Bradock Down on 19 January 1643 to provide a victory. At the Battle of Roundway Down on 13 July 1643 the Royalists' guns were so well handled that they were once more able to support the cavalry and even allowed the king's troops to seize the Parliamentarians' guns. Some Civil War actions saw only an desultory exchange of weapons' fire, but other engagements opened with an exchange of artillery. At the Battle of Marston Moor, 2 July 1644, the twenty-five guns fielded by the Royalist Army were soon rendered useless by a flanking attack from Cromwell's troops.

Speed was always of the essence and in some cases safety was compromised in order to bring the guns into action quickly. Indeed, records describe how iron ladles were used to scoop powder directly from wooden powder casks into the gun barrels in an effort to keep them firing at whatever cost but at great risk to the gunners. An average artillery piece could fire fifteen shots an hour, but beyond 300 paces was not very accurate and generally achieved better results in sieges.

Not everyone praised artillery. Artillerymen during the English Civil War declared that: 'The first shot [was] for the devil, the second for God, and the third for the king'. Ben Jonson, a soldier turned playwright, had earlier declared that artillery 'from the Devil's arse did guns beget'. John Milton, author of *Paradise Lost*, called artillery 'a devilish machination to plague the Sons of men'. In keeping with the age-old military penchant for black humour, the gunners in the Parliamentarian regiment of Sir John Meldrum nicknamed their largest artillery piece – a 32-pounder, 12 feet in length – 'Sweet Lips' after a well-known woman of ill-repute in Hull.

Other observations on artillery from this period included Colonel Slingsby's notes on its effectiveness: he claimed to have seen 'legs and arms flying apace' when infantry was engaged by artillery at ranges as close as 200 yards during the first Battle of Newbury, on 20 September 1643. (This and the engagement at Langport on 10 July 1645 were the only Civil War battles where cannon played a major role.) Other actions at which artillery fire inflicted casualties were recorded by Captain Gwynne. He saw: 'A whole file of men, six deep, with their heads struck off with one cannon shot of ours.' George Creighton, chaplain to Lord Ormonde's regiment, described the effect of artillery fire at the Battle of Ross, Wexford, in March 1647: 'I did see what terrible work the ordnance had made, what goodly men and horses lay there all torn, and their guts lying on the ground, arms cast away, and strewn all over the field.'

By the end of the war the New Model Army's artillery train could boast some fifty-six weapons, not including siege mortars; the force needed some

1,038 horses for transport and two companies of musketeers for protection. The Parliamentarians won the Civil War. They executed Charles I in 1649 and forced the rest of the royal family into exile, from which it was not to return until 1660, nearly two years after the death of Oliver Cromwell.

THE RESTORATION AND THE GLORIOUS REVOLUTION

In 1660, the year of Charles II's restoration, artillery was still being stored in the Tower of London. This was not an unusual practice: a number of countries kept their most important artillery in a well-guarded, centralized location which served as an arsenal. In France, for example, this was the Bastille and in Russia it was the Kremlin. The men in charge of the artillery at the Tower were really only custodians. Records from 1661 show there were only forty-eight gunners in England, but nine years later this had been raised to 103 paid gunners.

Between 1678 and 1680, Charles II commissioned Colonel George Legge to undertake a survey of the defences of the Channel Islands. Included in the report was the state of the fortifications on the formerly Parliamentarian-held island of Guernsey. Legge's survey records the weaponry as:

Plaiderie [possibly Le Tour Grand]	2 × iron sakers
West End of Town	1 × iron saker
Hougue a la Perre, bulwark	1 × demy culverin; 1 × iron minion (in need of a carriage)
North of above	1 × 6-pounder; 1 × iron saker; 2 × extra demi-culverins were recommended
At the Key de la Viatte facing to St, sans [St Sampson]	1 × iron demi-culverin
At the bulwark Cotamanse, facing Arme [Herm] and Jerau [Jethou]	1 × demi-culverin; 1 × falcon, iron 2 × 12-pounders were needed too
Belgrave Fort	1 × demi-culverin; 1 × iron falcon; 2 × 12-pounders also required
Vale Castle	1 × minion; 1 × falcon; 3 × demi-culverins needed too
Mont Crevet Mount	2 × iron sakers; 4 × 12-pounders needed too
Fort de l'Angle, east of Lancras [on the site of Fort le Marchant, it covered vessels approaching the harbour]	3 × 12-pounder needed on ship carriages

Nicq de herbe Lancras	1 × iron 8-pounder; another one was recommended
Le Corbiere de Lancras, a musquett shot, west of Nicqpounders	1 × iron saker; 2 additional 12-poounders were wanted
Middle of Lancras	1 × iron saker. Instead it was recommended there should be 2 × demi-culverins
Near above	1 × demi-culverins
Near above	1× iron saker. Another 12-pounder was required
Houmet nicol [on which stands Fort Houmet]	1 × saker; 4 × 12-pounders needed too
Vazon	3 × iron sakers; 2 × 12-pounders needed too
West of Vazon	1 × iron saker; to this should be added 2 × demi-culverin
Rocquaine Castle	1 × iron saker; this should be augmented by 3 × 12-pounders

Such a list of weaponry for an island of only 25 square miles emphasises the fact that England was anxious to secure its territories against France.

In 1685 the Royal Regiment of Fusiliers (sometimes spelled Fuzileers) was raised by James II of England as 'My Royal Regiment of Fusiliers'. The regiment was originally raised to march alongside and guard the artillery train; it was armed with firearms known as fusils, which were flintlocks as opposed to matchlocks. (Flintlocks used flint and steel to create a spark to ignite gunpowder. Matchlocks used continuously burning wick-like fuse to ignite gunpowder and were not considered safe.) Fusils were much more expensive than matchlocks but much safer to use in close proximity to gunpowder because no continuously burning match or smouldering fuse was required. A distinct uniform for the fusiliers developed over time and distinguished them as serving in a specialized role. At this time the daily rate of pay for a master gunner in the English Army was 14d and other gunners received 7d per day.

The reign of James II, as a Catholic king in a predominantly Protestant country, was by no means quiet. The first real test of his reign came in 1685 when he was forced to defend his kingdom against an invasion launched by the Protestant James, Duke of Monmouth, the illegitimate son of Charles II, who believed he had a rightful claim to the throne. Monmouth landed in the west of England from France at the head of a small force of only eight-two men and four cannon, but was able to raise many more followers in the countryside. In response, his uncle the king dispatched a force commanded by the Earl of Faversham. Second-in-command was John Churchill, a staunch Royalist, who had learned part of his soldiering in service abroad in Europe. The two sides met at Sedgemoor, Somerset, on 6 July 1685.

Churchill's forces experienced difficulties in moving their artillery and at one point were forced to use the coach-horses of the Bishop of Winchester, which were considered 'fitter for a bombardier than a bishop'. On the morning of the battle for a reason that has never been fully explained the gunners for Churchill's artillery were absent. Serjeant Weems of Dumbarton's (or Royal Scots) Regiment volunteered to fire the guns, of which he had some knowledge. Monmouth's guns could not equal the firepower of those on the king's side and after Churchill charged the rebels' position with his cavalry, driving off the gunners, they fell silent. For his part in the action Serjeant Weems was awarded a £40 gratuity 'for good service in the action at Sedgemoor in firing the great guns against the rebels'. It was a brief but bloody one-sided struggle which saw the defeat of Monmouth's forces. Monmouth was taken prisoner and executed, as were many of his followers.

However, James II's popularity continued to decline. In 1688 William of Orange, Stadtholder of the Netherlands, and his wife Mary, who was James II's daughter, were invited by Parliament to become monarchs of England in what became known as the 'Glorious Revolution'. They arrived in England in November 1688 and were proclaimed joint sovereigns on 13 February 1689. Meanwhile, James II had fled to France in December 1688. This whole episode in English history would mean nothing to the story of artillery but for the involvement of John Churchill, later to become Duke of Marlborough. Churchill was to achieve eminence during England's involvement in the War of the Spanish Succession, in particular because of his victory at the Battle of Blenheim on 13 August 1704. It was John Churchill who introduced significant changes in the conduct of land warfare and the tactics of weaponry, in particular the establishment of the 'artillery park'.

PETER THE GREAT

In Eastern Europe, Peter I, the Great, Tsar of Russia (1689–1725), followed the traditions established by his Western European royal counterparts, and displayed a great and very real enthusiasm for his army at every level, especially its artillery. Early in his reign Peter enlisted himself in a regiment of artillery at the lowly rank of bombardier, relishing the work and duties that the post demanded, even eating and sleeping with the crews and taking turns in standing watch. He reformed and modernized his army, having learned the trade of war the hard way from Charles XII of Sweden, his sworn enemy.

Throughout his reign Peter maintained an avid interest in the artillery, so much so that during the Azov campaign of 1695 against Turkey he personally inspected the artillery materials. The tsar also organized highly realistic military manoeuvres to train his army and in 1694 the largest, and last, exercise of its kind included 30,000 men from the cavalry, infantry and artillery. Although neither ball nor shot was fired there were still a number of casualties with faces burned and injuries sustained from the blast of the guns. This army was to expand Russia's empire, but at great cost, mainly at the hands of the Swedish Army. When he died in 1725, Peter the Great left behind a country that was exhausted but had an army of 212,000 experienced troops, who in turn were supported by a Cossack force of some 110,000 men and a strong navy.

FIVE

THE RISE OF THE GREAT GUNNERS, 1700–1800

T he eighteenth century opened with many of the leading European nations embroiled in hostilities. The Great Northern War, between Russia, Denmark and Poland on one side and Sweden on the other, was to last from 1700 until 1721. The War of the Spanish Succession opened in 1701 and did not end until 1714. England, France, the German states and Austria were the main protagonists and they were joined in the fighting by several other countries including, of course, Spain itself. In fact, throughout the century there were to be many conflicts, some of which had a profound influence on the use and deployment of artillery. Artillery was to become the 'force multiplier' that often decided the fate of armies and nations.

In the early part of the century there were few real changes to artillery. In 1742, Benjamin Robins, one of the most outstanding English mathematicians of his day, wrote in the preface to his work *The New Principles of Gunnery* that: 'The formation of artillery hath been little improved in the last 200 years'. The French, however, had continued to build on their earlier standardization efforts and abolished all mobile pieces larger than 24-pounders. Nevertheless, major efforts towards improvements in artillery were not begun until the War of the Austrian Succession, fought between 1740 and 1748. Many prominent artillerists emerged during this period, including Prince Joseph Wenzel von Lichtenstein, who continued the tradition of royalty becoming directly involved in artillery development. Lichtenstein not only limited Austrian artillery to 3-, 6- and 12-pounder guns and 7- and 10-pounder howitzers, he also standardized the design of carriages, wheels, battery forges and other artillery equipment. In the 1750s he had the foresight to establish experimental testing facilities near Budweis in Bohemia for the advancement of the science of ballistics – probably the first establishment of its kind anywhere in the world.

THE GREAT NORTHERN WAR

In the opening conflict of the century Peter I of Russia, Augustus II of Poland and Frederick IV of Denmark formed a triple alliance against Charles XII of Sweden with the aim of ending Swedish domination in the Baltic. This conflict, which lasted twenty-one years, became known as the Great Northern War and saw the employment of many and varied tactics, including attrition and scorched earth policies.

One of the greatest battles of the war was fought at Poltava on 28 June 1709. Manoeuvrings leading up to the fighting had been taking place since May and in its aftermath action was to continue until July. Charles XII of Sweden invested the Russian fortifications at Poltava with his army. In response Peter I marched his force of 80,000 men supported by 100 pieces of artillery to relieve the siege. The two sides prepared to give battle while minor skirmishes took place – Charles XII was wounded during one of them. The Swedish Army and the Russians met at Poltava, where Charles took the initiative and went on the attack. This surprised the Russians and gave the Swedish Army the upper hand for a short time. The outcome of the battle was decided when a Russian force of 40,000 fresh troops received the charge of only 7,000 Swedish troops. The Russians had lost 1,345 killed and 3,290 wounded. The Swedish Army had lost 9,234 killed and wounded and 18,794 taken prisoner. The use of artillery was decisive as it had been in other battles of the war, including Narva (30 November 1700) when the Swedish artillery bombarded Russian positions prior to an assault. The Swedes lost only 600 men, while the Russians lost 10,000 dead and wounded.

In 1718 Charles XII joined the list of notable artillery fatalities when he was struck and killed by a cannon-ball as he directed the siege of the Norwegian fortress of Frederikshald on 12 December. The Great Northern War was to drag on for a further three years until it was finally concluded by the last Treaty of Stockholm in 1721 and the balance of power was restored.

Under the terms of the Treaty of Nystad, 30 August 1721, (a preliminary to the Treaty of Stockholm) Russia acquired Livonia, Estonia, Ingria and a number of islands in the Baltic. Through the skilled use of its army and navy, including the power of its artillery, Russia had become the most dominant power in the Baltic and Eastern Europe.

WAR OF THE SPANISH SUCCESSION

In Western Europe from 1701 the War of the Spanish Succession was beginning to unfold. The Spanish Hapsburg Charles II had no direct heir, which meant that on his death the throne would be left open to two claimants. The first candidate was Louis XIV of France (son of the elder daughter of Philip III of Spain and married to Anne, the eldest daughter of Philip IV), who claimed the throne for his second grandson, Philip of Anjou. The second claimant was Leopold I, Hapsburg emperor, who was the son of the younger daughter of Philip III and was married to the younger daughter of Philip IV; he claimed the throne for his second son, the Archduke Charles. In theory the genealogy gave the two brothers-in-law an equally strong right to the throne. Neither Holland nor England, however, wanted to see a French or German claimant on the Spanish throne.

On 13 March 1700 France declared Philip heir to the Spanish throne and he was actually proclaimed Philip V of Spain on 1 November, following Charles's death. However, between March and November manoeuvrings had taken place that made war even more likely. The danger was compounded when French forces moved in to occupy fortifications in the Spanish Netherlands. The situation worsened and by 7 September 1701 a grand alliance against France had been established. This force included England, the Netherlands, Austria, Prussia, many of the German states, and later Portugal. France could count on Mantua and Cologne as immediate allies; Savoy initially supported the French but was to change sides later in the thirteen-year-long conflict and was replaced by Bavaria.

England declared war on 15 May 1702 and placed John Churchill, by now Earl of Marlborough and the darling of the English monarchy, in charge of the Anglo-Dutch force in Holland as captain-general. Regardless of the hindrance from the Dutch government, who had the power of veto over his use of Dutch troops in battle, Marlborough went on the offensive and invaded the Spanish Netherlands in June 1702.

There was enough space for the armies to manoeuvre and initially only desultory engagements took place. However, in 1704 the war entered a phase known as the Blenheim Campaign. In May that year Marlborough departed for the Rhine Valley with a force of 35,000 men, leaving a force of 60,000 behind to protect Holland. He chose not to reveal his intentions to his Dutch allies. On 2 July 1704, he fought and won the Battle of Schellenberg, but at heavy cost to his forces. Then on 13 August 1704 the first major English engagement of the war was fought at Blenheim. Marlborough commanded 52,000 troops and an allied Imperial force was led by Prince Eugene of Savoy. They faced a combined French and Bavarian force of 56,000 men led by Marshal Tallard, Marshal Marsin and Maximilian, the Elector of Bavaria. At about 10 a.m. there was a short exchange of artillery fire between the two sides to test each other's strength, preparedness and willingness to give battle. But even in this warm-up casualties were inflicted, including on the troops commanded by the Count de Merode-Westerloo, who lost two horses killed and a third injured as he sat post with his French comrades-in-arms. The battle did not develop properly until after midday when cavalry manoeuvrings by Brigadier Rowe's brigade were fired on by Imperial artillery.

The French artillery was commanded by a Swiss infantry officer called Zurlauben and was initially more accurate than the allied guns. The battle was essentially a cavalry engagement and the mounted arm was very much in evidence by 4.30 p.m. when Marlborough launched his squadrons against Tallard's centre. Eugene and Marlborough attempted to cut off the enemy forces in a double enveloping move, but through skilful handling Marsin and Maximilian were able to extricate their men.

Even though cavalry was the dominant arm during the battle, Marlborough wisely used his artillery as a mobile weapon – the first time this tactic was employed by an English force during a battle. In addition to serving as captain-general of the army, he was also the Master General of Ordnance. In this capacity he took a personal interest in overseeing the laying of every piece of artillery on the morning of the battle. As J.W. Fortescue, author of *A History of the British Army*, put it: 'For the other part, the artillery came out of the war with not less, perhaps with even more, brilliancy than the other corps of the army, and it is likely that no artillery officers ever worked more strenuously and skilfully in the face of enormous difficulties than the devoted men who brought their guns down to the south side of the Danube and then back across the river to the battle of Blenheim.' The battle was a victory for the alliance, which suffered 4,500 killed and a further 7,500 wounded. The French and Bavarian army had lost a total of 38,000 men killed, wounded and taken prisoner. Marlborough had also seized 117 cannon, 24 mortars and over 5,600 draught animals. The war now broke down into a stalemate as strategies were formulated and strengths built up once more.

Marlborough's next major engagement came during the Ramillies Campaign of 1706. The Battle of Ramillies was fought on 23 May. Like Blenheim it was primarily a cavalry action, but artillery did play a significant part. Again Marlborough and Eugene were in joint command of the allied artillery, which numbered 62,000 men with 120 cannon. The French, commanded by Marshal Villeroy, had only seventy cannon in their force. They were partially entrenched in defensive positions on high ground, but by using a feint against their left flank Marlborough was able to make the French move some men from their right flank to cover the left. Marlborough then ordered his men to charge the weakened French right flank and after heavy fighting the French were driven from the field. As the artillery was carried back from the line, the train was attacked and fifty guns were seized. The alliance had lost fewer than 3,000 men while the French had lost 15,000 killed and wounded and a further 6,000 taken prisoner.

The war continued with other various engagements and then came the phase known as the Malplaquet Campaign, which began in 1709. Once more Marlborough and Eugene commanded a combined force of English and Imperial troops, this time numbering 110,000 men with 100 cannon. The French under Marshal Villars numbered 80,000 and were supported by 60 cannon. The Battle of Malplaquet began at about 9 a.m. on 11 September 1709 with a preliminary bombardment by English guns. After two hours, this developed into a full bombardment by forty guns. During the ebb and flow of the fighting a unit of thirty Dutch battalions attacked the French right flank and was met by a hail of grapeshot fired by twenty cannon. In the face of this withering fire the Dutch succeeded in fighting through to their objectives, but French counter-attacks inflicted such heavy losses that they were forced to withdraw. On the French left flank the batteries of artillery were commanded by Marshal Villars, whose cunning positioning of his guns made them a dominant factor in the fighting. Indeed, he inflicted severe casualties on the German troops sent against him. As the battle developed, Marlborough and Eugene saw French infantry being drawn up in attack. In response, the Imperial artillery was arrayed to engage them from the flank. The firepower was decisive. By 1 p.m. the battle was going Marlborough's way and the French began to leave the field. The cost to the French was 4,500 killed and 8,000 wounded. But the bloody Battle of Malplaquet was a pyrrhic victory for the allies, who lost 6,500 killed and 14,000 wounded.

The war was to drag on until 1714, but England withdrew in April 1713 under the terms of the Treaty of Utrecht, which saw France cede Newfoundland and other areas of Canada to England. Philip V was recognized as the rightful king of Spain but it was agreed the two royal houses of France and Spain would remain forever separate. The treaties of Rastatt and Baden, drawn up in March and September 1714 respectively, finally brought peace to Western Europe. The war had established new royal dynasties and in the fighting artillery had truly been proven to be 'ultima ratio regum' – 'the last argument of kings'.

THE WAR OF THE AUSTRIAN SUCCESSION

The War of the Austrian Succession lasted from 1740 until 1748 and saw some very bloody fighting. Fighting began in January 1741, but it was not until four months later that its effects began to spread. Two years later in May 1743 George II of England gathered and led a force comprising English, Dutch and Hanoverian troops in support of the Habsburgs. The force was about 40,000 strong with an adequate artillery train and advanced into the Main and Neckar valleys along the Rhine. It met a French army of some 60,000 men commanded by Marshal Duc de Noailles on 27 June at Dettingen. This was to be the last time an English monarch personally led his troops into battle. The allied army was in the process of retiring to Hanau from Aschaffenburg when it found its passage blocked by a French force of 23,000 led by General de Grammont. Able to extract themselves from this dangerous situation, the allies then succeeded in fighting off a French cavalry charge. From their battle order the French were able to fire on the allies' positions. Cornet Philip Brown was to later write of the engagement that 'the balls flew about like hail'. Another eyewitness, Sam Davies, a footboy to Major Honeywood, wrote to a friend recounting how: 'our battel lasted 5 ours, the first they played upon our baggage for about 2 ours with there cannon . . . the balls was from 3 pounds and 12 pounds each . . . We stayed there till the balls came flying all round us. We see first a horse with baggage fall close to us, then seven horses fell apeace then I began to star about me, the balls came whistling about my ears. The I saw the Oysterenns [Austrians] dip there heads and look about them for they doge the balls as a cock does a stick, they are so used to them. . . . a twelve pounder came within tew yards of me. Then I began to stear indeed, it was about the size of your light puddings but a great deal hevyer.' Despite this pounding King George led his troops in a counter-attack which succeeded in breaking the French line and driving them off the field. After the battle the cost to the French was 6,000 dead and wounded.

Two years later the English were involved in the most serious battle of the entire war. The Battle of Fontenoy developed when the Duke of Cumberland, with an allied force of English, Dutch and Austrians troops numbering 50,000, was intercepted by a superior force of French as they tried to relieve the siege of Tournai. The French Army of 70,000 men under the command of Marshal Maurice de Saxe held the high ground and Cumberland ordered his men to attack. The objective was taken, but the Dutch troops, led by the Prince of Waldeck, failed to support Cumberland and when the French counter-attacked, fortunes were reversed. The allies were beaten back leaving behind 6,500 casualties. Cornet Philip Brown said of Fontenoy: 'I admire and adore that kind Providence who hath been my great protector and preserver of life and limbs during such a cannonading of nine hours as could not possibly be exceeded . . . there were three batteries (of cannon) continually playing upon our front and both flanks.'

The Battle of Fontenoy highlighted the need for a regular corps of drivers: Charles James Hamilton said: 'Each infantry battalion had two battalion guns [3-pounders] manned by gunners, dragged by hand in the front line of the attack to within thirty yards of the enemy infantry and gallantly fought as long as our infantry required support: while our 6-pounders engaged the French batteries, although heavily out-numbered by them. The fact that the civilian drivers disappeared with their horses early in the day limited the support these guns were able to give.' Hamilton, the third son of Lord Binning, was then aged about sixteen or seventeen and recorded his experiences at Fontenoy: 'We have had a most bloody battle with ye french; yesterday we bagan at 5 in ye morning & left off at 2 in ye afternoon, all wch time ye french kept cannonading us; I was forced to be very civil & make a great many bows to ye balls, for they were very near me . . . the foote were very sadly cut to Pieces, for ye french Put shot into their cannon & cut them down as just if they were sheering corn.'

Cumberland was called back to England to suppress the uprising of the Jacobite rebels, but returned to the continent almost without delay once the threat had been put down at home. Bitter and bloody fighting continued and the final campaigns of the war, which had also spread into Italy, were fought out in Holland. The status quo was restored by the Treaty of Aix-la-Chapelle on 18 October 1748, which saw all conquests, with a few exceptions, being restored to both sides.

The French commander Marshal de Saxe was an enigmatic figure. One of over 350 illegitimate children of Augustus II, the Elector of Saxony and King of Poland, he wrote a work entitled *Reveries upon the Art of War*. He was keen to adopt the new tactics that advocated the integration of the artillery arm with the infantry, but took current thinking a stage further by developing new all-arms formations called divisions.

FREDERICK THE GREAT AND THE RISE OF PRUSSIA

The Prussian king, Frederick II, the Great, is considered by many to be the father of either modern field or mobile artillery. He deserved both titles: he was the first to develop further the tactical artillery techniques of Gustavus Adolphus. During the Seven Years War, 1756–63, he created the concept of true horse artillery. Instead of operating conventional horse-drawn guns, Frederick implemented changes which ensured every cannoneer and ammunition handler was mounted on horse-back. This meant that for the first time light guns could keep up with the fast-moving, hard-riding Prussian cavalry.

Frederick also fully exploited the high trajectory angle of howitzers by using them to fire on his enemies' reserves, which were usually concealed behind some feature of the landscape. By developing this technique, he provided artillerymen with an insight into the concept of indirect fire. Frederick's use of this tactic came over 200 years after it was first employed and was really a reminder of the power which artillery could unleash.

Frederick the Great had not always been favourably inclined towards the large-scale use of artillery, but his experiments with fast moving, flying columns showed masterful initiative in using it as a mobile striking force. By keeping pace with the cavalry, it could also provide the latter with fire support. Of all Frederick's innovations, the greatest was the development of horse artillery. This branch of gunpowder weaponry was a new departure because, unlike the light field artillery, which used the same 6-pounder gun or the even lighter 3-pounder, the horse-artillerymen were all mounted. There were three drivers, each controlling two horses, riding postilion-fashion on the six-horse gun team, with each member of the eight-man gun crew riding his own horse.

The light artillerymen still had to march in the column with their pieces, which were pulled by horses, and were required to manhandle them with drag ropes and gunspike levers once they had been committed to battle. Before a gun can be laid on its target two essential adjustments are required: elevation and depression of the muzzle to either lengthen or shorten the range; and traversing left or right to bring the gun onto the bearing of the target, and in the eighteenth century this meant moving the whole piece on its carriage, there still being no facility to move the barrel independently of the carriage. Horse artillery was not exempt from these drills, but from this time onwards it was able to accompany cavalry units as they moved forward to make contact with the enemy. These mobile guns could also withdraw in good order and even be redeployed to another part of the battlefield where artillery support was urgently needed. Before this development, most European armies had possessed some form of mounted artillery, usually in the shape of galloper guns, which were light pieces drawn by one or two horses with the gun trail forming a pair of shafts. Each piece was usually accompanied by a light, two-wheeled tumbril drawn separately to carry the ammunition. But these were essentially weapons of close support under command of the cavalry units, to which they were attached either singly or in pairs. In small numbers they were not capable of delivering the same devastating effect as a full battery of guns suddenly coming into action.

The first Prussian mounted artillery units were raised in 1759 but were lost in battle due to a combination of being poorly deployed and the hot-headedness of the commanders in charge of this new arm. They were considered an elite force on the battlefield. By the end of Frederick's reign the horse artillery was organized into proper regiments of six troops, each equipped with nine cannon. Ever reluctant to be outdone, the British and French adopted the Prussian development.

Unfortunately, despite Frederick the Great's best attempts to improve the mobility of field artillery by lightening it and introducing horse artillery, it was still to remain a cumbersome force. During the early stages of the Seven Years War, he experimented with extremely light guns, which used chambered breeches and reduced powder charges. But these weapons lacked range and hitting power when pitted against the well-designed Austrian guns in the opening stages of the conflict.

The Austrian guns were the product of Prince von Lichtenstein's developments at Budweis. In 1765, following service with Austrian Army during the Seven Years War, a Frenchman by the name of Jean Baptiste de Gribeauval (1715–89), used Lichtenstein's system as a blueprint to improve the French Army's artillery, which only twenty-five years later would come into its own under the direction of Napoleon Bonaparte. It was not an easy process and the more reactionary of his colleagues successfully resisted his suggestions for a time. In 1776 de Gribeauval was presented with the opportunity to achieve his goal when he was appointed France's first Inspector-General of Artillery. With this position came the authority to carry out the improvements which have made him perhaps the most famous of all artillery commanders. Using his newly acquired knowledge de Gribeauval set out to standardize French field artillery into four types: 4-, 8- and 12-pounder guns supplemented by 6-inch howitzers. The 4-pounders were to serve in the role of regimental guns, while the 8- and 12-pounders and 6-inch howitzers acted as a reserve. It is interesting to note that a modern commander would probably consider the latter type his divisional artillery.

For garrison and siege use de Gribeauval organized 16- and 12-pounder guns, and 8-, 10- and 12-inch mortars. These were still the same smoothbore, muzzle-loading pieces of cast iron or bronze that they always had been. The programme of improvement was refined between 1802–3 using the de Gribeauval method to produce the 'Systeme an XI' (Year 11 System), whereby pieces of artillery were manufactured for lightness and strength by means of careful design, leaving out all embellishments and unnecessary ornamentation. The weapons developed by de Gribeauval were lighter than previous types but their carriages were stronger. The internal shape of the barrels of these new pieces was cast in the form of the drake-type guns, with shoulders on which the ball rested and a reduced powder chamber. The draught horses were harnessed side-by-side in pairs, instead of the usual tandem method, which gave better control of the animals on the battlefield. Drivers for the artillery wagons were now enlisted as soldiers. Separate, newly designed, two-wheeled limbers for the transportation of ammunition and powder charges were also provided, and increasing use was made of tangent scales and elevating screws, which eased the amount of effort required in laying the gun and also improved accuracy.

THE SEVEN YEARS WAR AND THE BATTLE TO BUILD EMPIRES

The Seven Years War, in which de Gribeauval had served, lasted from 1756 until 1763 and was precipitated by the rapid growth in Prussia's power, which alarmed Austria, France, Sweden and Saxony who formed an alliance to halt Prussia's emergence. At the time England was engaged in its own struggles for colonial power in India and North America, but that did not prevent it from eventually joining the war on Prussia's side. The Seven Years War was one of manoeuvre which was best performed by cavalry and infantry. Artillery did play a significant role in the major engagements of the war, such as the Battle of Rossbach on 5 November 1757 and the Battle of Leuthen on 6 December 1757 where Prussian artillery decimated Austrian formations. At the Battle of Minden on 1 August 1759 the English were present alongside the Prussians and Hanoverians. The French Army was 54,000 strong, under the command of Marshal the Marquis de Contades, with 170 cannon. The Prussian force, led by Ferdinand of Brunswick, numbered 42,500 men with 187 cannon. Over 7,000 Austrian men were killed and the Austrian Army lost 115 guns. The Prussians and their allies lost fewer than 2,800 men. At one point in the battle ten 12-pounders were rushed into the front line and a letter from a Prussian artillery officer, written after the action, describes what happened: 'We accordingly drew up our Ten guns close to the six regiments on the right and there waited undiscovered till the Enemy came almost within pistol shot, like a cloud, with numbers, and when they were just going to gallop down sword in hand among our poor mangled Regiments, we clapt our matches to the ten guns and gave them such a salute as they little expected, as they have since told us.'

England was also engaged in fighting Prussia's enemy France many thousands of miles away in India, in what might be called an extension of the Seven Years War. One of the most decisive engagements on this new sub-continent was the Battle of Plassey. Robert Clive commanded 1,100 Europeans supported by 2,100 native troops with only 10 pieces of artillery. The Indian Army of 50,000 commanded by Suraja Dowla and allied to the French was entrenched on the Bhagirathi River, and supported by 53 cannon. Clive crossed the river and entered a mangrove swamp; Suraja's forces were directed by the French to surround the English move. A sudden storm dampened the gunpowder of Suraja's men, but Clive had had the foresight to keep his powder covered and dry, and was able to discharge his weapons without coming under return fire. Clive predicted, correctly as it transpired, that a number of Suraja's troops were discontented and that as he approached to fire at close quarters he would not be attacked. The French artillerymen, under the command of St Frais, continued to fire until the last.

Success in the Battle of Plassey assured England's presence in the sub-continent. The fighting continued until 1763 when the Treaty of Paris saw Pondicherry restored once more to France. But it was to be an uneasy peace and within two years the First Mysore War broke out. This lasted until 1779, by which time the First Maratha War had started. The fighting between France and England, both supported by their loyal local troops, continued. The last of the four Mysore wars was fought in 1799, when the English Prime Minister, William Pitt, directed the Governor-General, Richard Wellesley, to move against the last areas of French influence in India. Assisting him in this task was his brother Arthur Wellesley, who distinguished himself in the campaign. Artillery was now being used by nations to forge overseas empires as well as to decide the fate of royal houses.

England was also fighting the French on a third continent, in the struggle for domination in Canada. Like India, this theatre can be seen as an extension of the rivalry that was to lead to the Seven Years War in Europe. The French had had a long-standing interest in Canada, but when they intruded into the Ohio Valley the American Colonials replied by dispatching Lieutenant-Colonel George Washington in 1754 to deal with the matter by building a fort at the confluence of the Allegheny and Monongahela rivers. Here he found the French had already erected a fort. War was now inevitable and both sides began to build up their forces.

Reinforcements arrived from France and local sieges and fighting in the woods became the normal mode of conflict in this inhospitable territory. Among the incidents during this period of fighting was the siege of Fort William Henry, when the Marquis Louis Joseph de Montcalm commissioned flat-bottomed barges to transport his heavy siege guns and mortars to blast the English-held fort into submission. The fighting between France and England, once again supported by natives loyal to whichever side they trusted or believed in, reached a peak in 1759. Troops under the command of General James Wolfe laid siege to the city of Quebec with a force of 9,000 men. The defenders numbered some 14,000 and were led by the Marquis de Montcalm. The resulting action saw both commanders killed during the Battle of the Plains of Abraham on 13 September 1759. It also saw the end of French dominion in Canada. While artillery had not been deployed to any great effect during the final stages of the fighting, it was to help in securing the newly conquered territory and keep it for England.

THE AMERICAN WAR OF INDEPENDENCE

Unfortunately for England peace in North America was not to last. By 1775 there had been a long-standing difference of opinion between England and the thirteen American colonies which eventually erupted into open hostilities on 19 April as English troops and Colonialists fired on one another at Lexington, Virginia. An army was raised under the direction of George Washington, who assumed command of all Colonial forces. In the beginning the new army of Colonials was no more than a rabble, but it was to be moulded into a cohesive fighting unit driven by self-belief and determination. It can be said that the American Continental Army was created on 3 July 1775, and along with it the artillery arm. The war did not always go well for the Colonials, who suffered a number of setbacks and defeats. There were no set-piece artillery duels along the European lines – in fact, the whole war was conducted along unconventional lines with the Colonials using hit-and-run tactics and giving battle only when it was unavoidable or on their own terms. For example, the Battle of Trenton on 26 December 1776, was fought out by Washington's forces who had crossed the Delaware River at night with 2,400 men. He mounted his attack at dawn and completely defeated the still sleepy Hessian garrison of 1,400 men. The attack gained a much-needed morale-boosting victory for Washington, but also won him a resupply of gunpowder and arms, along with a number of cannon. Fighting on land was to remain very much in this vein, with England continuing to pour in troops. The Americans were aided in their struggle by the French, who dispatched the Marquis of La Fayette in 1777. This young, energetic Frenchman held nothing but enmity for the English fighting man because his father had been killed at the Battle of Minden in 1759 by an English cannon-ball.

The tide began to turn for the Colonials during 1780 and 1781 and they achieved a victory over the English at the Battle of Cowpens on 17 January 1781. On 15 March 1781 at the Battle of Guilford Court House, North Carolina, the British commander, Lord Charles Cornwallis, acted in desperation in an effort to avoid defeat. At the height of the battle Cornwallis deliberately ordered his three guns to fire grapeshot into the close-quarter fighting between American Colonials and English troops, killing men from both sides. Only by ordering such an action was he able to drive off the Americans and save his army, which lost 93 killed and 439 wounded in the engagement. Deciding that he could no longer hold Georgia and the

Carolinas, Cornwallis retreated to Virginia. Cornwallis made another stand at Yorktown where he entrenched his positions with 6,000 men. He was faced by no less a figure than Washington himself who led a field force comprising 7,000 French under the command of Rochambeau and a Continental Army of 8,850 American Colonials.

The investment of Cornwallis's positions began in September 1781 and the siege was to last until 19 October when the English situation became untenable because of the temporary loss of command at sea. They were forced to surrender. At the start of the final phase of the engagement on 9 October Washington himself is understood to have fired the first shot from a heavy gun. Philip van Cortlandt, serving with the 2nd New York Regiment, described hearing the shot distinctly as it passed through the town striking several buildings on its way. This was the signal for Washington's artillery force of forty cannon and sixteen mortars to open fire. On the first day they fired over 3,600 rounds into Cornwallis's positions. Outnumbered and completely surrounded Cornwallis was left with no choice but to surrender. The war continued until 1782 when the Treaty of Paris recognized the independence of the United States of America and called on England to cease all hostilities once it had concluded fighting its current war with France and Spain. On 15 April 1783 the United States Congress ratified the treaty and by November that year the last of the English troops had embarked from New York. Artillery may have only been deployed in piecemeal units during the fighting, but it had helped a nation forge its destiny and win independence.

THE FRENCH REVOLUTION AND THE RISE OF NAPOLEON BONAPARTE

In Europe, de Gribeauval had started to reform the French artillery in 1774 and it now included mortars, which he considered the most useful of all arms. The new de Gribeauval 12-pounder was much lighter than the old cannon it replaced, and could be drawn by a team of only six horses. By contrast the Austrian 12-pounder in use during the time of Frederick the Great required the power of ten animals. With its large wheels and iron axletree, the new design gave de Gribeauval's 12-pounder a remarkable cross-country performance. He instructed that the wheels of all the carriages, both for guns and limbers, should be constructed to a single pattern, which meant the parts were relatively interchangeable. With such advances it was no wonder that copies of his 12-pounder gun and its derivatives soon became the mainstay of artillery parks across Europe. Reduction of the number of horses required for the artillery meant that less fodder had to be moved and less time spent by troops on blacksmithing, veterinary skills and grooming, which released them for other tasks.

De Gribeauval's most serious failure was his inability to persuade the French king of the value of the changes, which were not to be fully introduced into French service until 1791, almost two years after his death. By that time, however, Louis XVI had been overthrown in the French Revolution. But in a postscript to de Gribeauval's career, in 1791 his artillery improvements were adopted by the Swedes and two years later by the English.

In August 1793, in the midst of the chaos of the French Revolution, a captain of engineers, Lazare Carnot, eventually to become known as the 'Organizer of Victory', was elected to the Committee of Public Safety and put in charge of military affairs. He quickly established a cadre of young and energetic officers charged with building up the French Army. Their task was to embrace all three arms, infantry, cavalry and artillery, but to enable each of them to be capable of independent operations. In October 1795, during the period of the Directory when most French troops were in the field, the War Ministry believed there to be 29,000 troops in the artillery arm. Eventually these numbers were to double and horse artillery was to be introduced for the first time. The cannon used by the French artillery still had a very limited range and supply was in the hands of independent army contractors whose efficiency was limited by the carts, horses and mules that did much of the provisioning in the field.

In 1797 Carnot moved to Switzerland, but in 1800 he returned to serve as Minister of War under the rising star of a new, energetic and politically ambitious artillery officer, Napoleon Bonaparte. (Carnot's fortunes were mixed; he was eventually exiled by King Louis XVIII in 1815, when the country once more, if temporarily, returned to monarchy.) Trained as an artillery officer, Bonaparte was at his most militarily progressive in his attitude towards guns. He was no doubt inspired by the writings of the Chevalier de Teil, including *De l'usage de l'artillerie nouvelle*, in which de Teil expounded theories concerning the need for speed of movement on the battlefield and concentration of fire. It is known that the young Napoleon read this treatise during his time as a subaltern at the school of artillery at

Auxonne between 1788 and 1789, because at that time the institute was commanded by de Teil's brother and the works would almost have certainly been compulsory reading.

Napoleon was perhaps the first commander since the introduction of gunpowder artillery fully to understand the killing power of the cannon. To this end he would use it copiously throughout his career to inflict, at some engagements, over 50 per cent of the battle casualties suffered by his opponents. Under his direction artillery would once again reach the number of pieces used in the Thirty Years War and achieve the same level of tactical importance. He would write: 'Experience has shown, that it is necessary to have four guns to every thousand men.' Napoleon had a great many theories about the use of artillery, a number of which were taken up by his contemporaries and adapted to their own specific needs. Indeed, such was Napoleon's influence that it was to last long after his death in 1821.

The importance of de Gribeauval's reforms were to finally bear fruit for the French Army during the Wars of the Republic, 1792–1800. His tables of construction continued to ensure uniformity of manufacture, and the reduction in the weight of guns gave a mobility in the field that allowed artillery to be used with the greatest effect in Napoleon's new tactics. The final step in the field artillery's reorganization came in 1800, when a driver corps was established to put an end to the old system of using civilian contractors.

The first example of Napoleon's extraordinary skill as an artillery commander came during the siege of Toulon in 1793. A combined English and Spanish fleet had captured this important port, along with a third of the French fleet and the arsenal. The French Army opened the siege on 7 September and began the slow process of reducing the defences surrounding the port. On 16 September, Napoleon, then serving as a colonel, was passing through the region on his way to the Italian front when he was reassigned and took command of the artillery during the operation. He appreciated that the key to the success of the siege lay in commanding the two forts which were sited on the high ground overlooking the port. The English commander, Lord Mulgrave, also realized this and set about strengthening the forts. Napoleon directed that artillery with a plentiful supply of ammunition be brought up and ranged against the western fort. Laying the guns himself, he oversaw the opening barrage. By mid-November an assault was deemed to be possible, but the local French commanding officer withdrew. This action elicited from Napoleon an accusation of cowardice against the officer in question.

On the night of 17 December Napoleon himself led an assault on the fort, which was taken. The Allies, realizing the vulnerability of their position, evacuated the fort. For his part in this action Napoleon was promoted to brigadier-general and the path was set for his military career to flourish. Many volumes have been written on his tactics, both theoretical and practical, which preclude the need to recount the man's military career in full here. It is sufficient to say that the victories he gained over the next twenty-two years, and also his defeats and stalemates, have ensured that history looks on Napoleon as one of the truly great military leaders of all time.

Only a year before Toulon, the Battle of Valmy, the first of the Revolutionary War, had been fought on 20 September 1792. This action has been described as being 'an artillery contest'. The French Army of 50,000 men led by Charles Dumouriez and Marshal François Kellerman faced a weaker Prussian force of 35,000 under the command of the Duke of Brunswick. The Prussians were the more experienced of the two forces, but in the face of a deadly bombardment by fifty-four French cannon, directed by professional gunners, they were forced to withdraw. The Prussian guns fired at the French forces but at a range of over 1,000 metres round shot was not very effective. Casualties were between 300 and 500 on each side. The Prussian retreat was a boost to the morale of a previously untried army whose artillery was a dominant force on the battlefield.

INNOVATIONS IN DESIGN

During the eighteenth century a new type of artillery began to appear. It was called the howitzer, from the German *haubitze*, and soon became very popular right across Europe. Early types were similar to conventional cannon, being mounted on a two-wheeled carriage, but were capable of being elevated to higher angles than a normal gun. At first they were restricted by having barrels that could only be elevated to 20 degrees, but as time passed they became capable of higher trajectories. Mortars could fire shells at high angles of incidence, so that the defenders of a fortification could be brought under fire. Howitzers, like mortars, fired shells in a lobbing arc to reach over walls but could be used to fire heavy ammunition at a lower velocity and a shorter range than guns loaded with the same sized shot. Howitzers could be enormously useful on the battlefield, as had been proved by Frederick the Great. Until the introduction of this weapon reserve troops were immune to artillery fire when positioned out of sight and screened by trees.

The English Army at the time were using Cohorn mortars, named after Baron Meeno Van Coehorn, a Dutch military engineer. Many armies in continental Europe were also using mortars of various calibres, but all with the same purpose in mind – to lob shells at high angles of trajectory over defensive walls. The firing range for these weapons was adjusted simply by varying the charge of gunpowder. Mounted on a heavy-duty wooden base, they were ideal close-range weapons, fired at angles of elevation of between 45 and 90 degrees, providing the crews were protected from musket shot. The high 90 degree of angle for the barrel of the mortar would not have been used in normal practice for fear of the shell returning to earth in the vicinity of the crew who had fired it.

Mortars were also being cast for armies in India, such as the model designed for either Tippoo Sultan, 'The Tiger of Mysore', or his father, Hyder Ali. This weapon is believed to have been cast in Southern India in the second half of the eighteenth century and has the appearance of a crouching tiger, the wide gaping mouth forming the muzzle. It fired a shot of 240mm calibre and was captured by the English when they defeated Tippoo Sultan at the Battle of Seringapatam in 1799.

One of the more unusual designs was the so-called 'partridge mortar', which made its first appearance in about 1700. It comprised a large central bore around which were up to thirteen much smaller bores – a layout which allowed for one standard-sized mortar bomb and thirteen smaller shells to be fired in one salvo. This multiple firing was achieved when the flame produced on the discharge of the central barrel vented outwards into the surrounding smaller chambers, thereby firing them simultaneously. It was of French design and examples are known to have been used with some success during the defence of Bouchain in 1702 and again during the siege of Lille in 1708. An example of the 'partridge mortar' was illustrated in the *Memoires d'Artillerie* by Surirey de St Remy. It is described as being cast from bronze with a central chamber of 110mm (4.3 inches) and outer chambers each 30mm (1.2 inches). As an early example of area saturation weaponry it was really quite advanced.

The English experimented with new mortars from 1750 onwards. Weapons fitted with square collars on their chases, and elevation imparted by means of a brass screw working just under collar to achieve angles of up to 90 degrees, are known to have been trialled. During the same period English designers also experimented with mortars mounted on circular wooden beds in an attempt to achieve a full 360 degrees traverse for all-round fire.

Multi-barrelled guns were tried again at the beginning of the eighteenth century, but with only little more success than earlier attempts. Designs of triple-barrelled pieces were used by the French at a number engagements during the War of the Spanish Succession. Their design is attributed to an Italian priest and they were cast in bronze. The barrels could be fired independently or in a volley. Unfortunately for the French, this was one of their less successful experiments in artillery design; it proved very troublesome in reloading. A number of examples were captured by the English at Ramillies in 1706 and again at Malplaquet in 1709.

Standard artillery was now beginning to be referred to by the weight of the shot it fired and names that had been in use since the Middle Ages, such as saker, culverin and falconette, were dropped from military jargon. The giant wallbusters (*muurbraeckers*) disappeared as their role was taken over by a collection of much smaller guns firing balls weighing between 5 and 12 pounds. From about the 1760s the older-design guns, such as sakers and culverins, were replaced by horse artillery which made it possible for guns to be moved while in action, allowing them to be deployed as much as possible on ridges to give a clear field of fire. Siting artillery in such commanding positions gave it the capability to blow apart heavy formations of infantry.

Even with the new standardization, there were still five categories of artillery pieces in service: field, horse, mortars, siege and garrison. Guns of the last type had been developed to defend a fort or other vulnerable location from seaborne assault. They were basically the same as siege or field guns, but with a large calibre and were mounted on a heavy, four-wheeled wooden carriage similar to those in use on naval vessels at the time, and therefore not conducive to field operations. A unique garrison piece was developed in 1783 by Lieutenant Koehler of the Royal Artillery. He created a wooden carriage that allowed the barrel of the gun to be depressed to a low enough angle to fire on troops ranged at the base of hills and ships moored at the foot of the cliffs. Extra wadding rammed on top of the ball when the gun was loaded at the normal angle meant that it did not roll out when depressed to fire.

When used against ships, garrison artillery could also fire balls that had been heated in a brazier until they were red hot. After the powder was added and rammed down, a tompion of green wood was inserted so that the charge did not ignite when the red-hot cannon-ball was loaded. The gun was then fired in the usual manner. The heated ball was intended to cause a fire on board the target ship. Lieutenant Koehler's depression carriage is known to have been used against the floating batteries of the French naval commander d'Arcon's fleet and the Spanish ships on 13 September 1782 during the Spanish siege of Gibraltar.

At this time the infantry arm still made up the largest part of any army with cavalry strength averaging between 20 per cent and 30 per cent. Artillery formed a mere 2.5 per cent of the total military force, but by now it was showing it could be effective in deciding the outcome of a battle. It was being used to inflict a level of casualties out of all proportion to its comparatively small size. The emerging trend dictated a move towards lighter pieces of artillery. However, not all European armies accepted the trend and some continued instead to opt for heavy pieces, which could weigh up to 3 tons each. Resistance to change was to be found in some armies even as late as 1750, probably motivated by the cost of replacing existing serviceable artillery. In 1733 German 32-pounder guns with a calibre of 6 inches had a range of just under 3,000 metres, but required a crew of 14 men to operate them. Some examples of this gun were still in service much later and with a comparable sized crew, despite the belief that there should be an allowance of only one man for every 500 pounds (225 kilograms) of metal in the gun.

In 1734 Jean Maritz, a Swiss gunfounder from Geneva, entered French state employment and set about trying to convince the authorities that a better barrel could be produced if it were cast solid, rather than by the hollow, bell-casting technique still being practised. After the casting was complete, he would bore out the chamber. By using this manufacturing process Maritz believed a better fit between the ball and barrel could be achieved. In addition, Maritz argued his methods meant that powder charges could be reduced without compromising range and lighter guns could be manufactured.

The idea of boring out the barrel was nothing new. It had been in use since the sixteenth century, but no boring machine existed that could hollow out a barrel to the high tolerances Maritz believed were necessary. Unfortunately, he did not live to see his boring machine work and it was left to his successor to perfect the equipment, for which services the latter was appointed master of the royal arsenal at Ruelle and eventually all of the other French national

Recreated early form of field artillery in use around the time of the Hundred Years War. Known as serpentines, they were available in either breech-loading or muzzle-loading versions. (*Military Features & Photos*)

Muzzle-loading bombard, *c.* 1450, on display in Fort Nelson, Fareham, Hampshire, part of the Royal Armouries Collection. (*Military Features & Photos, courtesy Royal Armouries, Fort Nelson*)

Recreated breech-loading bombard of the fourteenth century, shown resting on a wooden trestle as it would have been during the Wars of the Roses. Note the large pot for the powder charge at the rear of the gun, along with wooden wedges to secure it in place. The wooden mallet resting directly on the barrel of the bombard is for hammering the wedges into place. (*Military Features & Photos*)

A recreated fourteenth-century bombard showing the barrel resting directly on a wooden trestle and the wooden tools used for loading the weapon. These tools include a swab for sponging out the barrel with water after firing to extinguish any smouldering powder embers, and a wooden ladle for loading powder into barrel. (*Military Features & Photos*)

Just after firing a recreated fourteenth-century breech-loading bombard, the smoke is just beginning to drift away. Smoke must have obscured vision on the battlefield and the noise of such weapons would have been deafening. (*Military Features & Photos*)

Re-enactment of a fifteenth-century gunner pouring fine powder into the vent piece of the gun to prepare it for firing. (*Military Features & Photos*)

Scene typical of a castle under siege by fifteenth-century artillery. The guns depicted here are bombards and appear to be muzzle-loaded types. (*Perigord*)

The siege of Ribodane, 1480. The artillery shown here is mixed, some pieces are quite large while others are smaller. Firing has been suspended while the attack goes on to the walls. (*Military Features & Photos*)

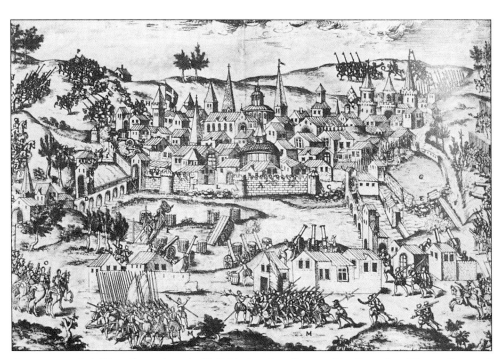

A very crowded fifteenth-century battlefield showing the combination of artillery, pikes and muskets and how each branch was deployed for battle. (*B.R. Hoay, Belfast*)

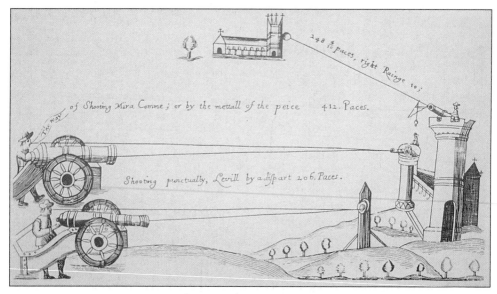

Illustration showing how gunners of the sixteenth century sighted and laid their pieces of artillery on to a target and to batter the walls. (*B.R. Hoag, Belfast*)

Large muzzle-loading bombard of the 1500s on display at Castelnaud, Dordogne, France. It is seen here mounted on a wooden frame and is protected from the defenders fire by a wooden screen. Note the large stone cannon-balls which were still being used in some areas in the sixteenth century as ammunition. (*Military Features & Photos*)

A sixteenth-century scene showing artillery firing from an elevated position to cover the advance of infantry. Artillery was now beginning to be used with some degree of imagination to support infantry on the battlefield. (*Grenelle Collection*)

A barrel foundry in the sixteenth century. This image shows molten metal being poured, while in the background barrels are being broken and added to the furnace for melting down and re-using. To the right an artisan is finishing the barrels with engraving. (*Grenelle Collection*)

Recreated falconet cast in Germany and typical of seventeenth-century artillery pieces. Note the sturdy design of the carriage and the stout wheels, designed to permit its movement around the battlefield and over long distances. (*Military Features & Photos*)

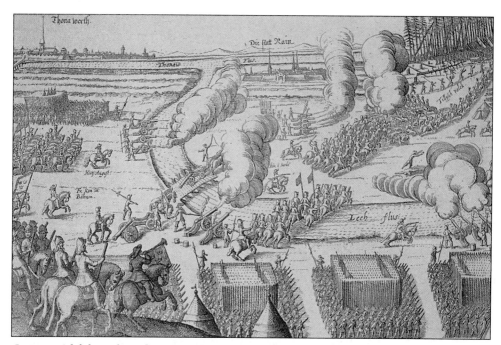

Gustavus Adolphus of Sweden on campaign during the Great Northern War, 1700–21. Note the advanced use of artillery to cover movements of infantry and cavalry during the battle. In the centre of the picture are at least two 'galloper' guns being moved by pairs of horses. (*Grenelle Collection*)

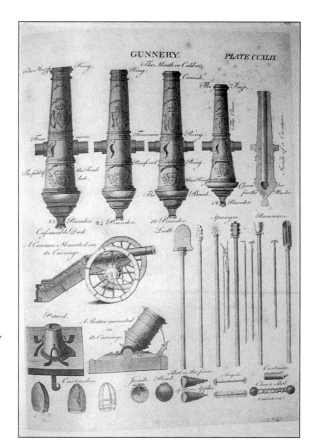

Barrels of different pieces of artillery in use during the seventeenth century, including a mortar on its firing mount. The engraving shows types of ammunition in use during the period and a range of wooden-handled tools. (*Ian Hogg*)

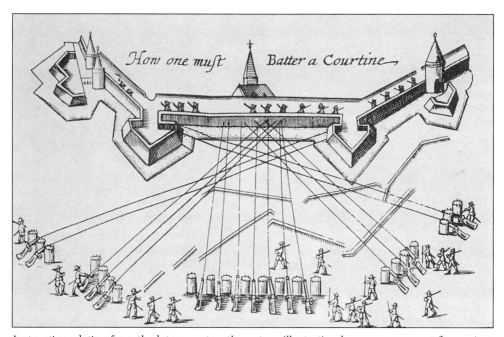

Instructions dating from the late seventeenth century illustrating how gunners must fire against defensive walls in order to batter a gap through which the infantry may assault. (*Ian Hogg*)

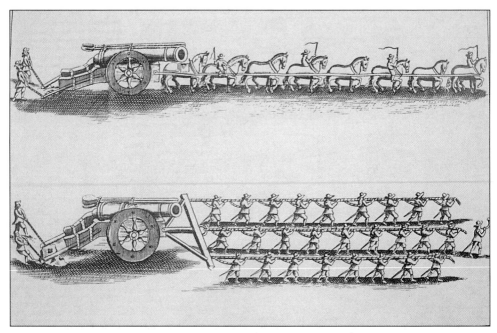

Methods of moving a large piece of artillery into position on the battlefield using either horse or manpower during the first half of the eighteenth century. (*B.R. Hoag, Belfast*)

A battle of guns in action at a siege, *c.* 1740. Note the barrels of gunpowder are kept well to the rear of the guns' position to prevent an explosion. The A-shaped device lying in the centre of the position is called a gyn and was used to remove the barrels of the guns from their carriage for either repair or replacement. (*Grenelle Collection*)

Workers at a barrel foundry beat the straw and rope mandrel solid and ready for the barrel casting, *c*. 1740. (*Ian Hogg*)

Re-enactor recreating the role of a Royal Artilleryman at the time of the American Revolution in 1776. He is shown here using a quadrant to set the angle of the barrel on a recreated galloper-style piece known at the time as a 'grasshopper gun'. (*Military Features & Photos*)

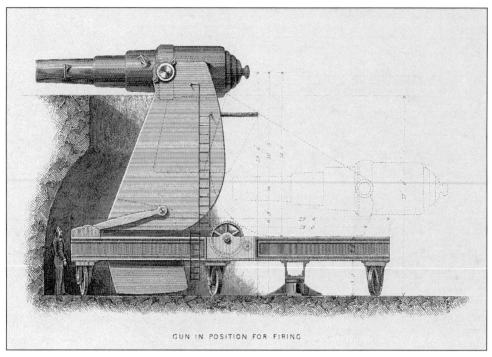

The Moncrieff disappearing mount for coastal artillery, *c.* 1870. The illustration shows the gun in position ready to fire. (*Ian Hogg*)

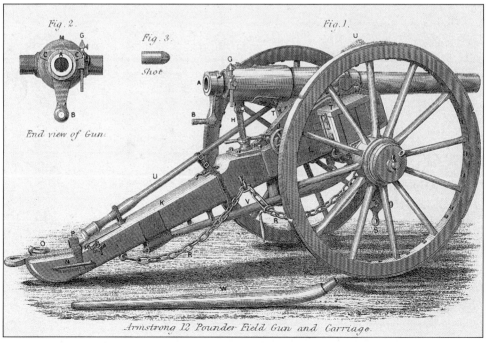

An Armstrong 12-pounder field gun on its carriage with detail of breech mechanism. (*Ian Hogg*)

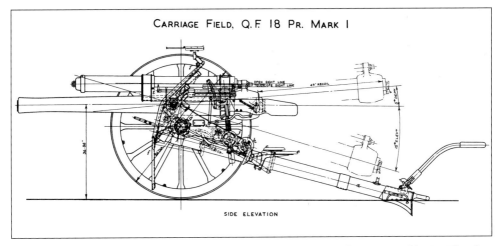

The 18-pounder 'quick firer' gun used by the British Army during the First World War. The plan shows angle of elevation and traverse along with length of recoil when fired. (*Military Features & Photos*)

German horses on the Russian Front during the Second World War being used to haul artillery. Despite much propaganda about the German army's mechanisation, each division still had some 5,000 horses for transport and to pull the guns. (*Military Features & Photos*)

American-built 155mm 'Long Tom' in use with Polish artillery group during the Italian campaign in the Second World War. The crew travels in the lorry, with ammunition transported in other vehicles. (*Military Features & Photos*)

Royal Artillery 5.5-inch medium field gun in action during the Normandy campaign in France during July 1944. Note the stack of shells which are kept separate from the bagged charges until the moment of loading. The 5.5-inch gun was in service with the Royal Artillery as a training weapon right into the late 1980s. (*Military Features & Photos*)

The new 105mm LG1 Mk II in current service with the French Army. Light enough to be towed behind a Jeep-type vehicle it can also be transported by air, for example, slung from a helicopter, for rapid movement around the battlefield. (*Giat Industries*)

The Royal Artillery's latest self-propelled gun, the 155mm AS90 which can fire high-explosive shells and smoke out to 30 kilometres range using special ammunition. (*VSEL Armaments*)

The British-designed ultra-lightweight 155mm field howitzer. The overall weight is only 3,745 kilograms as a result of the extensive use of titanium alloy in the design. It can be transported by air, using either helicopter or fixed-wing aircraft, or towed by truck. It can fire up to four rounds per minute and has a range of 30 kilometres using special assisted shells. (*VSEL Armaments*)

The American-designed and built 'Copperhead' terminally guided artillery shell. Seen here engaging a target tank, it is precision guided with lasers onto the target during the terminal or end phase of its trajectory. Such smart or intelligent munitions reduce collateral damage and civilian casualties and are perceived by many to be the way ahead in artillery ammunition. (*Martin Marietta, Orlando Aerospace*)

gun-foundries. The Maritz machine relied on hydraulic power to drive borers; before treadmills or horses had been used to turn vertical borers. This method of boring produced greater accuracy in the chamber and 'truer' piece than had been possible with the older boring methods. The Maritz machine was not to remain a French monopoly and before long it had been copied by other countries. It is known to have been introduced into England by 1774.

English mathematician Benjamin Robins' book *The New Principles of Gunnery* (1742), which was translated into German and French, was widely read by military thinkers. Among other ideas, Robins identified flaws in some of Galileo's and Newton's hypotheses, and made the first definite statements about the effect of air currents on the trajectory of the projectile. In 1749 his reputation as a military thinker led to his appointment as Chief Engineer for the East India Company, which employed him to oversee the repair and reconstruction of its forts in India. His research was mainly concerned with interior and external ballistics, which is to say the behaviour of the ball before and after it leaves the cannon's muzzle. By using an adapted version of Cassini's ballistic pendulum he produced new theories on the performance of projectiles. Robins' own ballistic pendulum was appeared in 1740 and was inspired by French research material. It comprised a heavy pendulum suspended in a metal frame with a solid target acting as the weight. If struck by a fired cannon-ball the pendulum was set swinging. By measuring the amount of movement it was possible, by knowing the weight of the target and the length of the pendulum arm, to work out the force of the ball when it struck. Because the weight of the cannon-ball fired was also known, and because the force was the product of weight and velocity, it was possible to work out the velocity of the ball. This method allowed an artilleryman to measure the effect of different formulations and charges of powder and determine which was the most effective for a particular weapon.

Benjamin Robins was not alone in writing on the science of artillery. Towards the end of the eighteenth century the theories of Swiss wagon-maker Samuel Johannes Pauly began to be known. By 1798, at the age of thirty-two, he was an experienced sergeant-major of artillery and had written a memorandum for the Swiss Army on the use, equipment and manning of 'galloper guns'. He also experimented with multi-shot firearms, including pistols.

The English regiment of Royal Artillery underwent a change at about this time when 'One officer and eighteen men of each regiment of cavalry and 34 infantry would be trained to serve with the "gallopers" in order to liberate the gunners for their heavier pieces.' This move was no doubt aimed at addressing the concerns of some artillerymen who took a dim view of so-called battalion guns being attached to the infantry. Headlam notes: 'We can imagine how the artillery fought against an arrangement under which their guns were frittered away simply to eke out musketry with case-shot, and their officers and men demoralized by being detached – sometimes for years – with the infantry.' There was some initial resistance to infantry taking control of pieces of artillery, even though they were only battalion guns; the move was to be forgotten – for the time being at least.

There were significant improvements in ammunition during the eighteenth century. The solid iron roundshot or ball was supplemented by canister which comprised a number of small iron or lead balls encased in a tin container nailed to a wooden base. This munition was designed to burst as it left the muzzle of the cannon on firing and was used against infantry and cavalry units in the open at ranges of about 457 metres. Other types of multiple projectile were used including grapeshot, which was similar to canister but used larger balls around a central axis netted together so that they flew in a regular pattern or scattered like shotgun pellets. Grapeshot was to prove the scourge of many an infantry advance.

Both fixed- and extending-bar shot and chain shot were reserved for sea service, where the jointed design of these projectiles wreaked havoc on the packed decks of ships and their rigging. Another difference between artillery on land and pieces mounted in warships was the use of flintlock mechanisms to fire the gun. The flintlock method of firing weapons, by means of striking flint against steel to create sparks to ignite the priming powder in the vent, had been known about for some time and was in widespread use on muskets. But for unknown reasons no attempt had been made to use it to fire cannon. In 1778, all this was to change when Sir Charles Douglas recommended the use of flintlock mechanisms for naval guns along with powder-filled quill tubes. These two innovations greatly speeded up the firing rate for naval artillery, and by 1790 they were in common use throughout the ships of the Royal Navy.

Artillery on the battlefield never took up the idea of the flintlock firing mechanism and instead remained with the port-fire and quick-match method of firing. In retrospect, had the Royal Artillery taken up the flintlock, it would have secured a huge advantage over any enemy because of the greatly increased rate of fire.

Already in use on the battlefield with howitzers and mortars were cast-iron shells filled with powder, the first designs of which were fitted with fuses ignited by the flash of discharge. In 1784 Lieutenant Henry Shrapnel of the Royal Artillery devised the artillery shell that would bear his name. It was a hollow-cast shell, termed 'spherical case-shot', which was filled with lead musket balls and a bursting charge. Designed to explode in mid-air, Shrapnel's shell spread its deadly hail over an extended area, being particularly lethal to infantry and cavalry troops in the open. Unfortunately, the irregularities that plagued fuses, powder and metallurgy made both common shell and shrapnel unreliable.

Indeed, only a few, rather small-scale improvements in artillery had been made by the middle of the eighteenth century. Lighter field pieces and carriages were being made and dispersed into separate brigades or batteries, and by about 1750, shells were made with a basic, if somewhat crude, fuse of beechwood cut to a length determined by the time it was expected to take to reach its target. Calculating the length of the piece of wood was still very much a hit-or-miss affair. If gunners were using a fuse against very short range targets, they had to accept the danger of either premature explosion in the bore of the gun or of the charge failing to ignite the fuse on firing. During the siege of Gibraltar between 1779 and 1783, the English defenders of the North Front faced exactly this dilemma. The Spanish lines were within the range of the English guns, but solid shot landed in sand, which caused few casualties. With no hard surfaces around the attackers' positions, the English defenders could not angle their guns to ricochet cannon-balls to cause casualties and collateral damage. Mortar shells, which dropped at a very steep angle, buried themselves in the ground before exploding, thereby causing only a few localized casualties. In an effort to break the deadlock Captain John Mercier of the 39th Foot evolved a system of 'calculated' fuses based on ranges to a target which the gunners knew to be exact within a few metres.

There were a number of benefits to Mercier's 'operative gun shell'. The fuse was made from wood which was 'ribbed' on the outside with each mark representing a period of time. It was simply snapped off at the required length for the time of flight, thereby allowing 140mm (5.5-inch) mortar shells and those fired from 24-pounders to be set to explode over the heads of the Spanish working parties. Most importantly, firing Mercier's shell from longer gun barrels gave greater accuracy. When combined with the shell's lighter weight this meant that less powder could be used for each shot. By the end of the siege, 129,000 of the 200,600 rounds fired had been shells.

It was to be another twenty years before the Royal Artillery accepted Mercier's device as more than a temporary measure suited only to Gibraltar's unique siege conditions. The spherical case-shot devised by Lieutenant Henry Shrapnel met with a similar dragging of feet. The young artillery officer's idea was not to be put forward for adoption until 1803, but the shell was to be highly praised by the Duke of Wellington during the Peninsular War and Sir George Wood at the Battle of Waterloo in 1815. The shell was only officially given Henry Shrapnel's name in 1852, ten years after his death.

The increasing use of artillery during the later eighteenth century gave rise to one further military development: the use of light infantry and light cavalry to protect the lengthening columns of artillery.

THE GUNNER'S ART

The men of the gun detachments, or the crews as they were now being called in some quarters, constantly practised the still complicated drill of laying and firing their pieces. First the loader placed a bagged charge of gunpowder in the bore, and then the spongeman rammed it home. Meanwhile, the ventsman had placed his thumb over the opening of the vent to prevent air being sucked into the chamber during the ramming actions as this could ignite any smouldering powder. This action by the ventsman was not necessary on the first loading, but after the first shot it was very important for the safety of the gun and the crew. The loader then rammed the ball down very tightly. When the gun was loaded the ventsman primed the vent with loose powder. After the piece had been laid to target by the 'Number One', the firer ignited his port-fire from the continuously burning slow-match, or linstock, and the gun was reported 'ready to fire'. On the word of command the firer applied his port-fire to the vent and the discharge sent the gun recoiling back on its wheels. It required at least three members of the gun crew to put the gun back in its firing position. No time was wasted in preparing the weapon for firing again. Almost at once the spongeman thrust his wet sponge down the bore to extinguish any smouldering remains of powder, and after the smoke from the discharge had cleared the gun was re-laid.

The extreme effective range of a 9-pounder field gun was about half a mile, but the cannon-ball could carry out to over 1 mile. Battle ranges were much shorter, on occasions often no more than 200 metres, and at ranges of 500 metres or less the gunners could fire canister shot into the densely packed ranks of advancing infantry. All laying was still done by lining the piece by eye – what today would be termed 'open sights'. Indirect fire was not really possible except with howitzers, and even then success was the result of luck more than judgement. For the best chance of a hit the target had to be in view of the gunners, which meant that they, in turn, were visible to the enemy. This left artillery open to retaliatory fire and in many cases gunners often got as good as they gave. Thus in the face of shot, shell and musketry, it was essential that detachments carried out their drill with instinctive, automatic precision.

The tools of the gunners' trade continued to be worms, rammers and linstocks. Some artillery crews were very good at coming into action and getting off a good number of shots – for example, the Bengal Horse Artillery at one engagement in India blasted its way through the fortress gates before the defenders could respond – but the average rate of fire still remained two to three shots per minute. The tangent sight, which provided the angle between the line of sight and the axis of the bore when the gun was laid, and wider use of the screw elevator improved aiming. During this period the ladle was abolished for use in loading heavy siege guns, which were now loaded with the ball mounted on a wooden sabot to fill the bore and reduce windage. Powder was loaded as a pre-weighed bagged charge, which made for safer handling of the compound, and this operating procedure also caught on with field guns.

THE CREATION OF STANDING ARTILLERY REGIMENTS

In 1693 France had started the process of raising special regiments of artillery and this was mirrored in England twenty-three years later when the Royal Regiment of Artillery was established on 26 May 1716. Previously, the almost universal practice had been to disband the artillery train once a war was over. This rule had been followed in 1713 after the signing of the Treaty of Utrecht which brought to an end England's involvement in the War of the Spanish Succession. Once again England's army was reduced to a minimum for home defence. This action was no doubt taken for reasons of economy, but in the long term the move was to prove militarily unsound. At various times between 1689 and 1746 factions in Scotland were to pose a threat to stability in England by attempting to return a Stuart king to the throne. This episode in the continuing saga of dynastic claim and counter-claim became known as the Jacobite Rebellion.

The first serious Scottish uprising of the Jacobite Rebellion came in 1715, when an army of some 4,000 led by John Erskine, Earl of Mar, marched south. On 13 November the Jacobite forces were engaged in battle at Sheriffmuir and Preston. The troops loyal to the king were led by John Campbell, the Duke of Argyll. They halted the Scottish advance and defeated the rebel army. The action was over so quickly that an artillery train could not actually be assembled in time to take part in the campaign and this fact made clear the inadvisability of disbanding the artillery after each war. The need for England to maintain a permanent standing force of artillery had never been more apparent or more acute.

The first two companies of artillery were created by royal warrant in May 1716. They were each commanded by a captain and quartered at Woolwich, near the gun factory. Each company comprised two lieutenant fire-workers, three sergeants, three corporals, three bombardiers, thirty gunners and fifty matrosses. But the establishment still lacked drivers and horses, these needs being supplied as before by civilians; nor were there any specific types of guns. Instead, the newly raised artillery companies were expected to perform garrison or field duties as circumstances required. Nearly eighty years later in 1793, after various proposals had been examined, the Royal Horse Artillery was raised by order of the then serving Master-General of the Ordnance, the Duke of Richmond, who ordered a unit with guns 'capable of accompanying cavalry into the field'. There were originally two troops in this unit, which was organized by the detachment system, with the gunners on horseback. This move was to be followed in 1799 by the establishment of a royal wagon train for the transportation of military equipment. In 1794 a 'Corps of Captains Commissairies and Drivers' was raised. It was renamed the Corps of Gunner Drivers in 1801 and then in 1806 became the Royal Artillery Drivers. However, it was not until 1822 that drivers were directly enlisted into the Royal Artillery. This was in sharp contrast to the Royal Horse Artillery where drivers were enlisted in a specialist role from the beginning.

Thus, by the time the next serious threat from Scotland in 1745, England had a ready-assembled artillery train. In August 1745 Prince Charles Edward Stuart, the Young Pretender, arrived in Scotland from exile in France. He landed in the Hebrides with only a handful of followers, but was quickly able to raise an army of 2,000 men. By September he had moved on Edinburgh, captured the city and occupied it, except for the castle which was still held by English troops. The clans gravitated to Charles's leadership and by November 1745 his ranks had swollen to 5,000 men. He marched south, defeating the forces of Sir John Cope at the Battle of Prestonpans on 21 September 1745 and seizing Preston, Lancaster and Derby. His advance continued for the rest of 1745 and into early 1746; it seemed unstoppable. But suddenly he halted only 150 miles from London. His advisers knew they faced an army six times their own strength.

Charles was all in favour of continuing to the English capital, but had to bow to pressure from his army leaders and went on the retreat. He was pursued by William Augustus, the Duke of Cumberland, son of King George II. Cumberland was fresh from fighting at actions in Dettingen in 1743 and Fontenoy in 1745, where he had experienced victory and defeat respectively.

Charles's army came to a halt at Culloden, east of Inverness, on the morning of 16 April 1746. The Young Pretender found the English drawn up and ready to give battle. The rebel Scottish troops were exhausted after a hard night's march but nevertheless formed themselves into battle order. The engagement began with an artillery bombardment from Cumberland's guns, against which the Highlanders charged fearlessly. Half of Cumberland's troops were experienced men, having served in the Austrian War of Succession, and were therefore well disciplined. The remainder followed the example of their battle-hardened comrades. Private Alexander Taylor, serving in the ranks of the Royal Scots on the right of the first line of Cumberland's army, later wrote: 'The Battle begun by Cannonading and continued for half an hour or more with great Guns. But our Gunners galling their Lines, they betook them to their small Arms, Sword and Pistol, and came running upon our Front-Line like Troops of hungry Wolves and fought with Intrepidity.' This account is supported by a letter from Will Aitkin, a young officer serving with Cumberland, who wrote home the day after the battle: 'Yesterday we had a Battle with the Rebels and have obtained a complete victory the two armies met in Culloden Moore Between Nairn and this place we Drew up in twines our Regt was in ye first we began the Action with cannonading on Both Sides which lasted some time and then they came up to us in a very Bold arry But we gave them such a Hot reception with our Small Arms that they could not Bear it long.' Further testimony of the efficacy of the artillery at Culloden is provided by Colonel Christopher Teesdale of the 3rd Buffs who wrote: 'The Royal army marched in three columns and formed battle in two lines and a corps d'reserve, with the dragoons on the flanks, and these moved forward with ten field pieces [short 6-pounders] in the front, and when we came within reach of cannon-shot our field pieces got into a bog, so that the horses were obliged to be taken off and the soldiers to sling their arms in order to drag the guns across the bog, which required some time. If the enemy thought our artillery could not be drawn across bogs their ground was certainly well chosen.'

It has been estimated that the battle lasted for only 25 minutes during which time the rebels lost 1,000 men killed and over 1,000 more taken prisoner, most of whom were later executed on the orders of Cumberland. The king's army lost only 309 men killed and wounded, a sanguinary affair indeed for Scotland. Charles Stuart returned to exile and Scotland never again raised an army to threaten England.

DEFENCE

In 1794, as Napoleon Bonaparte was rising up the ladder of command, an action took place in the Gulf of San Fiorenzo off Mortella Point on the island of Corsica. A Royal Navy fleet engaged a coastal fortification built in the shape of a round tower. It was of sturdy construction which withstood the battering of the naval bombardment, and was only subdued when heated shot was fired at it and started a blaze. The tower was manned by a garrison of thirty-eight men who served one 6-pounder and two 18-pounder guns. The design of the tower, the strength of which had so impressed, was copied in a building programme along the south-west coast of England. This was to be England's cost-effective counter-measure against a possible French landing during the Napoleonic Wars.

The original name of the site of the battle was corrupted and today these fortifications are known as Martello towers. They were very strong and could be built at minimal cost. England was to erect 164 such towers between 1803 and 1814, and they were each armed with a 32-pounder cannon mounted on a pivoting carriage to provide all-round defence. In the end the French invasion they were prepared to counter never materialized and the towers never had to prove themselves in action. However, rather than being dismantled, they were left standing and subsequently became part of England's defences during both world wars.

Coastal towers had long been in use in other parts of the world, including the Channel Islands. In fact Jersey is known to have had such fortifications as early as 1778, but they did not deter a short-lived French invasion in 1781.

Outside of England the greatest concentration of Martello towers is to be found in the Channel Islands; one of the last was built on Jersey in the 1830s, long after the threat of Napoleon had been removed.

The armament mounted in the Martello towers in the Channel Islands varied, but a favoured piece appears to have been the carronade. This was a short-range artillery piece developed by the Carron Company in Scotland and made in different sizes, including a 24-pounder. Having been first used on ships against the French in 1779, it remained in service with the Royal Navy, whose crews knew it by the nickname 'smasher'. At close-quarters it was devastating and could fire various types of shot, including grape and canister. While the carronade was used to arm some coastal fortifications the weapon was never pressed into widespread use and was certainly never taken into the field with other types of artillery.

RAW MATERIALS

Towards the end of the seventeenth century Britain had begun to see an improvement in its copper supplies. Commercially viable deposits of ore were discovered and mines opened in Derbyshire and Wales. The English Copper Company was founded in 1691 and by 1702 the first brass works had been built in Bristol. It should be remembered that during the reign of William III (1689–1702) most of the artillery for his army was made using copper from German and Swedish sources at a cost equivalent to 36 new pence per kilo. In about 1717, 1 kilogram of English copper cost about 30 pence but by 1791 this price had fallen to only 16 pence per kilo because Welsh and Derbyshire copper mines were producing high output. These mines provided Britain with a stable and reliable source of this valuable metal. At the time France was drawing its copper from sources as far afield as Armenia and South America. Universally there was also a huge increase in demand by the military for cheaper and more efficiently produced iron. In 1740 the total output of iron in Western Europe was 170,000 tons, but just 100 years later production levels were 123 times higher. There were great advances in metallurgical processes during the eighteenth century, many of which benefited artillery, for example the Darby and Huntsman processes for making cast iron and producing crucible steel respectively.

There were a number of indirect consequences of the increasing use of artillery, including the hastening of factory organization in the face of growing demands on craftsmen who produced the brass, wood and iron for weapons, and the need to standardize arms and equipment. In the closing years of the eighteenth century the world was entering a new era – that of mass-production where specialized weapons factories would operate. In 1796 the first flow-line production, the Soho Factory, was established by the English company Boulton & Watt, which specialized in turning and drilling. Two years later, in America, Eli Whitney set up a firm to mass-produce muskets, setting the trend for armaments companies in later years.

Over the next 100 years warfare and artillery were to be transformed. In 1794 a French officer, Capitaine Coutelle, was lifted above the Fleurus in a balloon to observe the battlefield. Enemy movements could now be observed from a different plane and artillery deployed to meet the potential threat. From that point onwards things were never to be the same again.

NEW DEVELOPMENTS AND THE GUNNER'S ART, 1800–1900

T he nineteenth century began as the eighteenth had finished: with Europe embroiled in wars that touched the whole of the continent from the coast of Portugal to Prussia. Later the conflict was to extend eastwards to include Russia and Poland.

The new century was also to be marked by a series of small wars that were really only side-shows to the major manoeuvrings of the empire-building nations as they expanded their territories into Africa and Asia. Although these were numerous and fiercely fought, they were localized and took second place to the larger conflicts of this period. Nevertheless, artillery in some shape or form was invariably to be found acting in support of troops who had been dispatched to establish a foreign power's rule in its colonies. After the Napoleonic Wars of 1800–15 Europe itself more or less settled down into an uneasy peace, punctuated by conflicts of national differences.

On 1 January 1801 the United Kingdom of Great Britain and Ireland was created by Act of Parliament. While this legislation has nothing directly to do with the history of artillery it meant that England's armed forces now became known as the British Army.

Over the next 100 years great strides would be made in the development of artillery. In 1810, for example, Friedrich Krupp established a small metal forging works in Prussia which would later supply weapons to armies around the world, including in France and Japan. In the United States men such as Robert P. Parrott, John A. Dahlgren and Thomas J. Rodman established themselves as armaments manufacturers. In England Willam G. Armstrong and Joseph Whitworth became almost household names as manufacturers of artillery. Henri Joseph Paixhans was to establish an arsenal and foundry in France, while on the island of Sardinia, Giovanni Cavalli was to do the same for Italy. Techniques now evolved that would lead to innovations and improvements in the manufacture of artillery which would, in turn, begin a revolution in the science of gunnery.

FROM 1800 TO WATERLOO

In 1803 Henry Shrapnel was ordered to report to the Carron Foundry at Falkirk, Scotland, where he was to oversee production of his 'spherical case-shot'. By the end of the year nearly 74,500 projectiles had been produced. The 'spherical case-shot' could be fired from all types of British guns, provided it was of the correct calibre. No soldier ever relishes coming under the effect of any fire, particularly artillery, and the 'spherical case-shot' was particularly dreaded by the French troops whose artillery had nothing comparable. British artillery equipment was further improved with a replacement design for the standard double-block trail carriage; this came in the form of a lighter and more manoeuvrable single-block trail carriage. The simple design alteration made the heavy British 9-pounder gun comparable in manoeuvrability to the French 4- and 6-pounders.

During his campaigns, the Duke of Wellington was to use his artillery selectively, often in small numbers and individual batteries but also at carefully chosen sites. He is known never to have held the weaponry in high regard but his strategically placed guns were intended to be called on at critical moments. They were sited all along the front of his deployments as support for the infantry and played a minor role in his defensive–offensive tactics.

The Duke of Wellington had gained much experience in India when he was still Arthur Wellesley. He used his artillery in a tactic that would become known during the First World War as the creeping barrage. This involved the guns moving forward towards enemy positions at a pace that allowed the infantry to walk behind, covered from the enemy's view. After initial setbacks the British Army, under Wellington, went on the offensive and routed the French from Spain and Portugal during the Peninsular War of 1807–14. The British pursued Napoleon's forces across the Pyrenees and back into France. As it went, the Royal Artillery loaded three 3-pounders onto the backs of mules to provide fire support during the campaign.

Some strategists point to this action as laying the foundations for the future development of mountain artillery, but the truth is that Napoleon was using pack animals as early as 1800 to move his artillery over mountains. On 8 March that year he assembled a force of 37,000 men at Dijon with an axis of advance into northern Italy which would take it through the St Bernard Pass; the journey was accomplished by 14 April. Then the French forces were reinforced by a further 20,000 troops who had made a similar march through mountainous routes. The terrain was deep with snow and the conditions terrible. Napoleon ordered his guns to be stripped down and loaded onto mules and sledges, which were each hauled by twenty men. Once through the mountains the artillery was reassembled. The force approached the fort at Ivrea, which guarded the entrance to the Plain of Lombardy, at a most dangerous time because the garrison was on the alert. The wheels of the guns and limbers were padded with straw, and using fifty men to manhandle each gun, Napoleon was able to advance his artillery to within close range of the fort's defences and completely surprise its defenders. While the foundations for this new style of warfare involving artillery had been laid, it was to be more than 100 years before mountain artillery came into its own as a distinct form of weaponry during the First World War.

During the wars of the early 1800s mortars were still in use. In England designs were being cast by producers including Francis Kinman who operated a foundry in Shoe Lane, London. He was effectively a civilian contractor working to supply mortars to the Board of Ordnance and was active during the Napoleonic Wars. Another manufacturer was Andrew Schlach, of Swiss origin. He was appointed the first Master Founder of the Royal Brass Foundry at Woolwich, which produced mortars of the Cohorn-type, a design which dated back to at least 1720. Some of the mortars were small enough and light enough to be carried by two men, but they would normally have been transported in a wagon. The compact weapons were used to fire shells weighing 3.5 kilograms out to ranges of 750 metres. Their ammunition and powder was transported on a separate wagon. One design of mortar from this period was referred to as 'Royal', a term that signified they had a calibre of at least 6 inches.

During the Napoleonic Wars, the garrison of Gorey Castle on Jersey in the Channel Islands comprised a company of infantry and fifty reserve or 'invalid' gunners. In 1804 it is known there were only three 24-pounders and a single 12-pounder cannon in the fortification's defensive complement. An inventory of artillery on the island of Guernsey reveals that in 1801 there were 116 pieces of various calibres, ranging from 6-pounders to 24-pounders. In 1816, only one year after the final Allied victory over Napoleon at Waterloo, another inventory indicates that this figure had risen to 187 pieces of similar calibres, which reflects how serious the French threat to the safety of the islands was believed to be.

The French Revolutionary Army had inherited de Gribeauval's excellent field-artillery system as a legacy from the days of the monarchy. The main feature of this artillery force, now in the hands of republicans, was its mobility. This had been achieved by reducing the length and weight of barrels and the weight of the gun carriage, which was equipped with iron axle-trees and large wheels. Designers now began to realize that without good wheels artillery could not be moved efficiently. By the nineteenth century wheels were constructed from spokes and felloes, which all had to be shaped exactly so that they would fit together to produce a perfectly circular wheel with a hub in the centre. An iron tyre was secured to the wooden wheel to create a hard-wearing surface and thus increase the serviceability of the wheel. Conical inserts for the hub, known as pipe boxes, had to fit the tapered arms on the axle-tree. Such attention to detail produced strong wheels.

The preferred wood for gun carriages was oak, but elm was sometimes used for the brackets. The latter was also used to make the wooden hubs, or naves, of the wheels because it had a strong resistance to splitting. The preferred material for use in the felloes was ash because of its flexibility and resilience. Artillery production still required the skills of many different artisans, including metalworkers and blacksmiths, carpenters and ropemakers, as it had done for hundreds of years.

Range and accuracy was improved by an increased precision in the manufacture of projectiles. Cannon-balls closer to being truly spherical and of a more accurately measured diameter were produced at the first specialized armaments centres. This made possible a reduction in the powder charge, because the problem of windage was not so great. There was also a marked increase in the use of prefabricated bagged charges, which replaced the old and dangerous method of handling loose powder and shot. The gun crews still had to go through a complicated loading process but improvements in gunnery techniques led to increased rates of firing.

Six or eight draught horses harnessed in double file could draw the lighter 12-pounder in good conditions. Teams of four to six horses were used to pull the smaller guns, such as the 6- and 4-pounder and the 6-inch howitzer. Napoleon constantly tried to increase the mobility of artillery still further. Like Frederick the Great, he sought to reduce the weight of pieces by shortening the barrel and using a chambered breech and smaller powder charge. But this French scheme, known as the System of Year XI (which was 1803, eleven years after the establishment of the republic), went the same way as the earlier Prussian idea and was ultimately a failure. After the changes were made, the pieces lacked range and hitting power. In an effort to redress its lack of effective weaponry the French Army deployed large numbers of Austrian and Prussian artillery pieces.

In Austria the Archduke Charles launched a series of reforms between 1805 and 1809 with a view to improving the battlefield effectiveness of his army. Charles restructured his general staff, dismissed inadequate and incompetent officers, and concentrated on artillery and the use of cavalry as a striking force. These reforms did go some way towards effecting the recovery of the Austrian Army, but it was nevertheless to remain what it had always been: an instrument of dynastic ambition rather than a mass army on the French model.

Austrian inadequacies were revealed during the Battle of Wagram on 6 July 1809, when Napoleon led an army of 154,000 men with 554 cannon against the forces commanded by Archduke Charles. The Austrians fielded 158,000 men with 480 cannon. Minor skirmishing had started on the evening of 5 July but battle did not commence properly until the morning of the 6th. It was a costly half-victory for Napoleon who sustained 32,000 casualties compared to the Austrians 30,000 men. Napoleon also captured 20 pieces of artillery, which could be used to replace his losses in the field without having to wait for resupplies to arrive from France. Charles's officers were indecisive, the Austrians suspended the attack and this, combined with the onslaught from the French artillery, forced them to withdraw.

At about this time the output in production of iron cannon in France increased from 900 barrels per year to a peak of 13,000. Seventeen new foundries were established with a combined yearly output of 14,000 bronze barrels. In addition French armourers produced 4 million muskets and pistols between 1804 and 1815. England's armaments manufacturers were also on a war footing, and it was not far behind in weapons production to feed the war effort.

Between 1812 and 1814 Russia used artillery pieces known as licorns. This name for the weapon was unique to Russia, but the design of the gun was basically the same as those in Western Europe and pieces of this type were manufactured in 10-, 20- and 40-pounder models. The interior bore of the barrel was tapered towards the breech end to produce a reduced chamber for the powder, but it was not like the drake design which used shoulders on which the cannon-ball rested. The Russian artillery train was very advanced for the time and even included a field forge to accompany the army and carry out repairs and maintenance on campaign.

Napoleon took full advantage of the manoeuvrability of the French artillery and turned it into one of his most important tools for conducting warfare. One of his favoured tactics, used particularly in later years as the quality of his troops declined, was to deploy the grand battery – massing artillery fire in support of his main effort on the battlefield. In this way he was able to literally blast the enemy line to shreds in order to allow his infantry to advance.

Napoleon was to write in his personal papers: 'It is with artillery that war is made.' He further said of his gunpowder weapons: 'My Artillery Guard decides the majority of battles. As I always have them at the ready, I can deploy them anywhere they are needed.' This credo was practised nowhere more fully than at the Battle of Friedland, 14 July 1807. The Russians with 46,000 men were deployed on the banks of the River Alle in Prussia and Napoleon fully intended to force them to give ground by skilful use of his artillery firing from the flanks. In command of Napoleon's I Corps artillery was General Sncarmont, who advanced his guns to close on the Russians' position. He opened fire at a range of 600 paces, which he shortened to 300 paces, then 150 until finally he was only 60 paces from the enemy front. The Russians retreated across the river, leaving 25,000 casualties behind them. The French had only lost 8,000 men out of a total force of 80,000. Two years later, reflecting on the outcome of the Battle of Valmy in 1792, Napoleon wrote: 'Artillery, like the other arms must be collected in mass if one wishes to obtain a decisive result.'

The British Army had learned many lessons in Spain and commanders like the Duke of Wellington were not prepared to sacrifice troops as 'cannon-fodder'. He practised a simple technique for preserving manpower: wherever possible Wellington would position his troops on the reverse slope of a ridge or hill so they were not in direct line of sight for the opposing artillery. When the time was right he would order the advance. This tactic was best demonstrated at the Battle of Waterloo, 18 June 1815, when his men were protected by this simple manoeuvre.

The significant part played by artillery in the total Allied victory at Waterloo has been well documented. Napoleon had abdicated as French emperor the year before and was imprisoned on the island of Elba off the west coast of Italy. In 1815 he managed to escape and return for a campaign now known as the 'Hundred Days', which culminated at Waterloo. The Duke of Wellington commanded an Allied force of more than 67,600 men with

156 guns. Facing him at the head of nearly 72,000 men was Napoleon with 246 guns and about 100 tons of cannon-balls. As the battle developed all branches of both armies were deployed – infantry, artillery and cavalry.

The French guns wreaked havoc in certain units, including the Dutch-Belgian contingent commanded by General Bylandt, which was posted east of the farmhouse of La Haye Sainte. So demoralized were they by the firepower of the French guns that they ran away. On another part of the battlefield, the Inniskillings were stoically standing their ground. Wellington employed his tactic of placing some troops on the reverse side of hills and they were protected to a large degree. Even in the thick of battle there was a temptation to engage in a little frivolity: Ensign William Leeke put his foot out to stop a seemingly spent cannon-ball. He was prevented from doing so by a sergeant who realized the danger. Only moments later the young officer saw four men in the file next to him fall victim to a cannon-ball.

Wellington had six troops of horse artillery available to him and they were deployed to various crisis spots throughout the course of the battle. Observing the movement of two troops led by Mercer and Bull, Wellington was heard to comment: 'That is how I like to see horse artillery move'. Captain Cavalie Mercer of the Royal Horse Artillery later wrote of one action:

Our first gun had scarcely gained the interval between their squares, when I saw through the smoke the leading squadrons of the advancing column coming on at a brisk trot, and already not more than one hundred yards distant, if so much, for I don't think we could have seen so far. I immediately ordered the line to be formed for action-case-shot! and the leading gun was unlimbered and commenced firing almost as soon as the word was given:– The very first round, I saw, brought down several men and horses. They continued, however, to advance. . . . A resolve strengthened by the effect of the remaining guns as they rapidly succeeded in coming into action, making terrible slaughter.

The French officer, General Foy, wrote of the British artillery at Waterloo: 'The English gunners are distinguished from the other soldiers by their excellent spirit. In action their handling is skilful, their aim perfect, and their courage supreme'.

Perhaps the unluckiest soldier serving on the battlefield that day was Carabinier Antoine Fauveau of the French 12th Division. His breastplate survives in the Army Museum, Paris, French, and shows he was struck directly in the right side of his chest by a cannon-ball. The entry hole is perfectly round and must have caused instant death.

In the end the battle swung the Allies' way and victory was complete. The French Army had sustained 25,000 casualties and the Allied forces about the same. In *The Art of Warfare on Land* David Chandler claims overconfidence and lack of originality cost Napoleon the battle. He fled the field only to be captured later and sent to the remote island of St Helena where he spent his remaining days. The threat of French military domination in Europe was over, but many lessons had been learned along the way. Even today, over 180 years later, Napoleon's battlefield tactics and theories are studied at military academies around the world, with particular emphasis on his ideas about the use of artillery.

WAR IN AMERICA

On the other side of the Atlantic Britain was once again forced to confront American troops and open a war on two fronts. The War of 1812 began as the result of an American invasion of Canada. This action had been launched in response to British and French warship attacks on American merchantmen with total disregard for their neutrality. It was a war fought partly by proxy, with the British making considerable use of people from Native American tribes. The conflict was also fought at sea and land operations were mainly hit-and-run actions with relatively few set-piece battles.

The war continued through 1814 until it was concluded by the Treaty of Ghent, ratified in February 1815. The climax of hostilities came at the Battle of New Orleans on 8 January 1815. The British infantry attacked General Jackson's entrenched army but was thrown into disarray by well-aimed American firepower. Twice the British attempted to carry the American positions, actions in which over 2,000 men lost their lives. In support of his riflemen Jackson had eight batteries of artillery sited on the eastern bank of the Mississippi River. Each battery comprised 4-pounder and 32-pounder cannon and at least one mortar of 13-inch calibre. On the opposite shore General Morgan and Commodore Petterson had some twelve 6-, 12- and 24-pounders under their command. These guns had been obtained by the Americans from the French during the Louisiana Purchase of 1803 and were in good order.

At the beginning of the conflict the British had been successful, but the Battle of New Orleans had taught them another lesson: they should never underestimate the power of the American fighting man, even if he was a militiaman or irregular. Once more America had used its artillery to help secure the country against outside aggressors.

LIEUTENANT-GENERAL GIOVANNI CAVALLI

Other countries in mainland Europe were also beginning to make changes to the artillery branches of their armies. In 1830 a Piedmontese artillery officer Lieutenant-General Giovanni Cavalli set out to improve emplaced artillery. He had a number of ideas, including theories on how best to use the space allotted to a gun position, a plan to simplify gun drills for loading and firing, and a scheme to minimize the number of men in each gun crew but still achieve optimum performance. One of his first moves was to create a force that used breech-loading guns. By carefully controlling the gun's recoil on firing he was able to reduce the amount of space required to operate it safely. The breech mechanism that Cavalli devised used a sliding wedge in combination with an obturating cup in order to gain a gas-tight seal at the breech end. The first gun to be manufactured to Cavalli's design was made at Piedmont. It had a cast-iron barrel of 90mm calibre and was trialled successfully between March 1832 and June 1833. These tests continued into 1835, but then the barrel burst. When cast-iron guns burst, the consequences were obviously dire for all concerned, and failure could result from stress fractures developing during continuous, often non-stop, firings.

Undeterred, Cavalli pursued his project. By chance he met Swedish industrialist Baron Martin von Wahrendorff in 1837. Cavalli explained the problems he had experienced and outlined his requirements to von Wahrendorff, whose factory at Aker manufactured some of the finest iron guns in Europe. The baron constructed a weapon to Cavalli's specifications and the resulting design was so well received that orders for 90mm weapons to the same standards came from Italy, France and Prussia. In fact, Italy continued to purchase guns in this manner from von Wahrendorff until 1845. Cavalli's name has often been overlooked in the story of artillery development in the nineteenth century but he designed and put into production the first successful rifled breech-loading cannon.

Cavalli achieved the rifling aspect of his design by using his own rifling machine, which cut two spiral grooves inside the barrel in a manner not dissimilar to those found on the Brunswick rifle. These grooves stabilized the

shell when fired. The elongated shells fired from Cavalli's weapon were fitted
with a series of raised lugs 6.4mm in height, which engaged into the spiral
grooves of the rifling, and thereby overcame some of jamming problems that
had beset Joseph Whitworth's unusual hexagonal bore system.

Cavalli continued to be involved in many aspects of artillery. He compiled
specifications for a two-horse galloper gun, but by the time it appeared in
1837, this type of weapon had been superseded by other designs. He even
devised a telescopic sight for artillery, and with the appearance of his
carefully calculated emplacement carriage, recoil was so accurately dampened
that military engineers were able to reduce the size of casemates and
therefore minimize the danger to gunners from high-angle fire.

THE SIEGE OF ANTWERP

On 27 October 1830 fighting broke out around the Belgian city of Antwerp
as a result of rising anti-Dutch feeling in the country. Earlier in the same
month Belgium had declared itself independent from Dutch sovereignty and
although the city of Antwerp proper was held Belgians, the citadel was
occupied by the Dutch under General Baron David Hendryk Chasse. A French
Army of 60,000 men led by Marshal Etienne Maurice Gerard entered
Belgium in August 1831 to counter a 50,000-strong Dutch army. In the face
of such opposition and local Belgian forces the Dutch were forced to retire.
The situation at Antwerp, however, remained unchanged and in November
the following year Marshal Gerard led his army, which included nearly 6,500
artillerymen, to besiege the city. His artillery train comprised 144 siege pieces
and 78 field guns. The Dutch occupiers of the citadel were still commanded
by General Chasse, who had a force of nearly 4,500 men with 144 pieces of
artillery of all calibres at his disposal and a plentiful supply of ammunition
and powder.

The attack opened on 29 November in the classic Vauban style with zig-zag
saps dug to approach the defences before parallels were excavated around the
city to seal it off. The besiegers used a combination of new artillery, including
a howitzer based on the Russian licorn, which had been improved by Colonel
Henri Joseph Paixhans, and a new model of mortar, both of which were used
to fire shells into the fortress. For direct fire Gerard was able to bring his
16- and 24-pounder guns as close as 50 metres from the walls. The Dutch
defenders could not reply and were completely out-gunned, but the siege

progressed slowly. The Dutch were gradually worn down but the French could not enter the city until 23 December, by which time its defences were in ruins. The Dutch had lost 561 men killed and wounded but the French had sustained just over 800 men killed and wounded during the operation. An armistice was drawn up in May 1833, but the Dutch did not fully recognize Belgium's independence until 1839.

This action offered important lessons about defence and the deployment of modern artillery. But armies never learn from one another's mistakes, only from their own. Many salient aspects of the operation were overlooked and because of this never fully understood. A little over twenty years later the British would have cause to regret the fact that they had not examined the action at Antwerp more closely when they entered into the great sieges of the Crimean War.

THE CRIMEAN WAR

In the European wars of the mid-nineteenth century artillery played a significant part. But the period was set apart by the fact that Britain was not drawn into these conflicts. Instead it was busy building an overseas empire and using troops backed up by artillery to control its new territories. The only exception to the Britain's rule of non-involvement in European conflict in this period was the Crimean War.

France and Britain fought as allies against Russia between 1854 and 1856, although hostilities had been developing as early as October 1853. What began as a minor difference of opinion over the protection of holy places throughout the Turkish Ottoman Empire soon degenerated into a war that demanded guns and ammunition. Turkey was considered the 'sick man of Europe' at the time and Russia moved in to dominate the country in order to secure an access point for its fleet into the Mediterranean. Britain and France mounted expeditionary forces to the Baltic against Russia. Although there were several actions, the conflict largely degenerated into attrition conducted through trench warfare. This was never more evident than at the siege of Sebastopol, on the southern tip of the Crimean peninsular, which was conducted for a year from October 1854. The Russian defences were formidable – the older coastal defences alone mounting 533 guns. The commander of the defences at Sebastopol was Colonel Frants Todelben. He oversaw the construction of earthworks to the north of the port and had 60 guns sited there with a further 145 guns to the south. Including the guns of the Russian fleet in Sebastopol harbour, Todelben had some 3,000 pieces at his disposal, most of which were kept in storage because of lack of space to site them. During the course of the siege he was able to replace losses from this reserve.

The siege began on the morning of 17 October 1854 when the Allies opened fire from 126 guns; by the end of this first day they had expended 9,000 rounds of ammunition. The Russians replied with 20,000 rounds, the greatest single day's bombardment to that date. However, this exchange was small beer compared with what was to come. In the eleven day-long 'Easter bombardment', between 8 April and 19 April 1855, the Russians replied to Allied artillery by firing 88,000 rounds. It was a wearing down process with Russian casualties running at an average rate of between 500 to 1,000 men per day by September 1855. Sebastopol finally fell on 8 September 1855. During the siege the Allies had fired 1.25 million rounds of ammunition, including shot and shell, that pulverized brick and soldier alike.

The British Army had gone to the Crimea with artillery unchanged since the time of Waterloo forty years previously, and the French equipment was not much better. During the course of the war, French and British armament manufacturers experimented with new artillery designs. Among these pieces was the British-designed oval-bored 68-pound Lancaster gun which was used at Sebastopol. It produced very poor results and the piece was discarded. Another British weapon was the Mallets mortar, named after its designer. This was made up of a series of longitudinal bars clamped together in a way that looked similar to early barrel construction. It could be broken down into sections weighing 12 tons. It was designed in 1855 and could fire explosive shells weighing 2,400 pounds; a lifting rig was required to load each round into the muzzle. The weapon was capable of hurling these massive shells 2 miles, but before it could be shipped to the Crimea the war finished. Today an example can be seen at Fort Nelson in Fareham, Hampshire, and another is outside the Royal Artillery Barracks in Woolwich, London, along with piles of ammunition.

Other developments made for use during the Crimean War included the first generation of illuminating rounds designed to be fired from mortars. They had large calibres, often of 6–13 inches, and deployed parachutes to slow their descent. These early parachute flares were used to light up the battlefield at night to deny the enemy the opportunity of making surprise night attacks, in much the same way as modern flares are used today.

It was also towards the end of the war that the first serious trials into rifling barrels were conducted with a view to increasing accuracy. The French rifled artillery, based on the system devised by Treuille de Beaulieu, was in service in sufficient numbers to prove its worth at the battles of Magenta and Solferino during the Franco-Austrian War of 1859. The barrel is only the means of directing a projectile towards the intended target and if its inner surface is smooth then the projectile can land almost anywhere in a target area. However if a series of spiralling grooves are engineered inside the barrel the projectile leaves the barrel with a spinning action which increases its accuracy. The rifling is engraved along a helical line and may be of either a constant or variable twist. Rifling also allows a weapon with a shorter barrel to be used without degrading the trajectory of the projectile.

Once the technique was proven to work, there was no going back. Rifling was to appear in different styles including hexagonal, micro-bore and oval. But the design that was eventually universally adopted is known as constant and is characterized by the constant slope of the grooves in relation to the axis of the bore. The latter is an imaginary line along the centre of the bore throughout the length of the barrel.

WILLIAM ARMSTRONG AND OTHER INNOVATORS

An account in J.D. Scott's personal papers of the events leading up to one of the significant advances in artillery at the time tells how William Armstrong (a solicitor by training who had turned producer of hydraulic equipment) sat in his London club reading an account in *The Times* newspaper of how British troops at the Battle of Inkerman on 5 November 1854 saved themselves by manhandling an 18-pounder smoothbore piece of artillery into position and fired it at the enemy. He was heard to exclaim that it was 'time military engineering was brought up to the level of current engineering practice'. He was appalled by the fact that a gun weighing 3.25 tons was required to fire a projectile weighing only 18 pounds. The story goes that he then set about drawing up plans for a revolutionary breech-loading piece which, rather than being cast of homogeneous metal, was built up from a series of metal strips wound around a central core and sheathed with an outer hoop heated to fit around it and then allowed to cool in order to exert tremendous pressure inwards.

Up to this point the methods of manufacturing gun barrels had hardly changed since the early 1800s – smoothbore, single-piece castings with integral trunnions. Armstrong manufactured the barrel of his new weapon from wrought iron over which he fitted tubes, or 'hoops' as he called to them, which were heated, shrunk in place and designed to give additional strength where it was most needed. The barrel was rifled and designed to accept a cylindro-conoidal shell coated in lead to grip the rifling, which would impart spin to the projectile. As he had planned from the outset, his new gun was a breech-loader. The breech was formed into what was known as the 'ring' into which a 'vent-piece' or breech-block could be dropped in a vertical action. A large screw was tightened to secure the gun for firing. To load the gun the operator simply unscrewed the securing action and the vent-piece lifted out. The lead-coated shell was then loaded into the breech and rammed in to engage the rifling and the powder charge inserted behind it. The breech was closed and a friction tube inserted into the vent. The gun was now ready to fire.

Not only was the prototype a success, but it has been pointed out that its strength-to-weight ratio was so superior to that achieved by traditional methods that it opened the way for guns vastly larger than those which could be cast as a single piece without exploding under the sheer pressure of the discharge when fired. The experimental model was a 3-pound gun, which was delivered for trials in July 1856, and proved itself over the next two years to be an unqualified success not only in terms of reliability but also in cost effectiveness in the manufacturing processes.

Sir William Armstrong was the first armaments manufacturer to have any success in making guns out of wrought-iron coils shrunk over one another in such a way that the inner tube was in a state of compression, and the outer under tension. His accurate calculations ensured that each coil gave the maximum resistance to the pressures built up in the barrel when the gunpowder exploded behind the shell. Armstrong's guns were ordered for service with the British Army. Production began in early 1860 and turned out 12-pounder models. Some of the other earliest Armstrong guns weighed over 20 tons and fired a projectile weighing almost 600 pounds with acceptable velocity, but his lighter designs were used all over the world wherever British Army was to be found in action, from China to New Zealand.

Towards the end of the nineteenth century, guns would be made using coils of wire or steel ribbon wound around the central tube to achieve the same results. But others in the field of artillery design must also be considered, including the American Daniel Treadwell, who had attempted to build up iron and steel barrels around a central core in the same manner as Armstrong. His experiments were conducted in the 1840s at a time when manufacturing expertise had not been developed sufficiently to allow such a process. In America Major Thomas J. Rodman, an ordnance specialist, devised a method of using a continuous stream of running water to cool the interior of the barrel during its manufacture. This placed the interior surfaces of the barrel under compression and produced a structurally sound weapon. Rodman-designed pieces of artillery were used during the American Civil War; some had a calibre of 20 inches and fired projectiles weighing nearly 1,100 pounds. This US Army officer also developed a new type of propellant powder described as 'progressive-burning', which was more efficient than the black powder compound still in widespread use.

The barrel of a gun comes under five different types of stress when fired: girder, radial, circumferential, longitudinal and torsional. Mathematical theory, as William Armstrong understood, showed that if one tube is tightly encased within another, the composite is much stronger than either of its component tubes alone. Extensive trials showed that the theory worked in practice and a new era of artillery was born. Gunmaking was transformed from an art to a precise science. Within twenty-five years guns weighing 5 tons were being replaced by designs weighing 110 tons and capable of firing shells up to three-quarters of a ton in weight. These new guns were built along the lines of Armstrong's design, with a steel tube encased in hoops and tubes of wrought iron.

As guns became larger, the difficulties in their manufacture increased. Massive steel tubes had to be made in one piece; red-hot strips of wrought iron had to be coiled on to them and welded together under powerful steam hammers. The demand for more powerful weapons led manufacturers to produce ever-larger hoops and tubes. The components had to be accurately machined in order to fit inside one another easily when red hot and be sufficiently secure when they cooled and contracted. Various methods of construction were adopted. Initially William Armstrong's system was widely used and great numbers of guns were produced at his Elswick Works, Newcastle-upon-Tyne, and in the Royal Gun Factory at the Woolwich Arsenal, London.

The Armstrong system at Woolwich was to be simplified by reducing the number of parts required for each gun. Later methods were devised which wound steel ribbon tightly around the barrel and then encased it in one or more jackets. These 'wire-bound' guns had strength to prevent bursting, but they lacked the rigidity of guns made with solid jackets and the long barrels had a tendency to droop at the muzzle under their own weight. This caused some concern but it was found that on firing the barrel straightened out momentarily and accuracy was not compromised.

Other pioneers of artillery, such as Joseph Whitworth and Alfred Krupp, had made guns entirely of steel in the 1850s but it was not until the late 1880s that such designs were accepted into service. The first all-steel gun of this new era was made by Vickers in 1888; other British steel-makers followed suit, including Cammel, Firth & Brown, who, along with Armstrong, soon came to dominate the heavy armaments industry. The transition from muzzle-loading to breech-loading artillery pieces was finally completed by the end of the nineteenth century, but not without serious debate about its operational reliability on the battlefield.

Refinements were also made to ammunition in the form of armour-piercing and lighter-walled anti-personnel projectiles. As early as 1822 a shell capable of being fired along a flat trajectory had been developed by General Henri Paixhans of France. Demonstrations had shown how these shells could destroy naval vessels, and their real test came in 1853 when they were used by a squadron of Russian ships at the Battle of Sinope to destroy a Turkish fleet. The consequences for coastal artillery was to be enormous.

Solid shot was to become a thing of the past as projectiles became elongated and streamlined with explosive charges detonated by improved fuses of both time and impact activation. The term fuse for artillery ammunition should not be confused with a fuse or cord that consists of a flexible fabric or plastic tube with a core of low or high explosive to set in motion a burning train. The latter is employed in demolition work and blasting, while the former is used to initiate the explosion or chain of events leading to the functioning of all types of ammunition, in particular shells.

By the end of the nineteenth century the smoothbore cannon, which was the predominant artillery type both ashore and afloat in 1800, had been replaced by the rifled gun, a change made more reluctantly, perhaps, in the world's navies than in its armies. The problem of recoil was also being redressed, first by ingeniously controlled springs, and later by more sophisticated hydropneumatic apparatus. In coastal artillery positions the guns were mounted on sloping 'runways', constructed from wood, which allowed the piece to roll back on being fired. Long spring coils were tried as were axle-spade recoil controls and recoil control 'shoes' that slid under the wheels during firing. But it was not to be until the close of the century that a truly satisfactory solution to recoil control was discovered.

THE AMERICAN CIVIL WAR

At the outbreak of the American Civil War in 1861 there was a rush to enlist in the infantry, and the artillery on both sides became the forgotten service. A small number of 'private' artillery companies had been raised before the war, such as the Washington Artillery of New Orleans, which was established in 1838 and had already seen active service in the war with Mexico. However, only twenty years later its roll-call of troops lists only thirteen names. Similar artillery units were to be found prior to 1861, including the Richmond Howitzers, the Washington Light Artillery of Charleston and the Norfolk Light Artillery Blues.

One of the reasons for the reluctance of men to enlist in the artillery service at the outbreak of war was the fact that recruits were required to have a greater degree of technical skill than infantrymen, especially in mathematics. Also the men knew full well that artillery fire attracts a return barrage from the enemy's guns and did not want to become targets for other cannon. It took a great deal of courage to watch a 12-pound ball travelling at over 1,400 feet per second. Artillery units also had to rely on state or federal government to supply equipment and for that reason it was not possible to raise many units locally. Despite these problems, by the end of the war in 1865 the Union Army had enlisted 432 batteries, which made up 12 per cent of all the forces that served. The Confederate Army raised 268 batteries, battalions and regiments of artillery which accounted for 18 per cent of the total armed forces. The reason for the disparity is that the Confederate Army was substantially smaller than the Northern forces. Both sides used siege batteries and these could be even more mixed than the field batteries. In addition to the guns used to batter fortifications, howitzers were employed in ricochet fire which Vauban had advocated two centuries before, while mortars lobbed explosive shells into defences which could not be reached by direct fire.

The American Civil War began on 12 April 1861 when Confederate artillery opened fire on Fort Sumter, Charleston, South Carolina, and the 'shooting war' started. The opening bombardment lasted thirty-six hours and but did not result in even one casualty. Only a mule lost its life in the barrage. The artillery's failure to have a significant effect says as much about the poor gunnery practices of the time as it does about the strength of the Fort Sumter's defences. The fort was to be held by Confederate forces until February 1865, barely two months before the end of the war. But that is not to say that Fort Sumter never took part in any subsequent action. On 7 April 1863 the Union dispatched several iron-clad Monitor-type gunboats to bombard the fort with a combined firepower of thirty-two guns. As they approached they passed tethered buoys floating in the water. What the buoys indicated soon became evident to the vessels' crews as the seventy-six guns in Fort Sumter opened fire. They were ranging markers which the Confederate artillerymen had positioned for use in just this kind of attack. The engagement lasted two hours and the Confederates used over 2,200 rounds in some of the most telling and accurate artillery fire of the war. The Union Monitor *Passiac* took thirty-five hits in as many minutes and only replied with four rounds from her own guns. The *Keokuk* sustained ninety hits, of which nineteen penetrated below the waterline and she later sank. In total the Union fleet fired only 154 rounds before retiring in total disarray. Other bombardments of Sumter, such as that conducted by General Quincy Gillmore with fifteen heavy siege guns, fared little better. It was another lesson from which the world could learn, but the situation was to be repeated again some fifty years later as the British and French tried to force the Straits of the Dardanelles in support of the Gallipoli landings against Turkey in 1915.

Early in the American Civil War, Benjamin Jones of the Surry Light Artillery wrote of manhandling ageing 6-pounder guns in training exercises: 'We are required to move the guns about by hand, over the field, to front and to rear in echelon and in line, to sponge and load in mimic warfare, until our arms ache, and we long for a rest.' The Northern states were stronger in both industrial output and manpower. Also the North had resources which the South was sorely lacking. For example, the North had nearly 4,500,000 horses compared to the South which had only 1,698,000, and of the 30,626 miles of railway track crossing the country only 8,541 lay in the southern states. Furthermore, in the North there were over 110,000 industrial establishments compared to only 18,000 in the South. The shortage of horses was only one of a series of crises to hit the Confederate Army in the field. The

Surry Light Artillery did not take delivery of two more smoothbore cannon until September 1861 and in December a further pair were added to their strength. They were not the only ones to lack equipment: a Mississippi battery departed for the war with sixty-five horses but only one cannon. It was to be March 1862 before it could make up a six-gun battery. An officer with an Alabama regiment wrote: 'Our church bells are being cast into field pieces, but they are useless without horses.'

It has been said that such was the commonality between artillery pieces in service during the American Civil War that gunners from either side could have changed places and continued to fire cannon without retraining. The loading drill was the same on both sides, mainly because they used the same drill book. First the number two gunner was handed a 'cartridge' (a measured charge of powder in a bag) to which the cannon-ball was fixed by the number five gunner who handled the ammunition. The number two then placed it in the barrel of the gun and the number one gunner rammed it securely down into the chamber. The number three served the vent, which is to say that when necessary he placed his thumb, protected by a leather thumb stall, over the vent hole to prevent premature ignition from any smouldering embers remaining in the barrel from previous firings. It was then his task to use a special 'pricking' wire to pierce the powder bag through the vent to expose the powder charge. Next the number four gunner inserted a friction primer into the vent hole to which he connected the end of a lanyard, a braided cord sometimes several feet in length. The gun was now ready to fire and on the word of command the number four would give the lanyard a sharp jerk.

The friction tube had been introduced into service as early as 1853 and was a much safer method of igniting the powder charge in muzzle loading artillery than older alternatives. It comprised a tapered tube filled with fine priming powder and was topped off by a peg running through the tube. This peg had a roughened surface so that when it was pulled by the lanyard it created friction, in exactly the same way as matches dragged on a rough surface, and the resulting sparking action set off the train to burn down the tube. When it reached the chamber the flame ignited the main powder charge and the gun was fired. This device soon replaced all other means of igniting the powder charge, including the percussion tube which was finally declared obsolete in 1866 having entered service in 1845. These devices now meant that slow-matches and other naked flames were no longer required.

After firing, the number one swabbed out the barrel with a wet sponge to extinguish any embers. The number two took another round of ammunition from the number five and whole process was repeated. The number six and number seven of the gun crew were tasked to serve the ammunition limber and when firing case-shot or shell, they had to cut the fuses to the required length. A well-trained gun crew could manage to fire at least two shots per minute. Even at this stage in the development of warfare, indirect artillery fire was still not practised.

In a typical battery each gun and each limber was pulled by a team of six horses, harnessed in pairs abreast with a driver to each pair. These pairs were referred to as lead, swing and wheel teams and a similar layout was used on the ammunition resupply wagons. This meant that a battery of six guns required seventy-two horses. Further horses were required to pull the field forge, battery wagon and other wheeled units. A full battery complement was 155 men, including officers.

During the American Civil War the idea of a double-barrelled cannon was resurrected once again. This time it was John Gilleland of Athens, Georgia, who tried to perfect the weapon. He devised a double-barrelled cannon in 1862 and even went as far as having examples cast at the local foundry for trials. The two barrels were set at an angle of 3 degrees and each was loaded with a 6-pound ball; the two balls were connected by an 8-foot chain. He held high hopes for the weapon but failed to convince even the desperate Confederate War Department of its effectiveness. Trials only reaffirmed what was already known: such a weapon could not be aimed with any great accuracy and, as always, the balls with their trailing length of chain in tow flew erratically. Like earlier attempts at firing chained shot simultaneously from two separate barrels this weapon failed because the basic firing techniques of the day did not allow the two barrels to be discharged with the exact timing required.

At the beginning of the Civil War there was little real appreciation on either side of the true role of artillery in battle. In Europe strategists had already learned that artillery was used to best effect when deployed *en masse*. Certainly at the beginning of the war generals on both sides still tended to disperse their guns in penny packets, often no more than a six-gun battery to each infantry brigade. The weakness of this system was never more fully exposed than at the action of Malvern Hill on 1 July 1862, when a concentration of sixty Union guns crushed each Confederate battery as it was brought into action 'almost like tin ducks on a shooting range'. Brigade batteries were often made up from a mixture of pieces and it was not uncommon for one to comprise four 12-pounder guns and two 24-pounder howitzers, or four 6-pounder guns with four 12-pounders. The weapons in these batteries could also be a combination of smoothbore and rifled. The Confederate artillery was less well supplied than the Union and a four-gun battery firing three different calibres of ammunition was not unknown because the guns were acquired from different sources. This must have created a logistical nightmare for the quartermasters who had to ensure the supply of ammunition to all these different types of artillery.

Because Confederate batteries were attached to individual brigades a general could withhold his guns from action even though they might be desperately needed elsewhere. However, by 1864 artillery was beginning to come under the direction of army corps commanders who in turn served under chiefs of artillery. The Union Army underwent a similar transition and began to use artillery to support the infantry.

One of the most efficient artillery pieces of the war was the 'Napoleon', which was officially designated the Model 1857. It was served by five or six men who could get off two aimed 12-pounder solid shots or four rounds of canister per minute. When the Civil War broke out the Union Army had only four Napoleons in service, but by the end of the conflict orders to foundries had increased this number to 1,157, making it by far the most widely used piece of artillery of its type. It cost an average of $600 to manufacture each piece. The Confederate Army also valued the Napoleon and manufactured some 535 pieces in a variety of metals, including bronze, brass and even cast iron. In addition to the output from its own foundries, the Confederate Army had other Napoleons and artillery pieces that it seized on the battlefield and was further supplemented by stocks supplied by blockade runners from Europe.

The design of the Napoleon is credited to Napoleon III, Emperor of France. It was first produced in 1853 cast from bronze. Small numbers of this gun had been on the American continent since 1857, and after extensive service throughout the war it continued to be used until the 1870s. The Napoleon was a versatile weapon and could be used to fire solid shot, spherical or conical shells (containing an explosive filling of black powder), grapeshot and canister. Both sides also used 6- and 12-pound field howitzers. They also began to use newly developed rifled artillery, some pieces of which were breech-loading. Indeed the American Civil War was the real testing ground for artillerymen who had to adapt themselves to this new technology.

The two sides acquired artillery from different sources, most notably Britain where armaments manufacturers such as Whitworth and Armstrong were making great strides into the development of artillery. Armstrong supplied limited numbers of guns to the Confederates in both 6- and 12-pounder designs. The 12-pounder was a 3-inch rifled piece, capable of firing three different types of ammunition – shrapnel, case and explosive, the last of which weighed 11.56 pounds. It had been in service with the British Army since 1859 and was one of the first breech-loading designs. Its shell was made from iron and covered in a layer of lead which was designed to grip the rifling of the barrel. But it was the guns that Whitworth supplied to the Union forces that proved to be more successful. They were more accurate and developed a higher muzzle velocity. General E.P. Alexander, the Confederate States' artillery chief, conceded: 'the United States three-inch rifle is much more generally serviceable'. In both the Armstrong and the Whitworth weapon the breech mechanism was operated by unscrewing the hinged breech and swinging it to one side to expose the chamber. The projectile was then inserted, followed by gunpowder charge, which was bagged. The guns were fired by means of a friction tube and lanyard.

The task of Union Army quartermasters was slightly easier than their Confederate counterparts when it came to supplying ammunition, because their gunners were usually more uniformly equipped with pieces such as the 2.9-inch and 3-inch 10-pounder rifled Parrot guns. These, in turn, were supported by the 3.67-inch 20-pounder Parrot gun and even a model with a 10-inch calibre which could fire a 250-pound shell over a range of more than 1 mile. The Parrot guns were manufactured by Robert Parrot at the West Point Foundry in New York. His design involved wrapping super-heated bands of iron around a basic cast-iron barrel. Parrot's techniques may have been influenced by a similar method for strengthening cast-iron barrels which had been devised by Sir William Palliser. However, in the British design the cast-iron gun was bored out to receive a coiled tube of wrought iron of the correct calibre, and this was thrust into the barrel and secured by a special collar at the muzzle. The gun was tested at this stage using water pressure, and then a second tube was fitted on by shrinking, after which it was rifled and proof-fired using a heavy charge. In between times trials were conducted by designers including Parrot in an effort to increase range and accuracy and these were matched by designs intended to improve rates of fire. Weapons designers realized that for the artilleryman the ideal gun would be one that could be loaded even faster than it could be laid.

Parrot must have known that cast-iron barrels were prone to fracturing, but he still believed his design would be serviceable. As the outer iron bands cooled they shrunk onto the barrel and provided extra support. A total of 534 ten-pounder Parrot guns in both 2.9-inch and 3-inch calibre were manufactured along with 300 20-pounder guns and number of the large coastal types. However, they were far from satisfactory. For example, in an action before Fort Fisher, near Wilmington, North Carolina, every single Parrot gun burst. Five ruptured in the first bombardment alone, killing or wounding forty-five men – eleven were killed or wounded by responding enemy fire. Admiral Porter of the Union fleet summed up the situation when he said of the Parrots that they were: 'Unfit for service, and calculated to kill more of our men than those of the enemy'. The Confederates, in a desperate act, copied the Parrot design and achieved results no better than their Northern counterparts. All models were prone to blow up at the breech end of the barrel.

Such was the Confederates' need for reliable artillery that at one point they even resorted to manufacturing barrels using the old hoop-and-stave method. This, it must be said, proved more reliable than the copies of the Parrot gun, but could only have been created out of despair.

Another Union artillery design was the 3-inch ordnance rifle, which is credited to Major Thomas J. Rodman. Nearly 1,000 pieces were used in battle during the course of the war. The accuracy of this piece (it gained its name from the fact that it was rifled and should not be confused with the modern word for an infantry firearm) was famous and even the Confederate forces held a grudging respect for it. A Southern artilleryman later wrote: 'The Yankee three-inch rifle was a dead shot at a distance under a mile.' Praise for the weapon was often overheard: one Union artilleryman claimed it could 'hit the top of a barrel at a mile'. The 3-inch ordnance rifle was issued to Union gunners from late 1863 and was soon copied by the Confederates who greatly prized pieces of this type which had been captured on the battlefield. The rifled barrel weighed 830 pounds and the carriage 540 pounds. It could fire four different types of ammunition over a mile. These included the ordnance shell, which weighed 7.5 pounds, and the ordnance case and ordnance canister, which weighed 10.5 pounds and 10 pounds respectively. The fourth type of ammunition available to the 3-inch was the Hotchkiss solid shot, which weighed 10 pounds and comprised a solid cast-iron round fitted with a broad lead driving band which was designed to grip the grooves of the gun's rifling. The variety of ammunition types meant that the same gun could be used in a number of roles, engaging infantry in the open and bombarding fortifications. Such was the reliability of the weapon that it remained in service with the US Army until the late 1890s, even being used in action during the short Spanish-American War of 1898.

At the other end of the range of artillery pieces developed by Rodman was the columbiad with a 38.1-centimetre calibre (about 15 inches). It was made using his water-cooling process. Examples of this gun were mounted in sites such as Rodgers Battery near Hunting Creek on the Potomac River where they could engage enemy shipping. The pieces were fitted in a special mounting which featured race-rings on which the wheeled mount could traverse through 360 degrees, to provide all-round defence if needed. The recoil of the weapon, which weighed over 22 tons, was absorbed through friction.

Casualty figures from any conflict can be telling and this was certainly the case for the American Civil War. Statistics on the causes of 144,000 casualties in the war were gathered by Gilbert Beebe and Michael DeBakey. Their studies reveal that of the original figure, 108,000 casualties were inflicted by small-arms fire and 13,000 by cannon-fired ball and shell (a figure approximately equal to 9 per cent), with the remainder being caused by other weapons, such as the bayonet. It has also been calculated that it took 900 pounds of musket ball to kill one man, although the exact weight of artillery power required to do the same job has never been determined.

THE RISE OF ALFRED KRUPP AND THE FRANCO-PRUSSIAN WAR

It might be thought that by this time European countries would have begun to settle their differences of opinion in ways other than declaring war. This could not be further from the truth. A number of conflicts broke out, some of which were over in a matter of weeks. The bloody Austro-Prussian War, often referred to as the Seven Weeks' War, was fought between 14 June and 23 August 1866. It saw Austria defeated by a far superior Prussian Army. Only seven years earlier Austria had been defeated in a conflict with France. The war objective – Austrian withdrawal from Italy – was secured in a little over four months and laid the foundations for a united Italy.

At this time a German armaments manufacturer came to prominence. Alfred Krupp's name was to become as synonymous with artillery as his

English counterparts, William Armstrong and Joseph Whitworth. He had unveiled his first gun barrel for a 3-pound weapon in 1847. What made his design so different was the fact that it was made from cast steel which is inherently strong. Initially there was little interest in the weapon, but undaunted he continued to design and exhibit many fine artillery ideas at his own expense.

Showcases for Krupp's weapons included the Great Exhibition held at the Crystal Palace, London, in 1851. However, he had to wait until 1857 for his first firm order for artillery, which came from the Viceroy of Egypt. In the wake of this, orders were placed by Prussia in 1859 and subsequently Krupp was much in demand from clients overseas, including Argentina, Spain, Sweden, Russia and Belgium. By 1860 German newspapers were calling him the 'Cannon King' and six years later his pieces were used by the Prussian Army during the Austro-Prussian War. The guns' presence at the Battle of Königgratz (Sadowa) helped secure a victory for the Prussians by inflicting 20,000 casualties on an Austrian army of some 170,000 supported by 600 guns. In the light of this action the world's press began to refer to Krupp's company as the 'The Merchants of Death'.

Krupp went on to develop further weapons, and at the Paris Exhibition of 1867 he displayed a 50-ton gun that could fire a shell weighing over 1,000 pounds. It was described in a French newspaper as 'a monster such as the world has never seen'. The purchase cost was in excess of $112,000. No wonder, then, that he could not find a buyer willing to pay the price. Instead he presented the piece to Kaiser Wilhelm of Prussia as a mark of his loyalty.

The French did not appear particularly concerned about the emergence of such powerful weapons from the Krupp foundries, but in 1870 they must have had cause to regret not trying to match Prussian developments sooner. The French Army was considered one of the finest in Europe at the time, after all it had defeated the powerful Austrian Army in 1859, but so too had the Prussian Army only seven years earlier. The Franco-Prussian War of 1870–1 was precipitated by a Prussian attempt to place a Hohenzollern prince on the throne of Spain. This was unacceptable to the French who considered it to be the act of a state attempting to establish European hegemony, and they could ill afford the possibility of fighting an enemy on two fronts.

The French declared war on 15 July 1870 and mobilized their army. The German states formed a coalition against France and soon had 380,000 men in the field. The conflict went badly for France almost from the outset. At the Battle of Weissenburg on 4 August the French found themselves outnumbered and were forced to give ground. Two days later at the Battle of Froschwiller the French started the fight well but were soon overwhelmed by Prussian superiority, particularly in artillery which outgunned the French by 312 pieces to 119. Further actions saw both sides sustain heavy casualties in several major battles and dozens of lesser skirmishes.

The Prussian advance was so swift that by 19 September they were able to lay siege to Paris. The Prussians were content to invest the great city and wear down its resistance by attrition. As the days passed more and more Prussian troops arrived and skirmishing became routine. The city attempted to remain in touch with outside centres of resistance by sending out balloons carrying messengers. To counter this the Prussians mounted 37mm Krupp guns on specially converted horse-drawn carts which they designated *Ballonkannones*. No balloons were ever shot down, but this development did show how artillery was capable of being adapted to cope with emerging technology on the battlefield or above it.

In the initial stages of the siege Paris had not been shelled, but Prussian military commanders in the field wanted to finish the war. Eventually permission was given for the artillery to open fire on Paris, which it did on 27 December. The bombardment intensified over the following week and continued for three weeks. The French finally surrendered on 23 January 1871. Both sides counted the cost of the war. Prussian guns had fired an average of 199 rounds per gun per day for the duration, but although over 12,000 shells had been dispatched against Paris only 97 people had been killed and a further 278 wounded. In contrast the artillery of the Parisian defenders had inflicted several hundred casualties on the Prussian batteries. However, ultimately Krupp's guns made Prussia the undisputed power in mainland Europe.

Krupp and other artillery manufacturers of the day would not have achieved their leaps forward in weapon design had it not been for the efforts of one man, Sir Henry Bessemer. In 1856 Bessemer devised a method of making mild steel by decarbonizing molten pig-iron by blasting it with air, a process which had taken eight years to develop. The result was the mass production of cheap steel for the first time. This cheap steel allowed the manufacture of barrels able to withstand the enormous pressures generated by the more powerful charges employed to increase range. Bessemer's breakthrough meant that weapons could be less bulky but still have great destructive power.

At this time some smoothbore cannon were still in use and had an average effective range of 900–1,100 metres, sufficient to maintain the superiority of these pieces over infantry small arms, and some countries continued to cling to old ways. The fine quality ores used in Scandinavian gun foundries persuaded the northern kingdoms of Denmark, Norway and Sweden to continue to use cast-iron for field ordnance, even though Prussia already had steel smoothbores in service, and Armstrong's design for a coil system was providing Britain with good guns that were economic to produce.

COASTAL DEFENCE

Artillery was now entering a new period where it would perform specialized roles. These included coastal defence, which required a class of artillery designed specifically to engage warships attempting to raid or bombard shore installations. Such guns had existed for some time, but it was only through the lessons learned during the American Civil War that this became accepted as a serious branch of the artillery. The need for such weaponry became more pressing with the advent of armoured warships, such as the Royal Navy's HMS *Warrior* and the French *La Gloire*, in the mid-nineteenth century. In an effort to combat such threats, there was a demand for heavier and more accurate weapons that could engage such ships at extreme range before they could bring their fire to bear on coastal fortifications. The new coastal guns would require protection from warship armaments, and there was a strong link between coastal artillery gun design and developments in fortification.

The first major designs for purpose-built coastal defences mounted heavy rifled muzzle-loading guns in special casemates, which were vaulted rooms set within a fort constructed from masonry. Some of the plans incorporated armour plate shields on the outer walls through which openings were pierced to allow the guns to fire. As time passed and the guns became more powerful the original casemate designs became too restrictive.

Experience from the American Civil War highlighted the fact that casemates made good targets and that guns in the open, protected with earth and concrete, stood an even chance of survival. At the beginning of the war, forts built in the days before rifled artillery were considered largely invulnerable to cannon fire. One such fortification, Fort Pulaski, lay at the mouth of the Savannah River on Cockspur Island. Originally built between 1829 and 1847, it was enlarged and strengthened until, by the end of 1860, it had consumed 25 million bricks and huge quantities of lead, timber and iron for additional protection – the cost of the project was some $250,000. The fort was manned by one ordnance sergeant and a caretaker who had charge of twenty out of a proposed 146 guns.

In April 1862, a year after the start of the war, Union batteries opened fire on Fort Pulaski, whose Confederate garrison had by now been increased to five companies totalling 385 officers and men. They had forty-eight guns, only a few of which could be brought to bear on the massed batteries on Tybee Beach. Within two days, two of the 84-pounder James rifled guns, firing from a range of only 1,600 metres, had reduced the fort's brickwork to rubble. Military engineers world-wide learned a valuable lesson from the Battle of Fort Pulaski and by 1868 massive shields of chilled cast iron were being used to supplement coastal defences in countries including France and England.

Bearing in mind what had been said about siting artillery in the open, designers began looking into the idea of developing a disappearing carriage that would allow guns to be emplaced in open-topped pits; their exact location would only be revealed when they fired. Laying the gun on to the target could be a trying process for the crew who could take as long as 2 minutes 20 seconds to traverse the barrel through an arc of 90 degree. It was only the very best crews that could fire more than just a single shot while a steaming warship was in range. The principal proponent of the disappearing gun was US coastal artillery. The gun mounting rose by means of counterweights and it could be be fired from above the parapet after which it fell back on itself by force of recoil, controlled by pneumatic brakes, and disappeared from the enemy's view. Even when they were firing, such guns would only reveal their presence for a few seconds, thereby greatly reducing the possibility of accurate retaliatory fire from ships.

In the late nineteenth century a number of disappearing mounts were developed, including the Buffington-Crozier, which was taken up by the US Coast Artillery between 1895 and 1917. One of the more successful designs was devised by Alexander Moncrieff. The son of an officer in the Madras Army, Moncrieff was born in Edinburgh, Scotland, and studied at the universities of Aberdeen and Edinburgh. He then spent some time in a civil engineers' office. In April 1855 he was commissioned into the Forfar and Kincardine Artillery (Militia) and made his way to the Crimea during a prolonged period of leave. During his time there he witnessed the Russian guns being destroyed in the Mamelon Fort on 6 June 1855. The damage inflicted by shots entering the embrasures prompted him to design a disappearing artillery carriage in 1868. It had a number of advantages, not least of which was protection from direct fire for the gun crew, who could take shelter under the solid parapet during loading and only raise the gun to fire when they were ready.

The mounting which bore his name stored the force of the recoil so that it could be used to raise the gun back from the loading to the firing position. Finally, the interposing of a moving fulcrum between the gun and its platform lessened the strain on the latter and allowed it to be of lighter construction. In the Mark II version of the mount, designed for a 7-inch or 7-ton rifled muzzle-loading gun, the recoil forced the gun backwards and downwards on its curved elevators to return it to the loading position. The energy of the recoil was sufficient to raise a heavy, cast-iron counterbalance weight, which could be used to return it to the firing position. Other designs of disappearing carriages were introduced using either hydropneumatic or hydraulic recoil buffers, but the effect was the same. Moncrieff later returned to Scotland and transferred to the Edinburgh Artillery (Militia) in 1863, being promoted major in 1872 while attached to the Royal Arsenal Woolwich. He became a colonel in 1878 and was knighted in 1890.

RAILWAY ARTILLERY

It was during the American Civil War that the use of railway artillery was first seriously considered. As far as can be ascertained the credit for recognizing the importance of rail-mounted guns goes to General Robert E. Lee, but he may have been influenced by his artillery chief General E.P. Alexander. The American Civil War was 14 months old when, in June 1862, at the Battle of Savage Station, a 32-pounder Rebel cannon was mounted on the bed of a railway flatcar and used to fire on the enemy. The cannon and its crew were protected by iron plates angled and bolted to a substantial wooden superstructure. It is understood that this system had been constructed at Lee's instigation, and while the cannon was confined to the railway track it could still be used to bring fire to bear on an unsuspecting target. It did not take the Federal forces very long to develop their own railway artillery. The Union Army's armoured railroad battery appeared and operated on General Grant's City Point Railroad, near Petersburg, Virginia. One of its pieces was designated a mortar and was known affectionately as 'The Dictator'. The weapon was in action at the siege of Petersburg, where it was used to fire shells weighing 100 kilograms over a range of some 2,000 metres into the town.

As the war progressed, the size of railway guns increased until by the end of hostilities a number of such weapons were being fielded by either side. It was realized that rail-guns could only be used in specific situations, for example at sieges where railheads passed close to the area of intended engagement. One of more unusual confrontations involving railway artillery survives in a rather sketchy account of how two trains mounting artillery engaged one another in a land-based duel of the type usually associated with battleships at sea. The outcome is uncertain and the veracity of the account should probably be doubted. Railway-mounted guns could also be used for coastal defence or on a static frontal defence, where the existing rail system was adequate to transport them.

In 1859, two years before the outbreak of the American Civil War, England had feared an invasion by France led by Napoleon III. No doubt prompted by this possibility, William Adams published an article in which he advocated mounting guns on eight-wheeled railways cars moved by locomotives to provide a mobile and inexpensive coastal defence system. This came at a time when Britain was also constructing a chain of specialized artillery forts, some built in mid-Channel waters to protect harbours such as Portsmouth from enemy attack. In the event the scare of French invasion soon passed and William Adams' suggestion was shelved, along with other defence ideas of the time. The coastal defences were nicknamed 'Palmerston's Follies', after the prime minister who had ordered their construction.

Ideas and theories about how more military use could be made of the railways persisted. One experiment conducted by the Indian Army in 1886 involved the use of a 40-pounder mounted on a standard railway car in an attempt to prove that railway artillery was a viable proposition. Unfortunately, nothing seems to have been done to take the project further and, like William Adams' idea, it fell out of favour. It was only eight years later, in the early part of 1894, that a unit of the Sussex Artillery Volunteers attempted to revitalize the development of railway artillery in the British Army. They enlisted the assistance of the local railway company, the London, Brighton & South Coast Railway, and a turntable was mounted on a railway car to give the gun a full 360-degree traverse. The locomotive superintendent supplied armour plating for the front and sides of the gun, with a slot left for observation. By May the unit had its version of the railway gun ready for official trials at Newhaven. The Sussex Artillery Volunteers fired a number of rounds at a target 1.5 miles distant and several rounds were fired with the gun at right angles to the track to prove stability. The railway car had been fitted with a cylinder which absorbed the shock of the recoil forces on firing and prevented damage to the track. In fact, so successful were these trials that the gun could be fired repeatedly without having to relay and resight on to the target.

THE BOER WAR AND ITS AFTERMATH

The Second Boer War of 1899 to 1902 proved to be the stimulus the British Army needed to consider the serious use of heavy calibre artillery pieces mounted on railway cars. No doubt taking the Sussex Artillery Volunteers' experimental success as a starting point, it was discovered that guns of a calibre larger than the 40-pounder could be mounted on railway cars. The Cape Government Railway in South Africa built two mountings using spare locomotives and tenders, and succeeded in producing two railway guns suitable for taking to the field. One had a calibre of 6 inches and the other 9.2 inches. The intention was to use the two guns in the siege of Pretoria, but the stronghold surrendered before either of the pieces could be brought into action. The 6-inch gun did, however, see brief action in the Battle of the Modder River, where it is recorded that it did not fire at angles greater than 16 degrees from centreline. The 9.2-inch gun arrived too late to be used in the action, but did serve as the prototype for future heavy rail-mounted guns used in the First World War. Indeed, it was during the 1914–18 conflict that railway artillery would rise to strategic prominence.

The Second Boer War saw British troops pitted against well-equipped irregular troops, farmers more often than not, in a brutal guerrilla conflict for South Africa. The Boer farmers were equipped with artillery pieces obtained from the French company Creusot and the renowned German firm Krupp. These weapons were modern in design but the Boers could never field more than a handful at a time and could certainly never hope to match the British Army quantitatively. One of the pieces deployed was the 1-pounder quick-firing gun which the locals gave the onomatopoeic title 'Pom-Pom' – a nickname that would remain in military use to describe such weapons for some considerable time. The British Army used field pieces such as the 15-pounder, 12-pounder and 5-inch howitzer, and while it enjoyed numerical superiority in artillery, its weaponry could not match the quality of the Boers' French and German-supplied guns. They deployed pieces nicknamed 'Long Toms' by the British troops. These tended to be of 150mm calibre and were of the type supplied by Krupp. Even though there was a great disparity in artillery complements, the Boers were able to pin down British forces in a number of protracted sieges, including those at Mafeking, Ladysmith and Kimberley.

At Mafeking the defenders made an improvized return to the hoop-and-stave gun design. The result was called the 'Wolf', after the nickname given to Baden-Powell, the commander of the garrison. The design produced a 5-inch howitzer which was built by Mr Coughlan of the South African Railway Workshop at Mafeking. It comprised a core of steel steam-pipe; around this were fitted bars of heated iron which were hammer-welded using a technique employed by early medieval gunsmiths. The weapon was of limited use tactically but its firing served to raise the morale of the defenders and gave the besiegers something to think about. The garrison of Mafeking was not alone in trying such improvization: at Kimberley the men of a mine workshop produced a gun called 'Long Cecil'. They had never before been called upon to produce such an item. Like the Wolf, this weapon was of limited use, but did give the defenders a means of reply against Boer guns.

At one point in the war British artillery even included naval guns of various calibres dismounted from ships, including HMS *Monarch* and HMS *Dora*, and fitted to wheeled carriages. These served well but overall the Royal Artillery left the conflict with the urgent impression that the British Army needed to upgrade its guns quickly.

New designs were drawn up. These incorporated gun shields to protect the crew from long-range rifle fire. Such devices had not appeared on artillery for centuries and served to illustrate how accurate weaponry had become. Long-range rifle fire, which American artillerymen had also encountered during the Spanish-American War of 1898, necessitated the development of indirect fire techniques. This method of firing on the enemy, who might be out of sight of the actual artillery position, also allowed guns to be fired from behind a natural obstacle such as a hill or copse of woods. Improved lines of communication in the form of field telephones, which had been used by the Americans in 1898, were also employed by the British during the Second Boer War. This technology allowed an observer to be placed forward of the firing line to observe the enemy and relay the fall of shot. He could also instruct the guns to alter their range and even direction on to target. Other methods of artillery observation included increased use of tethered balloons equipped with telephones to relay instructions to the guns. Nowhere on the battlefield, it seemed, was now safe from the attentions of the artillery.

TACKLING RECOIL

The French Army had learned a great deal about artillery during the war with Prussia and towards the end of the nineteenth century set about redressing its weaknesses. The first of these changes came in 1877 when France developed an improved time fuse for its shells. Next came so-called 'smokeless powder' in 1884. It was invented by Paul Vielle and its ingredients included guncotton and collodion (both nitrocellulose compounds), ether and alcohol. There are two theories about the origin of its title – 'Poudre B'. The first has it that the compound was named after General Boulanger in 1885. The second, and more plausible, is that it was named Poudre B to stand for 'Poudre Blanche', meaning white powder, to distinguish it from 'Poudre N', Poudre Noir, or black powder. Whichever is correct, the fact remains that by 1886 Poudre B was in use throughout the French Army. It was a versatile mixture, capable of being rolled and cut into all manner of shapes to facilitate improved combustion on firing. (In 1889 Sir Frederick Abel and Sir James Dewar perfected their smokeless powder for the British Army: it would become known as cordite because of its appearance. This compound was based on 58 per cent nitroglycerine, 37 per cent guncotton and 5 per cent Vaseline. It too meant an instant improvement in the way artillery functioned.)

In 1897 the French Army became the envy of the world once more with the introduction of the amazing 'canon de 75 de campagne a tir rapide', known variously as the *Puteaux* or *soixante-quinz*, the '75'. It was designed by Commandant de Port of the Ateliers de Puteaux and its development was a closely guarded secret. Early trials conducted with the prototype in 1894 produced a rate of fire of thirty-one shots per minute. This was faster than anything else in service at the time. It was quicker even than the Whitworth 12-pounder, which in 1865 had been shown to be capable of firing four shells before the first had hit the target. The combination of its breech mechanism and unique recoil absorption method placed the 75 ahead of its contemporaries.

Ever since the earliest days of gunpowder artillery recoil had been a problem and a variety of ways to reduce its effect had been tried, including friction beds, inclined beds, rubber buffers and carriages whose trails telescoped against a shoe that dug into the earth when the weapon was fired. The recoil system of this new weapon was based on a compact hydropneumatic design which used oil held in a cylindrical reservoir and nitrogen in a recuperator cylinder. On firing, the barrel moved back with its attached piston which increased the pressure of the oil in the lower chamber and thrust the floating piston forwards. This device closed the throttling valve to end the recoil and the nitrogen gas, now under even more pressure, pushed the piston back to its start point and oil flowed back into its reservoir. The gun was then returned to its firing position. The design team for the 75 used the Nordenfelt breech, which was simplicity itself. The mechanism was operated by grasping the handle and rotating it through 120 degrees to the left to open the breech ready for loading. Once a shell had been placed in the breech it was closed by rotating back to the right. A lanyard was used by the gunner to fire the shell and the whole process could be repeated rapidly and without having to reposition the gun. The 75 was fitted with a nickel-steel barrel capable of firing 6,000 rounds before it had to be returned to a depot for re-sleeving.

It fired brass-cased ammunition known as the 'fixed' type, which was available in high-explosive and shrapnel rounds. This led to the weapon being designated as a quick-firing, or QF, gun. Although the term refers to the gun, it is actually the ammunition which permits it to be designated as such. The ammunition for the QF gun is fixed, which is to say the propellant charge is contained in a brass case to which the projectile is fixed, in much the same way as a very large modern-day rifle bullet. The base of the cartridge case contains a primer which when struck by the firing pin in the breech mechanism of the gun fires the shell. The 75 was first used in combat by the French in China in 1900, and went on to provide sterling service throughout the First World War. It was not long before similar weapons appeared in service. The German equivalent, the Krupp 77mm Model 1897, had been developed in 1896. However, its rate of firing was much slower than the French weapon and it also lacked the 75's stability. After the crew of a

75 had fired the first shot to settle the trail spade into the ground, the layer and firer of the four man crew who served the gun could remain seated on the gun carriage.

The 75's shrapnel cartridge weighed 9.2 kilograms and scattered 302 hardened lead balls that were lethal out to 20 metres and still dangerous out to 160 metres. The projectile of the explosive shell weighed 5.3 kilograms, with the cartridge weighing 7.3 kilograms.

The 75 was taken into service by the US Army when it arrived in France in 1917 and the Singer Manufacturing Company was granted a licence to produce the weapon. It was only then that the secrets of the gun were discovered. At the start of the Second World War the US Army still had over 4,200 units of the 75. The 75 was also used by French troops during the Second World War when they engaged German tanks at Bir Hakeim, Libya, in 1941. But by then heavier armour plating and more powerful tank guns were proving too much for the small but powerful 75s.

INDIA AND THE FAR EAST

Artillery was now referred to collectively as guns. Howitzers remained a separate category – the term distinguished them for their specialized role of firing at high angles of trajectory. Barrels could now be traversed left and right independently of their carriage. The common shell was also being phased out of service and apart from a brief interlude when the British Army reverted to muzzle loading in 1869–70, all artillery was now of the breech-loading type with rifled barrels. For all these technological innovations, however, the actual guns themselves were still dependent on draught animals to haul them around the battlefield.

During the 1890s the British Army in India still fielded large guns and at one point had on its establishment four 'heavy batteries', each of which comprised four 40-pounders and two 6.3-inch howitzers. The latter type of weapon was re-distributed to two batteries in the Punjab, and one each in Bengal and Madras. Each battery, as far as the guns were concerned, was manned entirely by Royal Artillerymen (of the Garrison Companies). Their normal strength was one major (in command), one captain, three subalterns, two staff-sergeants, six corporals, six bombardiers and seventy-two gunners, with two trumpeters and one farrier. They employed twelve elephants for each battery, using two animals to each gun or howitzer. To look after the animals there was one jemader, twelve mahouts, and twelve assistant mahouts. For transporting the other artillery equipment the battery used 262 bullocks which were managed by one jemader, six sirdars and 131 drivers.

Artillery had not always been so well organized in India. During the Indian Mutiny of 1857–8 the regiments of Indian troops involved in the uprising managed to keep their artillery and used it in engagements, for example at Cawnpore in June 1857, where Captain John Moore of the 32nd Regiment said the defenders faced 'live shells [which] kept them in a perpetual dread; for nearly all night these shells were seen coming through the air, often doing mischief when they burst'. The British and mutinous Indian forces met at Cawnpore again in December. The British cavalry chased the native troops for 14 miles and succeeded in capturing thirty guns out of the thirty-six they held. Afterwards the British exacted an ironic but terrible retribution against the ringleaders of the mutiny by tying them to the muzzles of the guns and firing them, a form of execution known as being 'blown from the guns'. Thereafter, the artillery was only served by crews made up from British regiments.

During the 1880s some Far Eastern countries such as Burma (the modern-day Union of Myanmar) were capable of manufacturing 6-pounder cannon with a range of 1,500 yards.

The cannon-type weapons cast in China and India were comparable to those in use at the time of Waterloo and their designs remained virtually unchanged. While these were of limited effectiveness against armies in the region equipped with similar weapons, they were of little or no use against the superior firepower of European-style artillery. In 1854 the American naval officer Commodore Oliver Hazard Perry appeared off the coast of Tokyo, Japan, to encourage the country, which had been in self-imposed isolation from the outside world, to open up to international trade. The approach did nothing to soften Japanese attitudes but when Perry returned the following year with even more warships the Japanese were obliged to open up the country and enter into trading relations. Japanese gunpowder weapons in use at the time were grossly outdated as a result of their isolationism. However, the Japanese quickly obtained 4-pounder guns from the French and used them until the outbreak of the Franco-Prussian war in 1870. Then they acquired Krupp-manufactured guns. By 1872 the Japanese were in a position to manufacture their own 4-pounder field guns at the Osaka Arsenals. Less than thirty years later they would make the world's military powers sit up and take notice.

AMMUNITION

As the nineteenth century drew to a close, and minor wars and campaigns involving artillery continued, the development of ammunition was forging ahead. Solid shot had all but disappeared, except in coastal artillery where it was kept for use against armoured warships. Ammunition was now collectively called shells and individual projectiles were termed rounds – even though they were cylindrical in shape. Ammunition for the lighter field guns was now of the fixed-type, but larger guns, such as the coastal pieces, still had to be loaded using separate projectiles behind each of which was loaded a bagged charge of propellant. This same method applied to the large-calibre mortars still in widespread use at the time.

Obturation, that is to say gas-tight sealing of the breech behind the shell, was now achieved and all the gases produced from the propellant on firing were used to force the shell out of the barrel with no windage. This increased range and with rifling now universally accepted, accuracy was also much improved. New breech mechanisms and recoil control meant improved safety for the gunners, with only minimum risk of blow-back to injure the crew.

Ammunition was referred to by its 'natures' because there were now many types of shell available. These included: illuminating shells, which had been used as early as the Crimean War; high-explosive; and shrapnel, which had now evolved into a cylindrical shape and contained steel balls of equal size and weight around a central bursting charge to increase lethality. In 1883 General Kolmar von der Goltz of the German Army wrote: 'each new invention and each mechanical improvement seems somehow, in these days, to find its way into military service'. How right he was, and no more so than in the field of artillery.

By 1899 peace in Europe was strained, but it was to the Far East that all eyes would look as the twentieth century began.

SEVEN

ARTILLERY COMES OF AGE, 1900–2000

As the twentieth century began, the pace of artillery research and development quickened to meet emerging battlefield tactics. Each of these new designs was created to counter a new type of weaponry. It is therefore necessary to examine each of the new forms of artillery, such as anti-tank and anti-aircraft guns, on an individual basis in order to trace their history. Another form of weaponry that appeared in this century was the self-propelled gun, while advanced techniques of indirect fire using forward observation officers were developed. Some existing types of artillery, like coastal and railway guns, still had a role to play well into the twentieth century until they were finally supplanted by rocketry in the late 1940s and early 1950s.

RE-EQUIPPING THE BRITISH ARMY

During the Second Boer War, 1899–1902, the British Army is estimated to have fired 273,000 rounds of all calibres from the entire artillery force it deployed during the conflict. The expenditure rate of ammunition, while excessive for the time, was to pale into insignificance as the twentieth century progressed – in the First World War the opening barrage of a 'push' during an offensive campaign on the Western Front could see that amount of ammunition fired in a single day. The war in South Africa had been a steep learning curve for the Royal Artillery and had revealed a number of deficiencies. The Boer conflict had highlighted the fact that modern artillery had to be introduced to replace older equipment, some of which had been in service since the time of the Crimean War almost fifty years earlier. For this reason alone the development of the 13-pounder and 18-pounder field guns for the British Army makes an interesting case for examination. Even before the South African War ended in 1902, the Royal Artillery was expressing concerns regarding its ageing weaponry and a special field gun committee was set up, with the specific aim of laying out designs for new guns to arm the batteries of Horse and Field Regiments of the Royal Artillery.

Early on in proceedings the committee decided that the new gun should be 'quick firing', fitted with a shield and weigh no more than 28 hundredweight (approximately 1.5 tonnes). It had to be capable of accurately firing a 12.5-pound shrapnel shell out to 6,000 yards – the latter put it in the same category as the French 75. A small number of potential replacements for older weapons had been made ready for trials by three of the country's leading armaments manufacturers in 1902, but the trials proved inconclusive, with no one gun coming out overall as the best weapon. All of the pieces submitted had desirable features; this presented quite a dilemma for the committee which sought a compromise with the manufacturers. The committee approached the different manufacturers in turn and persuaded them to cooperate in order to incorporate the best features from their respective guns in an all-new weapon. Predictably, the process was not altogether straightforward and the committee came up with a plan to produce two types of gun: the 13-pounder and the 18-pounder. The companies concerned agreed to comply with the committee's wishes and the two new weapons were built from a composite design. The actual guns came from Armstrong and the recoil system from Vickers, while Woolwich provided the carriage – a classic case of joint venture long before this way of working became fashionable.

By 1903 one battery of the Royal Horse Artillery (RHA) and one of the Royal Field Artillery (RFA) were equipped with the 13-pounder and 18-pounder guns respectively and placed in readiness to participate in field trials. An argument now arose over how accurate the weapons were and it was suggested that the 18-pounder be dropped. The ballot was hung and Prime Minister Arthur Balfour was called on to use his casting vote and break the deadlock. Balfour was a politician without any military background, but he had enough sense to realise the benefits of having both guns in service with the Royal Artillery. And so orders were placed for both the 13-pounder and 18-pounder guns for service with the Royal Horse Artillery and Royal Field Artillery respectively.

The date that both guns entered service is generally given as 1904. Certainly by 1906 they were being issued to the regular RHA and RFA units for training and familiarization with new equipment. The weight in action of the new 13-pounder was just over 2,200 pounds, which fell well within the parameters laid out in the initial design briefings. It could fire a shrapnel shell of 5.7 kilograms out to a maximum range of 5,390 metres using a propelling charge of cordite to produce a muzzle velocity of 510 metres per second. The actual calibre of the gun was 76.2mm with a barrel length of 24 calibres; that is to say 24×76.2mm, giving a length of 1,828.8mm. Some sources, however, quote the barrel length as 23 calibres, which would mean it was 1,752.6mm long – the discrepancy is purely academic.

The 13-pounder gun was mounted on a two-wheeled carriage and drawn by a team of horses. It was served by six men and a well-trained crew could achieve a rate of fire of twenty aimed rounds per minute. This was possible because of the quick action of a sliding breechblock and the fact that the ammunition was of the 'fixed type'. The recoil system of the 13-pounder was simple, the barrel sliding on guide ribs on a bronze cradle. It was checked at the end of its backwards run by a hydraulic buffer placed above the gun, which was surrounded by metal recuperator springs. Although this recoil system worked well, it was to be replaced during the First World War by a new one based on the Schneider pattern air recuperator, as used on several artillery designs at the time, including the French 75.

The original 13-pounder was fitted with a tubular trail which restricted the maximum possible elevation to 16 degrees and the traverse to only 8 degrees. During the First World War all field artillery was horse drawn because this was the most expedient means of moving guns at the time. In fact, in 1914, the artillery element of the British Expeditionary Force (BEF) contained five RHA batteries which were equipped with 13-pounders and attached to the cavalry division.

At this time the 13-pounder only fired shrapnel shells, no high-explosive (HE) shells having been developed for it. However, towards the end of 1914 the War Office in London made the suggestion that high-explosive shells might be useful in both the 13- and 18-pounder guns. The General Headquarters of the British Expeditionary Force in France was not wholly convinced by the idea, but did agree to take delivery of 1,000 HE shells for trials with the 13-pounders. Later, the GHQ changed its mind for the good – a rare occurrence – and asked for further supplies. Initial ammunition deliveries consisted of 75 per cent shrapnel, the remainder being HE. But eventually the percentages were to even out at 50/50.

A typical brigade of Royal Horse Artillery comprised 19 officers and 651 other ranks, gunners, bombardiers and drivers. There were 275 riding horses and 480 draught horses to move the 12 guns, 4 carts and 64 wagons. A battery of 13-pounders comprised 6 guns, 1 cart and 38 wagons, with 102 riding horses and 122 draught horses, and a manpower level of 5 officers and 199 other ranks.

RUSSIA AND JAPAN AT WAR, 1900–3

In the main, European nations proved the worth of artillery on the battlefield, but it was the Japanese, emerging from years of isolation, who showed just how it could be used to bring an enemy to its knees. Japan had gained modern military experience during the Sino-Japanese War of 1894–5 and had proved its army could fight. However, its true potential was not demonstrated until ten years later when the country took on the might of the Russian Empire. Manoeuvrings between these two states had taken place between 1900 and 1903, during which time Japan made preparations to engage Russia in a war to end the latter's dominance in Korea and Manchuria. Hostilities broke out between the two countries on 8 February 1904 with a Japanese naval attack against the Russian fleet at anchor in Port Arthur, near modern-day Lushun, China. Initially Russia could only mobilize 83,000 troops and 196 guns from its formidable army of 4.5 million men. The Japanese would eventually mobilize their entire standing army of 283,000 troops with 870 guns and later on reinforce this with a trained reserve of a further 400,000.

The war was also fought at sea, but the real turning point of the conflict came with the six-month Japanese siege of the Russian defences at Port Arthur. The Russian Army had only recently been re-equipped with new quick-firing field artillery in the form of the Putilov M-1903 of 76.2mm calibre. It was an improvement on the M-1900, also in 76.2mm calibre, because it had a greater range and improved muzzle velocity but Russian artillery as a whole was no match for the huge siege guns that the Japanese would bring up.

The lightest piece of Japanese artillery used during the war was the Type-31 field gun firing a shell of 75mm calibre. This weapon dated back to 1898 and was unusual in the fact that it did not have a recoil system at a time when such devices were commonly incorporated into artillery designs. But this did not pose a problem to the Japanese gunners; in fact, they probably viewed this apparent deficiency as a benefit because in the extreme low temperatures experienced in Manchuria any recoil system could freeze solid. Aware of the extremely harsh conditions they would encounter, the Russians had used a recoil system manufactured from solid rubber on their M-1900 gun to counter the cold.

The light Type-31 gun did not perform as well as the Japanese had expected and its replacement design, the Type-38, also in 75mm calibre was not ready in time to see service during the war. However, when it was introduced, the Type-38 with its hydraulic buffer recoil system was practical enough to remain in service for more than forty years.

Japanese artillery was very advanced and much of the ammunition from the guns was discharged using indirect fire, which was controlled to pinpoint accuracy by forward observation officers skilled in map reading. This technique involved three or four men, including an officer, equipped with detailed maps and optical equipment, moving as far forward as possible and directing their artillery fire on to enemy positions. These forward observers could relay target corrections directly to the batteries and even bring fire to bear on targets of opportunity. Such tactics were not lost on observers from other nations who soon developed similar techniques for their own artillery force. The Japanese also used panoramic sights for observation, goniometers for measuring angles and even camera obscuras to observe the Russian defences from the safety of their own emplacements. They also used balloons for aerial observation and telephones to maintain contact with the gun batteries. In fact, when the artillery commander left his post he was followed by a signaller who unreeled telephone cables from a small drum so that the commander could remain in contact at all times.

In an effort to reduce Russian defences at Port Arthur the Japanese brought up nineteen siege guns with a calibre of 280mm and a range of nearly 10,000 metres. Their shells weighed over 300 kilograms and were devastating. The siege lasted from May until October 1904, until finally the garrison was stormed. Some 10 per cent of all Russian casualties were inflicted by artillery fire alone.

The lessons of artillery power had not been lost on the Germans, who, along with other European nations, sent observers to monitor the progress of the war. Germany was so impressed with the large Japanese siege artillery that the Krupp factory at Essen was set to work on designing pieces that could be used against the border fortifications of Belgium. At the end of the Russo-Japanese War and the Second Boer War, many armies began to upgrade and modernize their artillery, including the Germans and Austrians.

THE BEGINNING OF THE FIRST WORLD WAR

Many small conflicts were being fought around the world in the early twentieth-century but the main focus of trouble was the Balkans, where national unrest had been fomenting for some time. The Italo-Turkish war of 1911–12 gave way to the Balkan War of 1912–13. Then in June 1914 came 'the shot that was heard around the world' when the Austrian Archduke Franz Ferdinand was assassinated in the town of Sarajevo in Bosnia. A series of Austrian ultimatums directed at Serbia were rejected. The pace of moves towards a widespread conflict quickened as Austria declared war on Serbia and then Russia, allied to Serbia, declared war on Austria in return. The situation spiralled out of control as one European nation after another took up arms and joined either the Allied or the Central Powers' camp. Many countries, including Portugal, were dragged into the European theatre of the conflict; ulitmately it became a global war with fighting conducted in Africa, the Middle East and the Far East. This conflict was to precipitate the development of another dimension of warfare which artillery had to be adapted to counter: the threat of bombardment by aircraft.

In 1914 the German Army enjoyed a clear lead in artillery, particularly heavy guns of which it had 575 pieces. The Russians and French had 240 and 180 heavy guns respectively. But France had not always had heavy artillery and only five years previously the French Army totally lacked any type of weaponry in the heavy category. Indeed, in 1909 a staff officer replied to a question about this deficiency by stating: 'Thank God we don't have any! What gives the French Army its force is the lightness of it cannon.' Fortunately, hindsight can be a great motivation and by 1915 France had begun to equip its army with heavy guns to redress this imbalance. It is quite possible the programme was instigated after the Japanese success with heavy artillery at Port Arthur.

As the German Army advanced into Belgium it found its way barred at Liège by a ring of fortifications that could not be reduced by field guns alone. These defences were started by the engineer Henri Brialmont in 1888; they were partially subterranean and were protected by armour plating on cupolas housing the guns. The Germans responded in age-old fashion: they followed the maxim that nothing succeeds like excess. The German Army brought forward a pair of 420mm siege howitzers, which were moved by train from Krupp's factory at Essen to the front. Austrian-built howitzers of

305mm calibre from the Skoda works were also positioned and used to bring fire to bear on the forts. The Belgian commander, General Leman, said that when the shells from these monster guns impacted they formed a crater big enough 'to put a three-storey house in'. The bombardment lasted only four days, from 12 to 16 August, during which time the twelve main forts were reduced one after another, until finally the last one at Loncin fell. The large Krupp guns, nicknamed 'Big Berthas' were then moved to Namur where they were used to fire on more fortifications, which had also been designed by Brialmont, along with a pair of 305mm Austrian guns known as 'Schlanke Emma' ('Slim Emmas'). The bombardment of Namur took four days from 21 August until 25 August. Following this success another pair of 305mm 'Slim Emmas' joined the the guns at Maubeuge and reduced further Belgian fortifications to rubble. The German advance continued headlong; it was so quick that it outpaced its logistics resupply and the army had to slow down. This allowed the Allies to dig in and prepare defences in the form of a network of trenches. Both sides dug in as they attempted to regroup to build up their respective strengths.

But the combatants were like the long-distance runner who gives everything in one enormous effort to get ahead of the opposition, then never fully recovers and finally reaches the point where fatigue takes over. The armies facing each other across the shell-swept countryside of eastern France and Belgium settled into a routine of trench warfare and ordeal by artillery fire in a war of attrition. During the first six months of the First World War, from 15 August 1914 until 15 February 1915, the British Army was to fire 1 million rounds. It has been calculated that for each year of the conflict a typical German corps used 40 tons of ammunition per day and that during the first six weeks of the war each gun in the German Army fired on average 1,000 rounds per day. In the British Army ammunition had been allotted to the guns using the Mowatt scale, which in 1913 had allowed for 1,500 rounds for each field gun and 1,200 rounds for each howitzer. No one could have foreseen the massive expenditure of artillery in 1914 and the demand was only to increase as the war dragged on.

In October 1914, only three months into the conflict, the British and German armies faced one another across the battlefield in what has come to be called the First Battle of Ypres. Such was the initial rate of fire that British 18-pounder field guns were reduced to a daily firing rate of 80 rounds per gun from a reserve stock of 320 rounds per gun because supplies were running out. The Mowatt scale was shown to be a worthless piece of calculation that bore no relation to the true stocks of ammunition required to maintain sustained artillery fire power in a modern war.

As the war continued into 1915 the ammunition crisis worsened and a scandal of supply developed which was only tackled by very prompt action. Factories worked around the clock, work forces increased and national shell-factories were established. In March 1915 Sir Douglas Haig's First Army took the village of Neuve-Chapelle. The intensity of the artillery barrage was such that it turned the area into a scene resembling a lunar landscape flooded by a sea of mud. Conditions made it virtually impossible for the infantry to advance. This limited action lasted only three days but it had used up 100,000 rounds of ammunition, almost 20 per cent of the BEF's total stock. These rounds had been fired by 340 guns assembled to give cover to the infantry. The offensive was fought over a narrow front and the artillery was timed to fire a coordinated barrage to support the advances. This expenditure of ammunition in the first months of the war exceeded all expectations and, as commanders came to recognize the central role of artillery, the question of supply loomed ever larger.

The British Army was not alone in recognizing the pressing need for reliable stocks of ammunition. The French Army required 100,000 rounds per day just to keep the guns firing without additional stocks which had to be supplied when supporting an offensive: the guns were hungry beasts of war. An artillery presence was needed everywhere, it seemed, and the demand could only get more acute.

In January 1915 the Germans assembled 600 pieces of artillery ranging from 77mm to 100mm field guns along a 7-mile line facing Bolimow on the Russian Front. The barrage unleashed by this force was unique: for the first time in history artillery was used to fire shells filled with poison gas. Fortunately for the Russians, in the near-freezing conditions these shells had little or no effect. But undeterred by such a poor showing, the German Army continued to discharge gas shells. Then at the Second Battle of Ypres, the war took a new direction: the Germans released poisonous gas onto the battlefield from cylinders on 22 April 1915. The Allied armies soon followed suit and began to produce ammunition filled with gas for all sizes of gun except very large calibre weapons which fired shells filled with TNT explosive.

On its own TNT is an extremely volatile explosive filling for modern shells. The British mixed Lydite and later Research Department Explosive (RDX) to temper it. Experiments produced an explosive compound which produced vastly better results and was much safer to handle and fire. Shells filled with high explosives were used against troops in the open or were fired on trenches to collapse them and form breaks in the line. Shells filled with bullet-sized projectiles were now officially known as anti-personnel ammunition but the troops still referred to them as shrapnel, as indeed they did any fragment of shell. This type of ammunition was used against infantry in the open to break up an assault.

Gas shells were fired in great quantity from guns of various calibres, but mainly from field guns, such as the French 75, British 18- and 13-pounders, and German 77mm and 150mm. Shells were filled with gases including phosgene, chlorine and mustard but resulted in a relatively poor casualty rate for the actual amount of ammunition fired. While gas as a weapon inflicted a total of 1,205,655 non-fatal casualties, it only resulted in 91,000 deaths. Conventional shells were more versatile and by the end of the war nearly 70 per cent of all casualties had been inflicted by artillery.

Not all casualties caused by artillery fire were necessarily inflicted on the enemy. The French Army officer General Charles Percin, author of *Le Massacre de notre Infanterie*, believed that upwards of 75,000 French infantrymen were killed by their own artillery fire during the First World War. This is quite possible – shell fire could be indiscriminately directed. The German and British armies must have suffered similar tragedies but their casualty figures have not been calculated.

Expenditure of shells during the 'war to end all wars' reached quite startling levels. For example, in 1916 the British Army fired nearly 1,800,000 rounds in the preparatory bombardment of the Somme. In 1917, at the Third Battle of Ypres, also referred to as the Passchendaele offensive, the British artillery fired a continuous barrage of more than 4,282,000 rounds over a fourteen-day period but still did not suppress the German defences. The British Army's consumption of ammunition on this campaign has been calculated to represent a year's output by a force of 55,000 munitions workers. German armaments manufacturers had been at the forefront of weapons production when war broke out, and the Krupp works alone produced 9,000,000 artillery shells and 3,000 pieces of artillery per month, a figure which no other European nation could hope to match at the time.

Aircraft now began to replace tethered balloons for battlefield observation because they could fly over wide areas to report on troop movements and plot the positions of strategic installations, such as ammunition dumps and artillery sites. Initially their messages were dropped to the ground in weighted bags, but then early radio communications were developed and speeded up the process by making it possible to report directly to the ground at the time of observation. Aircraft could now be used to ensure artillery fire was directed with greater accuracy than ever before.

The level of importance attributed to aerial observation can be evaluated from the number of aircraft called on by the Germans to support the offensive against the French fortifications at Verdun which opened on 21 February 1916. The Germans had assembled 1,400 pieces of artillery over a 12.5-kilometre front with a stockpile of 2,500,000 rounds of ammunition for a six-day barrage. The artillery commander, Major-General Schabel, requested 166 aircraft, 14 balloons and 3 Zeppelins to provide battlefield observation. Despite the pounding, which did massive damage, it was three infantrymen who inveigled their way into Fort Douamont that opened it up for assault.

Artillery was used on all fronts of the war from Gallipoli in Turkey, to the Russian Front and the Alps, where the Austro-Hungarian and Italian armies were engaged in mountain warfare. But it was on the Western Front that it had the most profound effect on the way the war was conducted. Even today, more than eighty years after the Armistice, hundreds of shells are still uncovered annually by farmers as they plough their fields. These are deposited at specially designated pick-up points for the Belgian and French armies whose ordnance explosives teams dispose of them safely.

TACTICS

During the First World War specialized tactics were developed for the guns to allow them to perform specific tasks or missions, either when covering an infantry assault or providing counter-battery fire. The first of these techniques was known as the rolling barrage and was first employed in 1915 in an attempt to break the deadlock of trench warfare. It was a very discriminating tactic because each assigned battery fired down a path or line of fire about 200 metres wide. The first impact area was about 150 metres in front of the positions of the infantrymen, who were to follow in the wake of the barrage and then assault the enemy trenches. This area was called the 'danger zone' and was fired on for a period of between 3 and 10 minutes, which was the time calculated for the infantry to cross 100 metres of ground.

The barrage was then lifted or moved out to fire on ground at about 500–1,000 metres range. This was designed to provide support for the advancing infantry and keep the enemy in underground shelters.

The lifts or jumps in range could be made as many times as necessary, with the heavy artillery, such as 155mm and 8-inch calibre guns, firing high-explosive shells and the field guns, such as 75mm and 13- and 18-pounders, firing shrapnel, which could be up to one-third of any artillery force directed to provide a rolling barrage. It was terrifying for the Germans, but in their deep, bomb-proof shelters they waited until the artillery had lifted and then engaged the British infantry with machine-gun fire. Despite mixed results, the rolling barrage tactic continued to be used until 1918.

Another technique developed was the box barrage, which came rather late in the war and was designed to support trench raids by providing a cordon sanitaire fired by field guns supplemented by larger guns from the rear. The protective barrage was used by all sides from 1917 onwards and was designed to bring the maximum fire of guns to bear on the enemy's assembly point for an assault and thereby break it up; it was usually fired by the heavy artillery. The last main artillery tactic devised was the counter-preparation barrage, which was similar in some respects to the protective barrage, being directed against enemy trench systems and assembly points.

The First World War ended on 11 November 1918, with artillery still being discharged until the last minutes before the ceasefire. When the firing stopped it was almost as if the world had come to a standstill, so deafening was the silence.

THE SECOND WORLD WAR AND BEYOND

Over the twenty years after the Armistice artillery was used in a number of conflicts, including the Italian invasion of Ethiopia in October 1935. Developments were made: solid and spoked wooden wheels gave way to metal wheels and pneumatic tyres, and barrels could now be elevated and depressed separately from the carriage. Another refinement was the introduction of the split carriage trail which allowed the barrel to be traversed across an arc – some designs had a full 360-degree traverse capability, which for the first time permitted the gun crew to follow a target as it moved across the battlefield. These improvements would later result in better engagement techniques for specialized artillery operating in an anti-tank role.

Armies sought ways to gain combat experience, in particular using artillery and aircraft. For example, the support Germany gave to General Franco during the Spanish Civil War of 1936 to 1939 can be seen as the proving ground for German artillery and ground-support aircraft. The Sino-Japanese War of 1937 to 1945 tested the muscle of the latter's artillery branch, and further painful experiences were gained in disastrous border clashes with Soviet Russia. Meanwhile, Italian artillery gained experience during the war with Ethiopia in 1935.

America was able to distance itself from the global unrest of the 1930s and from the early stages of the European war after Germany unleashed its masterful *Blitzkrieg* and overwhelmed France and Belgium. But on 7 December 1941 its position was to change when Japanese aircraft attacked the US naval base at Pearl Harbor. Japanese armed forces mounted surprise attacks throughout the Pacific region and rapidly expanded eastwards across the ocean to establish an island-based empire. Such victories were to be relatively short-lived; the Japanese garrisons were reduced as one group of occupied islands after another became isolated and America fought back. Faced by the world's biggest industrial giant, Japanese forces would succumb to superior firepower.

Each of the occupied islands – for example, Tarawa, Saipan and Iwo Jima – had to be taken by amphibious assaults which were preceded by naval gunfire and then conventional artillery operated by the US Army or Marines. The weapons used by the artillery branches in this campaign were identical to those deployed by US forces in other theatres of war, including Italy and north-west Europe. They included 155mm 'Long Toms', 105mm towed and self-propelled and the lighter 75mm field pieces. The US Army had entered the Second World War with a relatively small artillery force but between 1941 and 1945 American ordnance factories were to turn out more than 500,000 pieces of all types, which were supplied not only to American forces but also to the Allied armies, including those of France, Australia and Britain.

During the Second World War the Channel Islands gained a new place in the history of warfare. In June 1940 the Germans seized and occupied the islands after some aerial bombing, despite the fact that they had been demilitarized by Britain. Within months the three main islands – Jersey, Guernsey and Alderney – were being fortified, at first with rudimentary defences in which artillery was mounted, but this programme gave way to massive concrete emplacements which far outweighed the islands' military importance. Over the next five years, until liberation in May 1945, Adolf Hitler ordered that this, the only part of British territory to be captured by the Germans, was to be defended. In the end the garrison on the islands surrendered without firing a shot, which must have been a great relief to the small force dispatched to accept the surrender, because by that time over 1,500 guns of all calibres were emplaced, including 88mm and 205mm pieces. On the island of Jersey alone the Germans had installed fourteen specialized batteries of artillery, in addition to other local sites, for which a supply of 27,000 tons of ammunition was held. The largest emplacement on the islands was the four-gun Mirus Battery sited at Le Frie Baton on Guernsey. The guns there had a calibre of 305mm and could fire 250-kilogram explosive shells out to ranges of 55 kilometres, and armour piercing shells of nearly 400 kilograms to a much shorter range. They were never used except to fire practice shoots. It has been estimated that had the islands not been fortified, absorbing thousands of tons of steel and hundred of thousands of tons of concrete, the much-vaunted Atlantic Wall, or *Festung Europa*, which the Germans erected to protect their occupied territories could have been 10 to 15 per cent stronger.

During the Second World War the British Army expanded the strength of the regiment of Royal Artillery to 750,000 men, which was an extremely marked increase from its complement of less than 200 at its formation in 1716. Britain was not the only country to reinforce its artillery arm. In Russia, for example, artillery had taken on a new importance in the 1930s after Marshal Josef Stalin declared it to be the 'God of War'. Between 1930 and 1940 the Russian artillery branch grew to include 67,000 pieces of all calibres, including mortars, and was to be immensely powerful by 1945. Between 1930 and 1940 the German Army expanded to be capable of putting 50,000 pieces of artillery and mortars into the field, but production was often compromised because a great deal of important factory space was given over to the development of so-called secret weapons. During the war the German Army used 200 distinct types of artillery in various calibres, not all of which were developed by German armaments manufacturers. In fact the Germans were not averse to using foreign artillery that had been captured in occupied territories, including Belgium and France, as either coastal guns or anti-tank guns.

While artillery played a significant part in the German *Blitzkrieg* in the Western Europe, it was on the Eastern or Russian Front that it was used to its full capacity. On the 19 June 1941 the German Army was ready to unleash 'Directive No. 21' or 'Case Barbarossa' against Russia. For this operation over 3 million men had been assembled along a 1,600-kilometre front. They were supported by 7,184 pieces of artillery and over 3,500 armoured fighting vehicles. Initially the war in the east went the German Army's way: huge numbers of Russians were captured and Hitler's forces penetrated hundreds of kilometres into the Russian interior. One of the greatest shows of German strength during the Russian campaign was the amount of artillery ranged at the gates of the city of Sebastopol where no fewer than 93 batteries of heavy artillery, 88 batteries of light artillery and 24 mortar batteries, along with detachments of self-propelled guns, were deployed.

Although the Germans used artillery well, it was the Russians who, having recovered from the initial shock of 'Barbarossa', began to restock and build up their stocks of artillery and fighting vehicles. In mid-1943 they were able to field between 70 and 80 guns per kilometre of front in counter-attacks against the Germans. For example, at the Battle of Kursk in 1943 the Germans had 10,000 guns and the Russians had 20,000. (In addition, the Germans had 2,700 tanks and the Russians 3,600.) It was the beginning of the end for the German Army in the east as the Russians emerged victorious. The Russians increased their superiority in artillery further and were ultimately able to put 200 to 300 guns on average into every kilometre of the front line. By April 1945 the Russians were inside the city of Berlin, which they ringed with 43,000 pieces of artillery and mortars to bring an end to the war. Artillery was used on all fronts during the Second World War and in some theatres, such as the North African Campaign, the barrages fired resembled the tactics of the First World War.

So successful were many of the new designs pressed into service between 1939 and 1945 that large numbers of weapons, including anti-tank and anti-aircraft guns, continued in service long after the end of the conflict. In fact a number of wars fought between 1945 and the 1970s saw a startling number of armies using artillery designs dating back to the Second World War. For example, the British Army used 25-pounders and 5.5-inch guns in a number of campaigns, such as Malaya (1948–60) and Aden (1964–7), and only finally retired them in the early 1990s from service with the Royal Artillery, where they had remained as training weapons. During the Korean War the Americans used 155mm 'Long Toms' from the Second World War, along with the 105mm M1, while the communist forces used much Russian-built equipment, such as the Su-76 self-propelled gun introduced into service in 1943. In the Korean War 35 per cent of the United Nations' casualties were inflicted by artillery dating from the Second World War, while their forces inflicted 75 per cent of all communist casualties using guns of a similar vintage. Such ageing weapons were not only directed against ground targets: North Korean anti-aircraft artillery, usually in the 37mm to 85mm calibre range, accounted for 87 per cent of all United Nations' aircraft lost in the war between 1950 and 1953.

FIELD ARTILLERY

Between the wars artillery had been classified into types and referred to by titles that specified the particular role in which the guns served. The term 'field artillery', for example, was used to identify weapons intended for use within the tactical structure of a mobile field army; these weapons were more specifically defined as guns which were organic to a division-sized unit. Field artillery in European armies during both world wars included guns and howitzers with calibres between 75mm and 105mm – in the British Army they were called either 13-, 18-, or 25-pounders. The importance of field guns can be judged by the fact that during the First World War British 18-pounders fired an estimated 100 million rounds. French and German guns of field artillery size expended comparable numbers of shells during the conflict. Ideally the guns in the field artillery category had to be capable of being served by a crew of six men and towed behind a light truck. On the outbreak of the First World War these field guns were still being hauled by teams of six horses in a manner not dissimilar to the gun teams of the American Civil War sixty years earlier. The use of horses in the British Army was not to be formally abandoned until 1939; in fact, some units used mules in Burma and Italy during hill and mountain campaigns because of the unique conditions in these theatres of war.

It was only with the advent of motorized transport that the horse was replaced as the means of moving artillery and other equipment around the battlefield. There was resistance to the move, with one side claiming that horses were more reliable. But the motorization lobby won the day with a number of arguments, including the fact that when its engine is turned off a vehicle does not consume anything, whereas horses have to be fed whether they are working or not. It made sound logistical sense to abandon horse-drawn artillery. However, during the Second World War the German Army still relied heavily on horses and the Italian Army even took mules into Russia with it in 1941 for the purpose of moving artillery and ammunition.

During the Vietnam War, 1965–73, the US Army established specialized battery locations for artillery in centres termed 'fire support bases'. These were located in positions from where the guns could fire barrages to support either infantry or another fire support base attacked by a numerically superior enemy. A typical fire support base was laid out in a circle and covered an area of 75 metres radius. It contained at least six M-102 guns of 105mm calibre, along with 81mm mortars and heavy machine guns for defence. It was surrounded by a barbed-wire perimeter and strengthened with sand-bagged positions. By maintaining radio contact with patrolling infantry and aerial reconnaissance these fire bases could engage enemy units with indirect fire across many miles of virtually impenetrable jungle. These sites were used throughout the war with variations on the theme – sometimes heavy artillery was deployed to provide fire support from a greater range. In the Malay Emergency of 1948 to 1960 the Royal Artillery of the British Army had developed similar fire support bases using 25-pounders and later Italian-designed 105mm M-56 pack howitzers, which could be moved by helicopters as underslung loads. In fact, it is quite possible that the Americans learned from the British experience and that it led them to develop the tactic for themselves in Vietnam.

Today field artillery is generally standardized to 105mm calibre, with some variation according to whether it is supplied by Western or Russian manufacturers, and while still towed by light trucks, it is now light enough to be moved as an underslung cargo load by helicopters. In fact, during the Falklands War between Britain and Argentina in 1982, it was common to see in news footage British 105mm light field guns being moved this way. This weapon was introduced into service with the British Army in 1975, to replace the Italian-designed 105mm M-56 pack howitzer, and was an obvious weapon to deploy in the Falklands to support the infantry. During the campaign some guns fired up to 400 rounds per day and helicopters were hard pressed at times to keep the guns supplied with stocks of ammunition. This design of gun proved so reliable that it is now in service in many countries around the world and equips specialized rapid reaction forces, including air-mobile and amphibious forces.

HEAVY ARTILLERY

In the twentieth century heavy artillery was classified as any gun or howitzer with a calibre of 155mm and upwards, although the description 'heavy' is still open to wide interpretation. Generally speaking it is applied to those weapons that are not organic to a division-sized unit, but are controlled instead by either corps or army headquarters, and are never expected to be deployed rapidly. The pieces that fall into the heavy category can include self-propelled guns, because the current trend is towards standardizing weapons with barrels of 155mm calibre. But guns with larger calibres – up to 203mm – are still in service with the US Army; Russia and China are also known to have towed pieces of this calibre in service. Heavy artillery was not always produced in such manageable calibres, but the guns in this category have always been intended for use in engaging enemy artillery in a tactic known as counter-barrage fire. Railway artillery fell into this class at one time, and today there are a handful of countries which, while not having heavy artillery in the true sense of the term, describe their pieces as being 'heavy by road' or 'heavy by rail'. This description can be misleading and only refers to the overall combat weight of the weapon, not simply its calibre of the weapon and thus the size of the shell it fires.

It might be thought that the railway gun was an anachronism in the twentieth century, but a place was found for it in both world wars. Prior to the outbreak of the First World War several French companies had manufactured and supplied a number of railway gun systems to South American countries, where they were intended as mobile coastal defences – exactly the role which had been foreseen in Britain more than fifty years previously. At the time Britain was having a change of mind and now considered the use of railway guns to be peculiarly suited to a continental method of conducting war, despite the ground-breaking field trials conducted in the closing years of the nineteenth century. The European continent had a widespread rail network which were considered an easy and quick method of moving heavy calibre artillery pieces.

The conditions that developed on the Western Front were unique in many ways, not least the long-range artillery duels. Despite the fact that the ground was churned up and was often no more than a sea of mud, the well-maintained network of railway lines on either side was able to serve the trench systems that made up the front line. Heavy railway artillery could be moved around fairly easily and used to the full to support different sectors as operations dictated. These guns were invariably of large calibre, such as the 9.2-inch weapons deployed by the British. After all, there was no point in putting a light field piece on a railway truck. Therefore, guns with calibres between 8 and 20 inches were placed on the rails.

Most existing rolling stock was not suitable for the job, which meant that trucks capable of bearing the weight of these huge guns had to be specially designed. However, they had to remain within the constraints of the gauge of the track and the width and height clearances of tunnels and bridges. The guns' massive recoil systems influenced the dimensions of the carriages and various ingenious means of controlling the recoil had to be developed to keep size to a minimum. Some of the carriages on which the guns were mounted had removable wheels, allowing the whole system to rest directly on to the track. Upon firing some of the recoil force pushed the gun back along the tracks but most of the force went directly into the ground. Other methods of recoil allowed guns simply to roll back freely on their wheels for a distance; they were then shunted back into the firing position by a tender. A number of hydraulic recoil systems to dampen most of the recoil force before the gun began to move on its carriage were also developed. However, since the objective was always to get the heavy gun into action quickly, a recoil control between the gun and the mounting was often thought to be unnecessary and simple sliding mountings were regularly used.

Long-range guns had been developed with the idea that they could be used to disrupt an enemy's rear area with harassing fire. For example, the tacticians believed that headquarters, supply dumps, railway junctions and troop concentration areas could all be targeted and thrown into disarray by a few shells fired at irregular intervals. In such a way chaos and uncertainty would be generated in those areas under bombardment, because no one would know when or from where the next barrage was coming. It was believed that such actions could be conducted with impunity by long-range guns because the enemy would have nothing powerful enough with which to retaliate. A number of these weapons were naval guns with a calibre between 12 and 14 inches, which had been specially converted to use on railway mountings.

At the outbreak of the First World War, the French possessed one of the most advanced railway gun programmes in Europe and had 300 artillery pieces classified as heavy guns. By 1918 this figure had increased to 7,000, of which some 400 pieces were mounted on railway trucks. During the course of the war they maintained their lead and even converted many ex-naval and coastal guns to suit railway mounts, all of which were used to good effect. The country's excellent railway system allowed the French Army to use these pieces for various roles including support fire, raking the enemy's lines of communication and long-range counter-battery fire. The only time these guns failed in their mission was when they tried to silence the German Paris Gun firing from a location in the St Gobain Wood. In this instance French failure resulted from the fact that the German gun, also moved by rail but sited in a fixed location, was more than 70 miles away, well beyond the range of even the heaviest French weapons. Rail guns were always seen as supplementary to other forms of artillery and were especially valued by the French, who were otherwise generally weak in heavy weaponry.

The US Army was largely unprepared for involvement in a European conflict in 1914–18. The first American troops entered the trenches of the Western Front with a mixture of British, French and US weaponry and equipment. Among the few artillery pieces the Americans did dispatch to the European theatre were three ex-US Navy battleship guns of 14-inch calibre mounted on special armoured railway carriages. These guns were crewed by US Navy personnel and are understood to have fired some 782 shells during the last days of the war in 1918. The guns are credited with destroying a German supply depot at Lâon and cutting the Metz–Sedan railway at several points. Thus, railway guns made an important contribution to the Allied war effort in Europe.

However, the age of the railway gun was not quite over and during the Second World War the British hauled out ageing 9.2-inch calibre guns, some of which were built to fight the Second Boer War. These railway guns were moved about on the Southern Railway and sited at Dover, where they were used to fire back at German long-range guns bombarding the town from sites in Calais, France. The British guns were shunted out to sidings from time to time, then secured with steel hawsers and opened fire with counter-battery fire. These actions were largely ineffectual and only really served to maintain the morale of the local populace who believed something was being done to hit back at the enemy. The Russians never developed railway artillery but they did build a series of highly advanced armoured trains. These could only serve the army in a limited way, for example to patrol long lengths of track across the Steppes and in thickly forested areas, despite the fact that the country also had a comprehensive railway network.

The largest calibre artillery pieces built during the Second World War were the two enormous 800mm railway guns, known as Gustav and Dora, constructed by Krupp. They were specifically intended to bombard the French Maginot Line. Of this pair only Gustav saw action, being used to bombard Sebastopol in 1942 and Warsaw in 1944. In his book *Lost Victories* Field Marshal Erich von Manstein, who commanded the German Eleventh Army in the operations against Sebastopol, described Gustav as: 'A miracle of technical achievement. The barrel must have been 27.45 metres long and the carriage as high as a two-story house. Sixty trains had been required to bring it into position along a railway specially laid for the purpose. Two anti-aircraft regiments had to be in constant attendance.' He went on to say of the Gustav railway gun: 'The effectiveness of the cannon bore no real relation to all the effort and expense that had gone into making it.'

The Gustav railway gun had been developed by Krupp in response to a personal query raised by Hitler in 1936 about what size of artillery piece would be required to reduce the Maginot Line. The German Army High Command had asked Krupp the same question; Krupp came back with the estimate that a calibre of 700mm, 800mm, or even 1,000mm would be needed. Despite the fact that no orders had been placed, the design team assumed that the weapon was required and set about designing Gustav and Dora. Drawings were prepared and presented in 1937 to the Army Weapons Office, which approved them, and the building programme started.

No one could have foreseen the difficulties in producing such massive weapons. The problems were so great that Krupp's schedules were soon in tatters. Instead of the guns being ready for 1940, as had been promised, it was 1941 before they could be assembled and test-fired for proof. Hitler was present at one of the field trials, along with Heinz Guderian, the Panzer commander. Dr Muller, a development engineer at Krupps, informed Hitler that the 800mm calibre Gustav could be used against tanks. Guderian was stunned at this statement and later said: 'For a moment I was dumbfounded as I envisaged the mass-production of "Gustavs".' He quickly explained to Hitler that the gun could be fired, but could never engage an individual target because it required 45 minutes to reload. Dr Muller probably meant to say that Gustav could be used to break up massed armoured attacks by tanks, rather than being used as a true anti-tank gun.

The Gustav gun was dispatched to Sebsatopol in 1942 to participate in the siege of the city. It required a crew of more than 1,400 men for its operation and defence, in addition to anti-aircraft units. The Gustav was formally known as '80cm K (E)' and was built in sections to allow it to meet the specifications of the railway loading gauge. The fully assembled weapon was 42.79 metres long, 7.01 metres wide and 11.6 metres high; it weighed 1,350 tonnes. It took three weeks to assemble the weapon and prepare it for firing. The Gustav was assembled using a four-rail double track, with two outer tracks for the assembly crane. The two halves of the bogie units were placed into position and the gun carriage built up on top. The barrel, which came in two sections, was assembled by inserting the rear half into the jacket and connecting the front half by means of an enormous junction nut. The whole assembly was mounted on the cradle. The gun was dismantled into breechring and block, the two barrel sections, jacket, cradle, trunnions and trunnion bearings.

All of the sections had to be transported on special flatcars. The mounting was split longitudinally for movement and dismantled from the top downwards. The sections were transported on additional flatcars hauled by trains. The Gustav could fire two types of shells: the 4,800-kilogram high explosive version had a range of 47 kilometres; the second type was the 7,100-kilogram concrete-piercing shell which could be fired out to 38 kilometres. To propel these massive shells a 2,240-kilogram charge was required. This was partly bagged and partly contained in a steel case 1.30 metres long and 960mm in diameter. During its deployment at Sebastopol and Warsaw the Gustav fired between 60 and 70 rounds in total. As proof of the destructive power of the weapon, one of Gustav's 7,100-kilogram concrete-piercing shells penetrated through 30 metres of rock at Severnaya Bay and destroyed a Russian ammunition stockpile. The Gustav was also moved to Leningrad, but the siege there had been lifted by the Russians before it could be made ready. In any case there is little likelihood that it could have made any difference in the face of the fierce Russian counter-offensive.

Although records for the equally large Dora exist, there is some doubt over whether it was ever built. After the war the weapons were still cloaked in secrecy and they were never completely discovered. Some parts of the Gustav were discovered by US troops in Bavaria in 1945, but like the Paris Gun of 1918, the Germans kept the better part of these massive weapons secret. Although these huge weapons are not the largest artillery pieces ever built, they do represent the largest ever railway guns to be constructed.

During the Second World War the Germans expended much energy on developing long-range, heavy artillery. This took up valuable factory space, manpower and machinery that could have otherwise been directed into producing conventional weapons of proven worth. The best remembered long-range artillery is that sited along the French coast at places including the Pas de Calais from where the guns fired across the Channel and into Dover in England. The first of these shells landed on the town on 12 August 1940, having covered the 34-mile range in about 1 minute. The British responded by wheeling out heavy artillery of their own, some of which dated back to 1914. Cross-Channel artillery duels were conducted much to the chagrin of the local populace. Throughout the Second World War German artillery positioned on the Channel fired at irregular intervals which made it all the more dangerous. At one time Dover was the most bombed and shelled place in the world and was given the nickname 'Hellfire Corner'. The long-range German guns were captured in September 1944; it was estimated that during their operation more than 2,200 shells had landed on the town. The results the pieces produced were far from war-winning: 148 people were killed and about 1,000 homes destroyed.

Today only a handful of countries still hold stocks of what could be described as very heavy artillery and its potential usefulness on the battlefield has to be doubted because aircraft or long-range cruise missiles can be tasked to perform the same function. If 155mm calibre guns are taken to be categorized as heavy artillery in modern terms, then there are a large number of such weapons in current service, both towed and self-propelled types. Russian Army trials have been conducted into developing battlefield tactics which involve bringing heavy concentrations of artillery fire to bear on targets in a softening-up process. These tactics involve heavy artillery, including self-propelled types. This firepower is designed to be unleashed before rapid assaults by heliborne and motorized infantry. This is a classic case of reinventing the wheel, because such tactics were used during both world wars, notably the German *Blitzkrieg*. The only difference is that heliborne infantry was not a part of the earlier technique.

Elsewhere during the twentieth century, the US Army made extensive use of heavy artillery in the Vietnam War and the wars in the Middle East during the 1970s and 1980s saw its continued deployment.

Without doubt the most potentially apocalyptic demonstration of heavy artillery was made on 25 May 1953 at Frenchman's Flat, Nevada, when the US Army fired the first nuclear shell from a heavy piece of artillery which had a 280mm calibre and was nicknamed 'Atomic Annie'. This trial proved that artillery could be used to deliver tactical nuclear weapons on the battlefield – the ultimate deterrent. The Russians followed in the arms race and within the space of only a few years the world's two postwar superpowers had built a stockpile of nuclear-armed artillery shells for guns ranging in calibre from 155mm to 203mm. Artillery pieces with calibres of 155mm and greater are still capable of firing nuclear armed shells, but treaties covering the use of such ammunition are reducing this capability.

These large weapons can also fire chemical shells filled with gas and biological agents. However, the latter form of filling usually involves the shell being used to carry a 'living' pathogen into a target area to contaminate the troops. While this remains an option, it is not entirely feasible because the kinetic forces and heat produced on firing could disrupt or destroy the viruses within the shell. Furthermore, the force of impact and bursting as the shell landed could also wipe out the agent.

Gas shells, however, have been widely used. They were deployed during the First World War but more recently were used during the Iran–Iraq War of 1980–8. While such shells produced casualties and generated alarm, on its own gas does not win a war. When gas shells impact on the target area the casing has to be ruptured to release the contents. If the charge is not powerful enough the gas is not released and so remains localized. Too much explosive charge and the gas is either dispersed too widely or incinerated which negates its effect. Such types of ammunition are recognized as a threat, but ultimately conventional high-explosive-filled shells remain the best option for use on the battlefield.

TERROR OR VENGEANCE WEAPONS

Throughout history some artillery pieces have been developed at enormous expense and pressed into service as so-called terror or vengeance weapons. The first such weapon to appear in the twentieth century was an extraordinary long-range gun deployed by the Germans between March and July 1918 to bombard Paris from a distance of nearly 80 miles. The calibre of this gun was only 210mm, so it was not the largest piece to be fielded by the Germans, but the range of the weapon made it unique. Known as the 'Kaiser Wilhelm Geeschutz', the piece had been developed at the Krupp's factory by Professor Rausenberger, who also designed the 'Gamma' and 'Big Bertha' guns. Rausenberger was an enigmatic figure who spent his spare time designing artillery pieces that could fire over the Alps. The Paris Gun, as this weapon is better known, was actually constructed from a series of composite barrels assembled to produce the 210mm calibre. The outer barrel was of 380mm calibre and had been bored out to accept a 210mm 'liner' barrel. The latter extended 14.5 metres beyond the muzzle of the outer barrel. The muzzle of the 210mm liner was lengthened by inserting a smoothbore barrel extension 6 metres in length, to give an overall barrel length of 40 metres. The whole was braced by a barrel girder to prevent excessive droop. The weapon weighed 145 tonnes. The front end of the firing platform was fixed in a traversing mount and the rear portion was fitted with railway-type wheels which allowed it traverse through 360 degrees to give all-round fire. The enormous amounts of powder required to propel the shell to its maximum range quickly eroded the chamber and barrel, which had to be returned to Krupp's works for reboring and rerifling to 240mm calibre after a number of firings. It is believed that in all three guns of this type fired on Paris. The full story behind the guns is still not known because the actual weapon itself does not survive, only photographs.

The Allies never had an answer to these long-range weapons. The ranges involved meant that even their most powerful guns could not fire back and aircraft failed to identify the German weapons' locations because they were looking in the wrong place. After the war, an Allied commission to Germany never found any trace of the pieces – they had completely disappeared. In all some 303 shells have been identified as being fired at the city, of which 183 landed within the confines of Paris itself. The shelling only produced 256 deaths and wounded 620 civilians. Such a weapon firing at extreme ranges could never be entirely accurate, but when firing at a target the size of a city this did not matter as long as the gunners hit something. As a war-winning weapon or 'terror weapon' the Paris Gun failed.

Firing at long range requires an understanding of more than just ballistics: a whole new science has to be applied which includes a grasp of geophysics. When a shell from a weapon such as the Paris Gun is fired to a height where it enters the stratosphere it enters a region of near-vacuum and as a result there is little resistance to slow it down. As the shell loses speed it begins to descend and gravity begins to exert its pull. Another factor to take into consideration is the Earth's orbit, which rotates it through space west to east. This means that if shells are fired at extreme range from a site in the east towards a target in the west the target may be further away than the maximum range of the gun. But when the shell has completed its flight, the Earth's rotation has brought it into range. The reverse is applied when long-range guns are fired from the west towards targets in the east; then the Earth's rotation would take the target out of range. To cope with this problem a series of complex formulae involving time and motion have to be worked out. The problem is not insoluable, but such a gun is more trouble than it is worth when intercontinental or intermediate-range ballistic missiles can achieve the same result today with better accuracy.

Such issues did not prevent the state of Iraq from trying to install long-range terror guns of 1,000mm calibre in remote desert locations. Iraq's objective was to be capable of firing on its neighbours, such as Israel. In the event the installation of these long-range, so-called 'super-guns' never happened. The technology to develop and produce the weapons was garnered from Western sources, including the late Dr Gerald Bull, a well-known figure in artillery development. The Iraqi super-gun programme, sometimes called 'Baby Babylon', was believed to be creating three weapons. They were to have been constructed by assembling a series of smoothbore sections bolted together to produce weapons of enormous power. Some of the sections for these weapons were fabricated in England, but customs officials uncovered the parts just before shipment and identified them as belonging to a weapon. Under the terms of an arms embargo prohibiting the licensed export of weapons to non-friendly nations, the items were seized and impounded. The sections look like innocuous parts of ordinary pipe-work, which leads to the suspicion that British customs were tipped off about their true purpose.

The smoothbore manufacture of the barrel sections, combined with the fact that they were to be bolted together, lends credence to the fact that these weapons would not have fired conventional shells but more likely rocket-powered projectiles. Their smoothbore design is interesting because it reflects the huge weapons used to bombard the walls of Constantinople over 500 years ago. The installations in which they were to be housed would have been in remote locations, but to orbiting satellites they would have been all too obvious. If the installation of these weapons had gone unobserved, once they had fired more than a handful of projectiles they would have become the target of an intense air-bombing campaign. Sections of these guns have been retained and can be seen today at Fort Nelson in Fareham, Hampshire, and the Royal Artillery Museum, London.

SELF-PROPELLED GUNS

During the First World War the French experimented with a new and innovative type of artillery described as 'self-propelled guns'. These weapons were developed by simply mounting the barrels and recoil mechanism of guns on motorized vehicles in an effort to enhance the mobility of artillery on the battlefield. The first designs comprised a gun barrel from a standard weapon mounted on a specially modified motorized vehicle which could be either tracked or wheeled. Self-propelled guns, SPG, were a success from the very beginning and were subsequently developed by other nations.

An interesting, but short-lived, trial of SPGs was launched by the British Royal Artillery in 1925 under the orders of the then Master-General of the Ordnance, General Sir Noel Birch. It involved a design comprising the barrel of an 18-pounder field gun, which could be elevated to an angle of 85 degrees to permit operation in an anti-aircraft role, mounted on the chassis of a Vickers medium tank. The first units of this new design were ready for trials in 1926 and allowed for seventy-five rounds of ammunition ready for use to be carried. Each vehicle was served by a crew of six. The trial crews were formed into a six-gun battery in 1927 and called the Experimental Mechanized Force. Field-firing trials proved the performance of the design and in 1928 a third version of the SPG was mooted. This was to incorporate a gun shield to protect the crew but, with the high angle of elevation removed, could only be fired in the field role. Despite all the signs that this weapon could be a success the War Office scrapped the idea and disbanded the Experimental Mechanized Force.

However, that was not the end of the SPG. Indeed the idea was taken up by a number of armaments manufacturers in various countries who experimented with their own designs, with the result that during the Second World War the main belligerents all had some form of self-propelled artillery in service.

Self-propelled guns can generally be said to fall into two groups. The first includes pieces serving purely as direct fire weapons used to accompany infantry; in this role they are sometimes referred to as 'assault guns' and actually look like tanks, a role in which they frequently serve. During the Second World War this category included the Russian Su-76, ISU-122/152, Su-85 and Su-100 and the German SdKfz 164 and SdKfz 184 self-propelled units. Some of the Russian types were still in use during the Korean War.

A handful of such designs are still in service but this category of SP artillery has largely given way to light field guns and anti-tank missiles.

The second category of self-propelled guns encompasses those that fire indirectly and act as fire-support weapons, but have been given mobility in order to improve their tactical flexibility. This form of SP artillery is used in the same way as towed, wheeled equipment, but has the advantage of quicker, independent movement across country and is generally faster into and out of action. Most modern artillery in this category is mounted on tracked chassis and today is almost exclusively of 155mm calibre. Examples included the French GCT, British AS90 and the American-designed M-109 in use by many countries. The only exception are weapons built by countries including Russia; it has standardized its gun designs around the 152mm and 122mm calibres, which are used on the M-1973 and M-1974 SP units respectively.

In 1981 Czechoslavakia stood the whole defence industry on its head by producing a wheeled self-propelled gun. Known as the 'DANA', it is based on an 8×8 wheeled chassis and carries a 152mm gun which can fire conventional high-explosive-filled shells out to ranges of more than 17,000 metres and rocket-assisted shells out about 24,000 metres. Another innovation came in 1983 when South Africa unveiled the G-6 general support gun, which not only moved SP design further away from the recognized form, but was also significantly lighter than other guns in this category. In additon, it could fire 155mm shells out to ranges of 39,000 metres, a distance unprecedented at the time. The towed version of this weapon, known as the G-5, was deployed by the Iraqi Army when it confronted the Allied Coalition forces in 1990–1, and at one point it was feared that the Iraqis might arm these weapons with shells filled with nerve gas such as Sarin or Soman to fire on Allied emplacements. When one considers that the legendary Dr Gerald Bull has been linked to the development of the G-5 and G-6 its capabilities are not quite so surprising.

MOUNTAIN ARTILLERY

Mountain artillery in the modern sense of the term is a gun or howitzer specifically designed for operations in mountainous terrain. For this purpose it should be capable of being broken down into its main components and transported by mule or in some cases even man-packed. The concept had been born during the Napoleonic Wars, but little was done to develop the full potential of this type of artillery until the beginning of the twentieth century. Mountain artillery was used extensively during the First World War. Some units of German troops sent to assist General Franco's forces during the Spanish Civil War took with them a number of Krupp-designed 75mm mountain guns. This taught them valuable lessons which they would later apply during the Second World War when deployed against partisans in the mountains of Yugoslavia. Mountain weapons saw a resurgence during the Second World War when specialized troops, such as the German *Gebirgsjager*, used guns with calibres of between 75mm and 105mm.

Some components of mountain guns are designed to be light enough to be carried by a man, but not for long periods and certainly not over long distances. It was much more common to use horses to carry the weapon and reserves of ammunition. One of most important aspects of mountain artillery was that it had be lightweight, and yet at the same time capable of firing a shell with a useful weight out to a reasonable range. Some German guns could fire shells weighing between 7 kilograms and 15 kilograms out to ranges of 10,000 metres and 13,000 metres, which was a much better performance than the standard 81mm mortar of the day. The barrels for pieces of mountain artillery had to be capable of being elevated to high angles, because in mountain warfare guns had to be discharged over ridges and peaks to reach the enemy using indirect fire. The German Geb H40 gun of 105mm calibre, for example, could elevate its barrel to 70 degrees. It was capable of being dismantled into twelve parts for man-handling and was towed in three special carts.

One successful postwar development was the Italian-designed M-56 pack howitzer of 105mm calibre. It weighed 1,290 kilograms and could be broken down into eleven loads, the heaviest of which was 122 kilograms. This weapon was taken into service by a number of countries, including Australia, Spain, Germany and Britain.

Mountain artillery has fallen from use in modern armies whose troops now use mortars with calibres of at least 81mm or call in air support to perform the same job. Should troops operating in mountainous regions require the fire support of artillery, then helicopters are more than capable of transporting in light field guns, such as the British Army's 105mm or French LG1, quickly and easily. They can also bring in crews who would not be tired by the exertions of climbing and fly in a steady supply of ammunition to maintain a battery's combat readiness.

COASTAL DEFENCES

The disappearing gun remained one of the main coastal defence weapons until the early years of the twentieth century. Even then it became obsolete only when it was realized that increased ranges of engagement, due to advances in gunnery tactics, meant that a weapon mounted in a relatively exposed position could be hit by fire from a warship. This prompted the introduction of barbette mounts, whereby the gun mechanism was largely protected by a concrete emplacement, but the barrel remained above the parapet. This system remained standard until the Second World War when the increased use of air power showed that such artillery positions were vulnerable to air attack. Some sought to re-introduce overhead protection and in other cases the casemate was reverted to, but in an highly improved form. Some countries began to use armoured turrets, similar in design to those used on warships, in an effort to protect the guns.

The types of artillery used for coastal defence varied but often included light, quick-firing guns of between 57 and 120mm calibre for use in the close defence of harbours against attack by torpedo boats and similar light craft. Heavier howitzers were emplaced in defences sited behind crests, and were not visible from the sea. This put them in an ideal position to fire armour-piercing shells at high angles of trajectory where their plunging effect would allow them to pierce the armoured decks of the warships. Later fire control became a major concern. The warship was a moving target and did not always travel in a straight line; instruments had to be designed that allowed the target to be located and tracked. These pieces of equipment also calculated gun data and transmitted this information to the crew.

The most important advantage that coastal artillery enjoyed over other forms was virtually unlimited space in which to deploy observation posts and range-finding apparatus, and to accommodate the large mechanical calculators used to work out gun data. This was improved on even further with the introduction of radar to coastal artillery fire control in the early 1940s. Conventional coastal artillery was abandoned between 1946 and 1956. In its place came guided missiles as guns were moved out of their emplacements and away from the coast. Despite this move, however, some countries have retained their coastal artillery defences, most notably Sweden, and there are signs that other nations are planning to revive their conventional coastal artillery, but using missiles rather than guns.

ANTI-AIRCRAFT ARTILLERY

Anti-aircraft artillery pieces are guns specifically designed for attacking aircraft in flight. They are generally characterized by an unrestricted traverse capability and can elevate their barrel to at least 80 degrees. They must also have a high velocity in order to deliver the shell to the target in the shortest possible time and be capable of high rates of fire. Guns on extemporized mounts were used against balloons by the Prussian Army as early as 1870 during the war with France. However, it was only between 1908 and 1909 that the first true anti-aircraft guns were developed by the German companies Krupp and Rheinmetall. These weapons were usually of a calibre between 65mm and 77mm, for example the German 77mm 'Ballonen-AK' introduced in 1914. They differed from previous attempts at anti-aircraft artillery because they were mounted on motor vehicles. It was believed that they would be able to pursue a slow-moving balloon or airship. Early attempts at developing a successful anti-aircraft gun included an experiment to put British 13-pounder field guns and 3-inch guns fitted to pedestal mounts on the back of lorries, such as the Thorneycroft 3-ton J-Type.

The main protagonists in the First World War had some form of anti-aircraft gun by 1914, but it was Germany that took the lead with the development of the 88mm Flak in 1918. This was to serve as the benchmark from which the mighty, dual-purpose 88 of the Second World War would be developed. The French adapted their famous 75mm to an anti-aircraft role, but such guns were only in service in small numbers at first because aircraft were not initially regarded as a priority target. The British Army referred to anti-aircraft guns as 'Archie' or 'ack-ack', which was the phonetic radio term of the day for the letter 'A'; the latter nickname persisted into the Second World War. The German term for this type of artillery was *Flugzeug-abwehrkanone*, usually shortened to 'Flak' and meaning anti-aircraft cannon/gun. The Allied air crews held this branch in awe and used the word flak more frequently than ack-ack to refer to these weapons.

The rapid development of military aviation during the First World War was matched by an equally rapid development of anti-aircraft guns. Over the thirty years after the Armistice calibres up to about 120mm were developed for this specialized role. There are a number of difficulties in developing an effective anti-aircraft weapon, one of the most significant being accurate and reliable fire control. This was initially tackled by fitting sights to each of the guns in a battery – some were extremely complicated to use. Later, a single 'central post sight' was adopted in the middle of gun groups; the firing data would be worked out there and the orders passed to the guns by means of telephones. Even with such advances the individual guns still retained their sights out of force of habit.

Ammunition was another area that required a great deal of development because artillery was now operating in a whole new way. This new target moved in three dimensions; forwards, up and down, and laterally. The problem came in trying to obtain a direct hit on an aerial target to initiate the point of detonation of the early range of anti-aircraft explosive-filled shells. A great deal of time and money was spent on refining ammunition. Over the years fuses were developed that allowed the gunners to predict with a fair degree of accuracy the height at which a shell would detonate.

During the First World War, on average some 3,000 shells had to be fired to either damage or destroy an aircraft. By the Second World War this figure had risen to 40,000 rounds to achieve the same result. The reason for the disparity is aircraft had become faster and flew at higher altitudes; in addition, the guns increased their rate of firing during the interwar years.

An anti-aircraft shell is fired towards its target area and once in flight cannot be corrected, which means the gunner must take into account any movement the aircraft is likely to make after the gun has been fired. Such calculations can only be estimates, because the man on the ground does not know what the pilot is thinking or what the atmospheric conditions are at 30,000 feet. The most sensible approach to the whole anti-aircraft problem is to assume that the aircraft will continue to fly at a constant speed and fixed height with no deviation from its course.

Once the position of the aircraft had been determined, it was necessary to calculate its course, speed and height, and work out the gun data which allowed the guns to fire at the optimum moment to give the shells the best chance of finding their target. At first the work of plotting the aircraft's course had to be done very quickly by men using charts, tables and mathematical calculations. They relayed their solutions without hesitation to the gun batteries. In the 1920s the task of these mathematicians was made slightly easier by the appearance of the first 'predictors', in effect mechanical computers, which were devised to solve the problem rapidly and repeatedly. By the 1940s these machines had begun to give way to electronic predictors capable of producing results much faster and with great accuracy.

During the Second World War Britain was equipped with a formidable range of modern anti-aircraft guns, including the 3.7-inch and 4.5-inch calibre weapons. Defending the cities against the bombers was a priority and many guns were sited along paths which approaching bombers were predicted to fly. London had a comprehensive range of anti-aircraft guns deployed in its defence. It was here that Professor Sir Archibald Hill of the Air Defence Research Committee made a calculation which he believed would eliminate the idea that a 'London gun barrage' was what the capital needed in its defence. Sir Archibald claimed:

> One cublic mile of space contains 5,500,000,000 cubic yards. The lethal zone of a 3.7 inch shell is only a few thousand cubic yards and exists for only about $\frac{1}{20}$th of a second. The idea of a 'barrage' of anti-aircraft shells is nonsense. The word ought to be dropped; it gives a false impression, and is based on sloppy thinking and bad arithmetic. Nothing but aimed fire is of any use. In order to give a one-fiftieth chance of bringing down an enemy plane moving at 250 miles per hour and crossing a vertical rectangle ten miles wide and four miles high (from the barrage balloons to 25,000 feet) about three thousand 3.7in shells would be required a second.

Fortunately for all concerned it was Sir Archibald's calculations that were flawed and not the belief in a gun barrage. Many hundreds of guns of all calibres were deployed.

As the Allied air forces gained the upper hand they were able to take the fighting deep into the heart of Germany where cities, factories and other strategic targets were bombed. In order to counter this threat the German home defences had to develop a layered anti-aircraft defence which incorporated guns ranging in size from 88mm to 120mm. Just like their British counterparts these guns were able to take a steady toll on aircraft, but they could never defeat the massed squadrons of bombers. Between 1927 and 1942 the Germans developed about twelve anti-aircraft guns of their own design, to which they added many captured weapons seized from occupied territories, including France, Belgium and Russia. The German-made pieces included the standard 88mm Flak 41, the 105mm gun (which appeared as either the Flak 38 or Flak 39) and the massive 128mm Flak 40 which was introduced in 1942 and had a service ceiling of 14,800 metres. As the war progressed and the Allies grew stronger, Germany was forced to remove anti-aircraft weapons from the front line and to commit them to vulnerable areas such as cities and industrial centres. The Germans constructed special Flak towers on which batteries of anti-aircraft guns were sited; the towers were placed in elevated positions which allowed them to operate clear of ground clutter. The Allies swamped these defences but at considerable cost to themselves. Not only had the guns been diverted away from the front lines, but thousands of troops and millions of rounds of ammunition had also been denied to the artillery arm in the theatres of fighting.

Different countries developed anti-aircraft guns to suit their specific requirements and incorporated such designs into a layered air defence, which in Britain also included early warning radar. Specialized anti-aircraft units, designated either light or heavy according to the type of guns with which they were equipped, now began to appear. The units classified as 'light' were usually equipped with weapons of a calibre between 20mm and 40mm. These guns had high rates of fire – from 100 to 120 rounds per minute – and could be sited around airfields on the coast where they could intercept low-flying intruders (they used computing sights as opposed to predictors). Light anti-aircraft artillery invariably fired shells which were impact-fused and in that role they took a steady toll of the slow-moving German V1 flying bombs in 1944. The 'heavy' units were equipped with guns firing time-fused shells which had a calibre of 75mm and upwards. The heavy batteries were integrated with predictors.

During the Second World War the larger anti-aircraft guns were reclassified: weapons of 75–100mm calibre were now described as 'medium' anti-aircraft weapons and anything above that was called heavy. A fourth, not so widely used, class of weapon – the intermediate anti-aircraft gun – was also designated. The guns in this new category were of 55mm to 57mm calibre and were intended to provide fire to an altitude beyond the reach of the light guns but still too low for the medium and heavy guns. Both Britain and Germany tried to develop guns that would operate in this range, but without much success and the whole concept of intermediate anti-aircraft weapons was shelved for the rest of the war.

The main technological advances in anti-aircraft gunnery during the Second World War came with the introduction of powered loading and fuse-setting, which greatly accelerated rates of fire. Mechanical time fuses improved the practical ceiling of shells but eventually gave way to proximity fuses, which could detect the presence of a target by radio signals and required no setting. Once the target had been detected the fuse detonated and the shell exploded in a range lethal to the aircraft.

Postwar developments in anti-aircraft defences had to confront jet aircraft flying at supersonic speeds and at high altitudes. Weapons designers focused on developing weapons with a higher muzzle velocity in order to reduce the shell's time of flight, thus increasing the lethal radius of shells as they deflagrated and increasing the gun's rate of fire. Solutions to these problems just beginning to appear when the first generation of guided anti-aircraft missiles were developed. These marked the end of medium and heavy anti-aircraft guns, and by the 1970s the transition to missiles was complete.

However, the introduction of missiles did not mean the end of anti-aircraft artillery: light or intermediate guns still feature on the battlefield, despite the fact that shoulder-fired missiles are becoming more common. Anti-aircraft guns of 20–30mm calibre are still held by a large number of modern armies and the Bofors 40mm gun is widely used, though in a much upgraded and modernized version. These weapons are primarily deployed for the protection of front-line troops against ground-attack helicopters and slow-moving, fixed-wing aircraft. Nowhere was the effectiveness of these guns proved more convincingly than in the Falklands in 1982. British pilots had great respect for this type of anti-aircraft fire which at times was extremely fierce. In fact, such were the lessons learned from this brief conflict that the British armed forces reintroduced light anti-aircraft guns into their arsenal.

During the Allied Coalition's war against Iraq in 1990–1 after the invasion of Kuwait, nightly raids over the Iraqi capital, Baghdad, produced reaction from the anti-aircraft gunners who blazed away with conventional ammunition but without result. This type of gunfire was termed 'Triple-A' (anti-aircraft artillery) and while it was frightening, the use of anti-aircraft missiles created the most Coalition casualties, underlining the fact that missiles are more potent than light-barrelled weapons against fast moving aircraft operating at high altitudes.

ANTI-TANK GUNS

Anti-tank guns, as their name indicates, are designed to attack all types of armoured vehicles, but tanks in particular. Such guns have a number of special design features, including the firing of fixed ammunition at very high velocities and a high rate of fire. Anti-tank guns in the truest sense of the term are identified as being fitted with split trail carriages to permit the widest possible arc of traverse for target engagement. Some anti-tank gun designs, such as the mighty German 88 and the much lighter British 2-pounder, both of Second World War vintage, were mounted on cruciform and tripod platforms respectively to allow a complete traverse through 360 degrees for all-round fire.

The first true anti-tank gun – which is to say a gun designed specifically to destroy tanks, and not simply one created for another purpose but then utilized in an anti-tank role – appears to have been a small 37mm weapon built by the Germans in 1918, and mounted on a two-wheeled carriage. It was created out of necessity in response to the use of tanks by the Allies, who had fielded these armoured vehicles in an attempt to break the deadlock of trench warfare. Tanks were first deployed on the battlefield in November 1916 and the Germans responded by engaging them with direct fire from pieces of artillery including 77mm guns. These did produce results but later purpose-built guns were to make a bigger impact in anti-armour warfare. Few of the newly developed 37mm guns were manufactured, with too few actually being used on the battlefield to have any significant effect. The new weapon had made armies realize that specialized artillery was needed to engage the tank and defeat it.

The interwar period served as one of rearmament for most countries, and this process included building up strength in anti-tank guns. As with anti-aircraft guns, weapons of various calibres were developed and adopted according to each country's requirements. By and large the ammunition fired by this first generation of true anti-tank guns ranged in calibre from 20mm to 37mm. Such small calibres were used because they could be developed without the need to produce excessively large rounds and the targets themselves carried relatively poor armoured protection. Most of the early weapons were mounted on two-wheeled carriages towed behind a vehicle, and were small enough and light enough to be deployed and operated by a crew of three or four men.

During the Second World War tank designs underwent radical changes and armour protection became thicker. It was obvious to weapon designers that small calibre anti-tank guns would be useless against such machines. In an effort to redress the imbalance in the gun versus armour race, anti-tank weapons of ever-increasing calibre were developed and introduced into front-line service. Once again the Germans took a very quick lead with the introduction of a 50mm gun in 1940. They referred to these specialized weapons as *Panzerabwehrkanone* or simple *Pak* guns and devised the tactic known as *Pak fronts* which presented a wall of anti-tank guns to resist armoured thrusts, especially on the Eastern Front against massive Russian tank assaults. These guns exacted a high toll on tanks but in the case of Russia sheer numerical superiority helped overcome this new obstacle.

The British Army gained an edge in 1941 with the introduction of the 6-pounder gun, which had a calibre of 57mm and could penetrate 74mm of armour at nearly 1,000 metres range. It was designed to replace the older 2-pounder gun which fired a projectile of 40mm calibre – the British Army had abandoned over 500 units of this weapon on the beaches of Dunkirk during the evacuation in 1940.

As the calibre of anti-tank guns became larger, heavier projectiles were required with more powerful charges to propel them at velocities sufficient to penetrate thicker armour. The 17-pounder anti-tank gun was introduced into service with the British Army in May 1942 and from the beginning it proved its worth as a hard-hitting anti-tank gun. The decision to proceed with the development of the 17-pounder was taken in November 1940. Its design was based on a 3-inch gun firing a 17-pound shot. In keeping with British Army practice the gun was known by the weight of the shell it fired, which in this case was a 17-pound armour-piercing shell with a calibre of 3 inches. The weight of the propelling charge was 8.2 pounds. The 17-pounder gun was served by a crew of five and weighed 6,700 pounds in its travelling mode and 6,445 pounds in its firing mode. It could fire either high-explosive or armour-piercing shells which had a muzzle velocity of of 950 metres per second with a maximum range of 10,516 metres. A good gun crew could manage a rate of fire in excess of ten rounds per minute, but this level was not practical in an anti-tank role, where targets had to be selected and engaged with effective fire. The 17-pounder was mounted on a split-trail carriage. It could be elevated to +16.6 degrees and depressed to -6 degrees and could be traversed through an arc of 90 degrees, which allowed the crew to track a moving target and engage it at the most opportune moment. The 17-pounder was capable of penetrating armour thicker than 9 inches at ranges of 3,300 feet. The weapon was 24 feet 9 inches in length, and the barrel was fitted with a double-baffle muzzle brake to reduce recoil, which was a prominent feature in the design. The gun was 7 feet 2.5 inches wide and had a low profile of only 5 feet 6 inches, which meant that it could easily be concealed and could avoid a fair amount of counter-battery fire. A gun shield was fitted for the protection of the crew and was based on the spaced armour design to give the optimum level of protection. Despite its large size and heavy weight the gun was a popular weapon with the troops, even the airborne units valued its effectiveness to fight off armoured attacks after they had landed by glider. In fact the British 6th Airborne Division had 17-pounders air-landed by Horsa gliders, which could accommodate them comfortably. Other airborne units to use the 17-pounder anti-tank gun included the specialized 2nd Airlanding Anti-tank Regiment, which deployed the weapon from gliders after crossing the Rhine in March 1945. In addition to its use by specialized troops, the 17-pounder was attached to standard infantry and armoured divisions. These formations had strengths of over 18,300 and nearly 15,000 men respectively, and in each case an anti-tank regiment was equipped with forty-eight 17-pounders backed up the 25-pounders for fire support.

The 17-pounder was versatile enough to permit its being mounted into armoured vehicles which took advantage of its excellent penetrative power. The Firefly was an ordinary Sherman tank into which had been fitted a 17-pounder in place of a standard 75mm gun. By 1944 this design was so established that one in four of the tanks used during the Normandy campaign in 1944 was armed with it.

Another 17-pounder vehicle was the Archer self-propelled anti-tank gun, which was something of an oddity. It comprised a 17-pounder gun mounted in an open-topped gun mounting, but set in reverse so that the gun overhung the rear engine decking. Some 655 of these vehicles were constructed and saw considerable service after their introduction in early 1944. Another experiment with the 17-pounder was the Straussler: the gun was fitted with a motive unit from a Bedford QL lorry in an early attempt to provide an artillery piece which was capable of moving short distances over the battlefield using its own auxiliary power. The benefit of this design was that a prime mover vehicle did not always have to be present to transfer the gun from one location to another. However, it was thought that the design left the crew exposed to counter-fire and the Straussler was never taken into service.

Without doubt the 17-pounder in its towed version had a significant impact during the closing stages of the North African Campaign after it arrived in sufficient numbers to allow the Allies to take an exacting toll of the German Army's powerful Tiger tanks. Throughout the war the 17-pounder saw service in most theatres, including Italy and north-west Europe.

Postwar, the 17-pounder continued in service with a number of armies, including those of Egypt, Pakistan, Israel and South Africa, who saw a need for such a weapon in their anti-tank arsenal until it became apparent that missile technology was taking over in the gun–armour race. The Israeli Army, for example, is known to have used 17-pounder guns in 1948 in its war with the Arabs, and although the crews were relatively inexperienced with little training, their presence on the battlefield did force the attacking Syrian armour to withdraw from areas such as Degania B, which had been their designated objective.

The most feared anti-tank gun of the Second World War was without doubt the German 88. Like the British 17-pounder it appeared in several forms, including mounted as a main armament in the turret of tanks like the German Tiger. It was originally an anti-aircraft gun designated Flak 36 (because it appeared in 1936) and could fire a shell weighing 9.4 kilograms up to a serviceable ceiling of nearly 10,000 metres. During the German invasion of Western Europe the gun was pressed into service as an anti-tank weapon and produced instant results. It is unclear whom the credit should go to for using it in this role: some claim it was General Erwin Rommel and other sources cite different German commanders. But whoever ordered the 88 to be used as an anti-tank gun set it down as a benchmark by which other armaments manufacturers' work would be judged.

When America deployed its forces overseas in 1942, it was obliged to equip its army with a towed version of the British-designed 6-pounder, until it adopted a 90mm gun on a self-propelled mounting. By the end of the war the British were in the process of developing a 94mm anti-tank gun and the Germans had started a programme of trials of a massive 128mm anti-tank gun, which would have been overkill by any standards. The US Army then deployed and standardized the highly versatile 105mm calibre, around which would be developed the M1A1, another of those weapons that would serve for many years after the war.

The anti-tank guns developed in the later stages of the war evolved in a way that was counter-productive for the fighting man in a combat situation. The main problem lay in the fact that the weapons were in danger of becoming too heavy to be of any practical use in a mobile war. The way in which armour is attacked and defeated is the subject for a discourse on ammunition, but the problem must be outlined here so that the manner in which specialized anti-tank guns developed can be understood. The first real method devised for defeating a tank was to use a solid steel shot with a pointed nose – a cylindro-conoidal projectile that looked like a very large version of a modern rifle bullet. But it was soon discovered that there was an upper limit to the velocity at which such projectiles could be fired at an armoured target – in the order of 853 metres per second (2,800 feet per second). It was found that at velocities beyond this the steel would not penetrate the armour, but would instead shatter on impact. New projectiles using a core of tungsten steel were developed. They needed more powerful cartridges to produce the velocity required for armour penetration and this was one reason why anti-tank guns started to increase in size.

In the early 1940s the shaped charge was perfected. This provided the means to defeat armour by penetrating it using directed explosive force, or chemical energy, from a shaped warhead charge. In postwar years many nations would go on to develop their own range of weapons to fire this new type of ammunition. In the British Army, for example, two types of chemical energy round were taken into service:, the high-explosive squash head, HESH, and high-explosive anti-tank, HEAT. These were of 120mm calibre and could be fired from infantry-operated recoilless guns, such as the now obsolete Wombat. In their time such weapons were allocated to the support companies of infantry battalions, and therefore were not artillery in the true technical sense of the term.

The new anti-tank projectiles did not require high velocities, which prompted a return to lighter guns, but this time along the path of recoilless weapons. By the 1950s the anti-tank gun in the true sense of the word had all but disappeared from the arsenal of the front-line fighting man, leaving the way open for the development of single-shot, disposable anti-tank projectiles which were fired from the shoulder. But even then there were a number of countries that decided to retain anti-tank guns of the more traditional type, including Switzerland which held at least two types of anti-tank gun in front-line service until the late 1990s. Russia still holds a number of traditional anti-tank guns, but in self-propelled mounts for deployment with airborne forces. Even in such a role their usefulness on the modern battlefield must be doubted, given the light calibre of the guns and the fact that they would be deployed against tanks with reactive armour. Shoulder-launched missiles are the proven way forward and it is only a question of time before the last remaining types of anti-tank artillery are consigned to storage where they belong.

MORTARS

Mortars have been mentioned throughout this book to indicate the importance of their role in supporting artillery. Strictly speaking mortars are pieces of ordnance designed to fire only at angles of elevation greater than 45 degrees and thus have a higher barrel elevation than the howitzer. Today's mortars are usually short-barrelled weapons of 60mm, 81mm or 120mm calibre. They are used by the infantry and therefore no longer come under the title artillery. Although outside the scope of artillery in the true sense of the term, it is interesting to note that some Russian mortars of 240mm calibre have a performance almost equal to field artillery of the same calibre. ·

Like railway artillery, large-calibre mortars remained in use long after their actual benefit on the battlefield had been challenged by more accurate guns and howitzers. Mortars, in the sense of artillery pieces, were still in use during the First World War and it was during that conflict that the idea of the trench mortar was introduced. Among the first to see the potential use of such weapons was German Army, which had reached the conclusion as a result of observations made by German observers during the Russo-Japanese War. As early as 1914 Sir John French of the British Army called for 'some special form of artillery' for the infantry, and by the end of the war the mortar had been transformed from heavyweight bombardment weapon to lightweight, close-support weapon for the infantry. The Americans retained mortars of large calibre sited at specially constructed strategic locations, such as Corregidor in the Philippines, mainly to provide coast defence. The advantage of such designs was that they delivered shells in a steep downward trajectory to attack the deck of a ship, which is a great deal thinner than the armoured belt surrounding the hull.

As warfare changed from static to mobile there was no longer any need for large-calibre mortars. Their use in the First World War had been instrumental in levelling border defences constructed from steel, masonry and earth ramparts. But later developments, such as increased overhead protection and fortifications sunk deep into the ground, such as the Maginot Line in France and the Siegfried Line in Germany, would counter the effects of mortar fire.

Naval vessels could never really be defended against mortar fire from coastal batteries which is probably why America maintained the large-calibre mortar long after most countries had abandoned it in favour of other forms of artillery. Finally, by the end of the 1950s, most conventional coastal artillery, including the heavyweight mortar, was declared obsolete.

MANUFACTURING

Barrels for modern-day artillery pieces are manufactured using a process known as monobloc, which means they are created as a single forging without any jacket or liner. This technique allows a barrel of 105mm calibre to be forged in 10 minutes. Another barrel manufacturing process is called swaging; here an oversized mandrel is passed through the barrel by an hydraulically operated ram to exert the pressures required to overstrain the inner surfaces of the barrel. This allows the manufacturer to autofretage only that length of the barrel which requires pre-stressing in a modern-day version of Rodman's technique developed nearly 150 years ago.

These new processes allow a barrel with an external diameter 50 per cent greater than the diameter of the bore to be strengthened using the autofretage technique to a level that would otherwise require an increase in wall thickness approaching 50 per cent in a non-autofretaged monobloc barrel. Barrel wear and fatigue, which could lead to the weapon bursting on firing, is also greatly reduced. In fact, the life of a barrel can be more than doubled by using this method. The autofretage process involves pre-stressing the barrel by stretching the inner layers of metal beyond their elastic limit but at the same time stretching the outer layers within their elastic limit. The effect is that the outer layers compress the inner ones. Advances have led to artillery becoming more efficient than ever before and with improvements in propelling charges barrel life has been further extended.

With the introduction of muzzle brakes to the end of barrels in the mid-nineteenth recoil was reduced to a tolerable level. There are many different types of muzzle brakes but they all operate in the same manner – deflecting the propelling gases through at least 180 degrees as the shell leaves the muzzle of the gun.

Ammunition for modern artillery has also been refined to the point where it comprises mainly high-explosive filling, but guns can still fire other types including smoke and illuminating rounds, when called upon to do so. Ammunition is today streamlined to reduce drag and most types are 'boat-tailed' in shape, which is to say they have a slight taper towards the base end. The range of modern ammunition has also been increased to include rocket-assisted projectiles and a system known as base-bleed. This last type involves a small smoke-generating device fitted to the base of the projectile and activated when the shell is fired. During its flight time the smoke fills the vacuum created behind the shell during its trajectory and reduces the drag on the shell. This simple idea has allowed conventional shells to increase their range by about 10 per cent without redesigning the shell or increasing the weight of propellant charge.

Another type of shell is the terminally guided munition, for example the American-designed 'Copperhead', which is a 155mm calibre projectile fired like a conventional round of artillery. It is fin-stabilized and is used to engage targets such as tanks or specifically identified buildings. After following its normal ballistic trajectory the Copperhead projectile locks on to its objective with a laser tracking device; this guides its terminal or last course corrections towards the target which has been 'illuminated' by an artillery observer using a laser designator. Such types of ammunition are mid-way between conventional artillery shells and missiles.

Ammunition remains a mix of fixed and semi-fixed types for light field guns, and separately loaded bagged charges and projectiles for larger guns of 155mm calibre. In the case of self-propelled guns, this division of powder charge and projectile is a logical move because it reduces the risk of fire and sympathetic explosion should the carrier vehicle be hit by counter-battery fire. Ammunition can now be transported to the guns in the front line by helicopter, truck or the specialized armoured ammunition resupply vehicles. The logistic movement of ammunition has come a long way since it was first transported around the battlefield by a man with a wheelbarrow.

THE FUTURE

Wars will still be fought using conventional artillery, both towed and self-propelled, which will continue to remain in service with the armies of the world. In all the time artillery has been in service it must have proved its worth because its basic principles remain the same today as they were hundreds of years ago: barrels are still used to aim and direct a projectile towards the target with the highest degree of accuracy possible.

During the Gulf War of 1990–1, the Allied Coalition Forces facing the Iraqi Army deployed more than 1,600 pieces of artillery into the combat area and had many more to call on. It was believed at the time that the war could degenerate into artillery duels of the type seen only ten years earlier when Iraq faced Iran. In the end such a situation did not develop, mainly because aircraft of the Coalition Forces destroyed large numbers of identified artillery batteries and because of the mobile flexibility of the Coalition artillery, which also included a number of multiple launch rocket systems (MLRS).

These systems are viewed in some quarters as the way forward for artillery. Although rocket weapons are powerful in their own right, it is doubtful whether it will ever fully replace tubed artillery on the battlefield. Changes are being made to conventional tubed artillery as a result of emerging technology. For example, new alloys will reduce the weight of weapons and increase their operational readiness for better deployment via helicopters. Electronic technology is being used by the artillery spotters to make artillery a 24-hours-a-day, all-weather weapon system. Aerial observation has been refined to the point where small unmanned airborne vehicles (UAVs), sometimes called drones, can be sent out to 'spy' on the forward edge of the battlefield. Furthermore artillery observers can use satellites to locate a target to within metres and thereby greatly reduce collateral damage to surrounding areas.

As armies enter the twenty-first century it is unlikely that conventional tubed artillery as we know it will disappear – a fact borne out by its continued use in combat zones around the world.

BIBLIOGRAPHY

Baumgartner, Frederic J., *France in the Sixteenth Century*, Macmillan, 1985

Beebe, Gilbert W., and Michael DeBakey, *Battle Casualties*, Springfield, Mass., 1952

Bennett, Matthew et al, *Hutchinson Dictionary of Ancient and Medieval Warfare*, Helicon, 1998

Brereton, J.M., *The British Soldier: A Social History from 1661 to the Present Day*, Bodley Head, 1986

Bull, Stephen, *An Historical Guide to Arms and Armour*, Studio Editions, 1991

Carlton, Charles, *Going to the Wars*, Routledge, 1992

Carver, Field Marshal Lord, *Seven Ages of the British Army*, Weidenfeld & Nicolson, 1984

Chandler, David G., *The Art of Warfare on Land*, Hamlyn, 1974

Cole, Hubert, *The Wars of the Roses*, Granada, 1973

Comparato, Frank E., *The Age of the Great Guns*, Stackpole Books, 1965

Davis, William C., *The American Civil War: An Historical Account of America's War of Secession*, Salamander, 1996

Duffy, C., *Siege Warfare: The Fortress in the Early Modern World, 1494–1660*, Routledge, 1979

Earle, Peter, *The Life and Times of Henry V*, Weidenfeld & Nicolson, 1972

Fortescue, Hon J.W., *A History of the British Army*: 13 volumes, Macmillan, 1899–1930

Hewitt, John, *Ancient Armour & Weapons*, John Henry & James Parker, 1855

Hime, H.W.L., *The Origin of Artillery*, Longmans & Co., 1915

Hogg. Ian V., *The Illustrated Encyclopedia of Artillery*, Quarto, 1987

Johnson, Curt, *Artillery: The Big Guns go to War*, Octopus, 1975

Keegan, John, *The Face of Battle*, Jonathan Cape, 1988

——, *A History of Warfare*, Pimlico, 1994

Koch, H.W., *Medieval Warfare*, Bison, 1978

——, *History of Warfare*, Bison, 1987

Lawford, James, (ed.), *The Cavalry*, Roxby Press, 1976

Macksey, Kenneth, *Guinness History of Land Warfare*, Guinness, 1973

Manstein, Fritz Erich von, *Lost Victories*, edited and translated by Antony G. Powell, Methuen & Co., 1958

Massie, Robert K., *Peter The Great: His Life and World*, Gollancz, 1981

Needham, Joseph, *Science and Civilisation in China*, 6 volumes, Cambridge University Press

Nicolle, David, *Medieval Warfare Source Book: Volume I: Warfare in Western Christendom*, Arms & Armour, 1995

——, *Medieval Warfare Source Book: Volume 2: Christian Europe and its Neighbours*, Arms & Armour, 1996

O'Connell, Robert L., *Of Arms and Men*, Oxford University Press, 1989

Reid, William, *The Lore of Arms*, Purnell Book Services, 1976

Roberts, Michael, *Profiles in Power: Gustavus Adolphus*, Longman, 1973 and 1992

Rogers, Colonel H.C.B., *Artillery Through the Ages*, Military Book Society, 1971

Rybot, N.V.L., *Gorey Castle (La Château Mont Orgueil)*, Société Jersiaise, reprinted 1978

——, *Elizabeth Castle*, Société Jersiaise, ninth edition 1986

Temple, Robert C., *China: Land of Discovery & Invention*, Patrick Stephens, 1986

Townsend, Charles, (ed.), *The Oxford Illustrated History of Modern War*, Oxford University Press, 1997

Tuchman, Barbara, *A Distant Mirror: The Calamitous 14th Century*, Papermac, 1978

Wheatcroft, Andrew, *The Ottomans*, Viking, 1993

INDEX